MODELS FOR THINKING AND WRITING

MODELS
for
THINKING
and
WRITING

WARREN TAYLOR
Oberlin College

THE WORLD PUBLISHING COMPANY
Cleveland and New York

Published by The World Publishing Company
2231 West 110th Street, Cleveland, Ohio 44102

Library of Congress Catalog Card Number: 66–18465
Printed in the United States of America

Acknowledgments

For permission to use material in this book grateful acknowledgment is made to the following:

Robert H. Baker. *An Introduction to Astronomy,* 1941, p. 89. Reprinted by permission of Harper & Row, Publishers.

Carl Becker. Reprinted from *Progress and Power* by Carl Becker, pp. 87–102, by permission of Alfred A. Knopf, Inc. Copyright, 1949, by Carl Becker.

John M. Berdau. *Early Tudor Poetry.* New York, 1931, p. 127. By permission of The Macmillan Company.

Isaiah Berlin. *The Hedgehog and the Fox.* London: Weidenfeld & Nicolson, 1953, pp. 1–4; 39–42; 81–82. Reprinted by permission of the publisher.

Bruce Bliven. "The Traffic Catastrophe," *The New Republic,* LXXXIX (1937), pp. 296–297. Reprinted by permission of the author.

A. C. Bradley. *Shakespearean Tragedy.* New York: The Macmillan Company, 1929, pp. 253–254. Reprinted with permission of The Macmillan Company of Canada Ltd. and Macmillan & Company Ltd., London.

Sir William Bragg. *The World of Sound.* New York: E. P. Dutton and Company, 1922, pp. 83–85; 97–98. Reprinted by permission of G. Bell & Sons, Ltd., Publishers, London.

Waldo R. Browne. *Altgeld of Illinois.* New York: The Viking Press, 1924, p. 1.

Holger Cahill. "America's Art Today." From *America as Americans See It,* edited by Fred Ringel, 1932, pp. 258–259. Reprinted by permission of Harcourt, Brace & World, Inc., Publishers.

Rachel Carson. "The Gray Beginnings." From *The Sea Around Us* by Rachel Carson, pp. 6–15. Copyright © 1950, 1951, 1961 by Rachel L.

Carson. Reprinted by permission of Oxford University Press, Inc.

Rachel Carson. *Silent Spring*. Boston: Houghton Mifflin Company, pp. 46–51. Reprinted by permission of the publisher.

Alfred Cobban. *Dictatorship: Its History and Theory*, pp. 234–237. New York: Charles Scribner's Sons, 1939. Reprinted by permission of the publisher.

Charles Horton Cooley. *Life and the Student*. New York: Alfred A. Knopf, Inc., 1927, p. 74.

Thomas Craven. *Treasury of Art Masterpieces*, 1939, p. 11. By permission of Simon and Schuster, Inc.

Karl K. Darrow. *The Renaissance of Physics*. New York, 1936, pp. 146–148. By permission of The Macmillan Company.

John Dewey. *Human Nature and Conduct*, 1928, p. 39. Reprinted by permission of Holt, Rinehart and Winston, Inc.

Georges Duhamel. *America the Menace*. Boston: Houghton Mifflin Company, 1931, pp. 152–161. Reprinted by permission of Houghton Mifflin Company.

John Charles Duncan. *Astronomy*, 1935, pp. 89, 165, 194. Reprinted by permission of Harper & Row, Publishers.

Loren Eiseley. From *The Mind as Nature* by Loren Eiseley, pp. 45–52. Copyright © 1962 by Loren Eiseley. Reprinted by permission of Harper & Row, Publishers.

Wilford J. Eiteman. "Two Decades of Depression," *The New Republic,* LXVII (1931), pp. 222–225. Reprinted by permission of the author.

Richard Theodore Ely and Ralph H. Hess. *Outlines of Economics*. New York: The Macmillan Company, 1937, p. 258.

Wallace K. Ferguson and Geoffrey Bruun. *A Survey of European Civilization*. Boston: Houghton Mifflin Company, ed. 1936, pp. 19–20; ed. 1947, p. 420.

E. M. Forster. "Sinclair Lewis." From *Abinger Harvest*, 1938, pp. 129–136; copyright, 1936, 1964, by E. M. Forster. Reprinted by permission of Harcourt, Brace & World, Inc., Publishers, and Edward Arnold (Publishers) Ltd., London.

James Frazer. *Man, God, and Immortality*. New York: The Macmillan Company, 1927, pp. 380–385.

R. Buckminster Fuller. *Nine Chains to the Moon*. Philadelphia: J. B. Lippincott Company, 1938.

Morris Ginsberg. *Reason and Unreason in Society*. Harvard University Press, 1948, pp. 193–195. Reprinted by permission of Heinemann Educational Books, Ltd., London.

George W. Gray. *The Advancing Front of Science*. New York: Mc-

Graw-Hill Book Company, Inc., 1937, pp. 233–234. Copyright, 1937, by George W. Gray. Used by permission.

George W. Gray. "The Problem of Influenza," *Harper's Magazine*, January, 1940, p. 166. Reprinted by permission of *Harper's Magazine*.

Theodore Meyer Greene. *The Arts and the Art of Criticism*, 1940, p. 38. By permission of Princeton University Press.

Coleman R. Griffith. *General Introduction to Psychology*. New York: The Macmillan Company, 1923, p. 21.

Francis Hackett. *The Invisible Censor*, 1921, pp. 160–164. Copyright 1921 by B. W. Huebsch, Inc. All rights reserved. Reprinted by permission of The Viking Press, Inc.

Robert W. Hegner. *College Zoology*. New York: The Macmillan Company, 1931.

Lancelot T. Hogben. *Retreat from Reason*. New York: Random House, 1938, pp. 58–59.

R. M. Holman and William Robbins. *General Botany*, 1928, p. 74; *Botany*, 1939, p. 20. By permission of John Wiley & Sons, Inc.

Harry N. Holmes. *Introductory College Chemistry*. New York: The Macmillan Company, 1939.

Robert Maynard Hutchins. *The Higher Learning in America*, 1936, pp. 66 and 98. By permission of Yale University Press.

Aldous Huxley. "Music at Night" from *Music at Night and Other Essays* by Aldous Huxley. Copyright 1931 by Aldous Huxley. Reprinted by permission of Harper & Row, Publishers; Chatto and Windus, Ltd.; and Mrs. Laura Huxley.

Aldous Huxley. *Two or Three Graces*. Doran, 1926, pp. 11–12. Reprinted by permission of Harper & Row, Publishers.

William Ralph Inge. *Outspoken Essays: Second Series*, 1922, p. 163. Reprinted by permission of Longmans, Green & Company, Publisher.

William James. *The Principles of Psychology*, 1890, II, pp. 365–366; 368–369. Reprinted by permission of Holt, Rinehart and Winston, Inc.

Howard Mumford Jones. "Education and World Tragedy," the first of the 1946 Rushton Lectures. From *Education and World Tragedy*, Cambridge, Massachusetts, 1946, pp. 3–7; 17–20; 27–28; 34–35. Reprinted by permission of Harvard University Press and Howard Mumford Jones. Copyright 1946 by the President and Fellows of Harvard College.

W. T. Jones. *The Romantic Syndrome*, 1961, pp. 15–16; 20–36. Reprinted by permission of the author and Martinus Nijhoff, Publishers of The Hague. Copyright 1961 by Martinus Nijhoff, The Hague, Netherlands.

Arthur Kallet and F. J. Schlink. *100,000,000 Guinea Pigs,* 1932, pp. 47–48. By permission of Vanguard Press, Inc.

Immanuel Kant. *Critique of Pure Reason,* trans. Norman Kemp Smith. New York: The Macmillan Company, 1929.

Arthur Koestler. *The Act of Creation.* New York: The Macmillan Company, 1964, pp. 121–124. Copyright © Arthur Koestler, 1964.

Joseph Wood Krutch. "How Dead Is Liberalism?" *The Nation,* CXLIII (1936), p. 297. Reprinted by permission of *The Nation.*

Suzanne LaFollette. *Art in America.* New York: Harper and Brothers, 1929, p. 106.

Ring Lardner. "The Golden Honeymoon." From *The Golden Honeymoon.* New York, 1926. By permission of Charles Scribner's Sons, Publishers.

Harold J. Laski. From *The Dangers of Obedience* by Harold J. Laski, pp. 112–119. Copyright 1930 by Harold J. Laski; renewed 1958 by Frida Laski. Reprinted by permission of Harper & Row, Publishers.

D. H. Lawrence. *Apocalypse,* 1932, pp. 73–82. All rights reserved (Copyright 1931 by The Estate of D. H. Lawrence). Reprinted by permission of The Viking Press, Inc.

Leslie Lipson. From *The Democratic Civilization* by Leslie Lipson, pp. 589–594. Copyright © 1964 by Oxford University Press, Inc. Reprinted by permission.

Chester R. Longwell, Adolph Knopf, and Richard F. Flint. *Geology,* 1939, p. 12. By permission of John Wiley & Sons, Inc.

R. M. MacIver. *Leviathan and the People,* 1939, pp. 12–13. Reprinted by permission of Louisiana State University Press.

Alexander Meiklejohn. Reprinted from *What Does America Mean?* by Alexander Meiklejohn, pp. 20–31. By permission of W. W. Norton & Company, Inc. Copyright 1935 by W. W. Norton & Company, Inc. Copyright renewed 1963 by Donald Meiklejohn.

George Meredith. *An Essay on Comedy.* New York: Charles Scribner's Sons, 1897, pp. 82–84.

Truman Jesse Moon and Paul Blakeslee Mann. *Biology for Beginners.* New York: Henry Holt and Company, 1921, p. 3.

Douglas Moore. *Listening to Music.* New York: W. W. Norton & Company, Inc., 1937, p. 39.

Edgar Ansel Mowrer. *The American World.* London: Faber and Gwyer, 1928, pp. 79–81. Reprinted by permission of Faber and Faber, Ltd., Publishers.

H. H. Newman, ed. *The Nature of the World and of Man:* Julius Stieglitz, "The Nature of Chemical Processes," p. 143; H. H. Newman,

"The Nature and Origin of Life," pp. 189–191; W. C. Allee, "Evolution of the Invertebrates," p. 275; Fay-Cooper Cole, "The Coming of Man," p. 365; H. H. Newman, "Causes of Adaptation," pp. 406–408; Elliot R. Downing, "Human Inheritance," pp. 438–439. Reprinted from *The Nature of the World and of Man*, edited by H. H. Newman, by permission of The University of Chicago Press. Copyright 1926 by The University of Chicago Press.

Oxford English Dictionary: definition (9) of the word *crystal*. By permission of The Clarendon Press, Oxford.

Henry Bamford Parkes. Reprinted from *The American Experience*, pp. 4–11, by Henry Bamford Parkes, by permission of Alfred A. Knopf, Inc. Copyright, 1947, 1955, 1959 by Henry Bamford Parkes.

Charles John Pieper, Wilbur L. Beauchamp, and Orlin D. Frank. *Everyday Problems in Biology*. Chicago: Scott, Foresman and Company, 1932, pp. 420–422. Copyright © 1932 by Scott, Foresman and Company. Reprinted by permission.

V. S. Pritchett. Reprinted from *The Spanish Temper*, pp. 50–53; 64–69, by V. S. Pritchett, by permission of Alfred A. Knopf, Inc. Copyright, 1954, by V. S. Pritchett.

Herbert Read. *To Hell with Culture*. New York: Schocken Books, 1963, pp. 171–177. Copyright © 1963 by Herbert Read. Reprinted by permission of Schocken Books, Inc.

Julia Ellen Rogers. *The Tree Book*. New York: Doubleday, Doran and Company, ed. 1931, pp. 9–10.

Francisco Romero. "Man and Culture," in *Ideological Differences and World Order*, edited by F. S. C. Northrop, 1949, pp. 403–406. By permission of Yale University Press.

Richard Rovere. "The Importance of George Orwell." © 1956 by Richard Rovere. Reprinted from his volume *The American Establishment and Other Reports, Opinions and Speculations* by permission of Harcourt, Brace & World, Inc.

William G. Roylance. "How Big Should the Farm Be?" *The New Republic* CI (1939), pp. 137–138.

Rollin D. Salisbury. *Physiography*, 1907, 1931, pp. 412–413. Reprinted by permission of Holt, Rinehart and Winston, Inc.

George Santayana. "Emerson," *Little Essays*, edited by Logan Pearsall Smith. New York: Charles Scribner's Sons, 1924, pp. 199–203. Reprinted by permission of Daniel Cory, Esq.

Ferdinand S. Schevill. *A History of Europe*, 1938, pp. 221 and 428; 1951, p. 238. Reprinted by permission of Harcourt, Brace & World, Inc.

Preface

The material in this book was brought together with the conviction that thinking and writing are inseparable and deeply personal. Indeed, to know what a man thinks and how he says it can reveal much about him. Thus, the habits the student develops in grasping and holding ideas and in expressing them are of primary importance. If an individual is to emerge mature and intelligent from his college years, much of his work should be directed toward the formation of sound habits of thinking and writing. The text of this volume offers a study of substance and method—twenty-six essays or models of prose in Part I, and ten chapters on specific ways of developing ideas in Part II.

Each essay in Part I represents the serious reflection of a recognized and respected twentieth-century writer on a subject of unfailing interest to anyone wishing to become broadly educated in the humanities—in literature, painting, music, history and civilization, and social, scientific, and philosophical thought. Neither omnibus coverage of all human issues and ailments nor accents on controversy are here undertaken. A writer of the highest quality has written his piece; let it stand alone before a young writer. The young writer will find a careful study of it excitingly instructive if he is intent on reading analytically and critically and expressing himself clearly. He will find some of the older writer's personality in the essay and he in turn will reflect some of his own in what he thinks and says about the essay.

All the models are short enough to invite concentrated, thorough study, and all should prompt effective discussion during class. Several are cross-disciplinary in emphasis; others, largely informative; still others, deliberately opinionated and critical. The only classification of the models has been their arrangement by advancing degree of difficulty.

Each essay is followed by questions for study that encourage close, analytical reading for both substance and method. An emphasis on summarizing sentences and outlining should give the student command over the essay as a whole—its ideas and its structure. Other questions encourage the enlargement of vocabulary, inquiry into the origins and multiple meanings of words, and precision in the use of words. Subjects for original papers stemming from the essays are frequently suggested.

The essays or models of Part I are followed in Part II by analyses of various methods of presenting and developing ideas. Each chapter consists of a detailed study of one method—

Ideas: Sentences and Paragraphs
Illustration
Analogy
Analysis
Comparison and Contrast
Classification
Definition
Cause
Proof

Specific ground rules for the use of each method are amply illustrated with samples of both good and bad usage, showing effective applications as well as pitfalls to be avoided. Most important are the examples from the types of writing the student encounters daily and therefore must learn to read intelligently and critically: from textbooks and periodicals. Practice exercises appear not only at ends of chapters, but also at appropriate places in the text following discussions of particularly important points.

The two parts of the book are separate, and either can be used as desired. The models in Part I can be read simply as essays for study, and the discussion in Part II is in no way dependent on Part I. But if the essays are integrated with a study of the methods (see list of Correlations, pp. xvii–xix), each essay can complement the text as a finished example of the various methods by which the student can express and develop his own thoughts.

Contents

PART II   ON DEVELOPING IDEAS

Correlations Between Models and Ways of Developing Ideas

Carl Becker *The Last Three Centuries*
Leslie Lipson *The Criticism of Democracy*

CAUSE

Rachel Carson *Water and the Chains of Life*
Morris Ginsberg *Causes of Modern Wars*
Edmund Wilson *Arthur Rimbaud*
Howard Mumford Jones *Education and World Tragedy*
Alfred Cobban *Government and Higher Education*
Herbert Read *Civilization and a Sense of Quality*

PROOF

Rachel Carson *Water and the Chains of Life*
Alexander Meiklejohn *Spirit: Ancient and Modern*
Alfred Cobban *Government and Higher Education*
Carl Becker *The Last Three Centuries*
Leslie Lipson *The Criticism of Democracy*

List of Illustrations

Introduction

When he stops to reflect on the *how's* and *why's* of what he is doing, the student who goes to college to get an education today soon discovers that the word *education* may be jargon, without precise meaning. He realizes that he himself has to define it. He himself has to learn the meaning it will have for him. For the word, in common usage, may signify any of the varied or contradictory purposes and pursuits that those who use it without defining it intend it to mean. And they may have buried that intention in the shadowy and echoing recesses of their own awareness. The alert and inquiring student must ask himself: "What kind of education am I here to get; and what difference will my getting it make in my life? Can I tell a really educated person when I see one?"

The student lives in a tendentious age. Today, he hears much talk and, indeed, sees many manifestations both of technological change in the external world and of ideological conflicts on economic and political issues in the world of human affairs. He cannot detach himself from them. No sensible person expects him to; he lives in his age.

The chances are great, however, that he will miss getting a full and meaningful education if he permits the tidal waves of depersonalized technological and ideological movements to sweep him wildly from anchorage in his own developing personality. The student will concern himself, of course, with questions of science, technology, and society; but if he is to achieve fullness and richness of personality, judgment, and vision, he will show no less concern for man's more directly personal and expressive disciplines: art,

literature, religion, and philosophy. He will discover that his
education is within him and that all disciplines are but reflections
of man's enduring interests in himself and in the world.

The student's education centers in how much of the world and
of life he sees and in the interpretations and values he himself
places on what he sees. To be a genuinely educated person is to see
and understand the wide ranges in perspectives and choices that
give life its fullest meaning. If he is to educate himself, the student
must seek confrontation and command of these ranges, no matter
whether he makes the effort prior to or concurrently with training
in some area of specialized study or skill. Confront and command
he must, if his life is to be personally full and rich and socially
constructive and useful.

The genuinely educated person has attained maturity and
competence in the perspectives, choices, and decisions that affect
him both privately and publicly. Defined as a personal ability to
choose perceptively and wisely in one's confrontations of experience and to make those choices effectively known and shared,
intelligence is, therefore, the governing faculty the serious student
seeks. His intelligence is reflected in his command of facts, ideas,
and language; it is inescapably a major part of his personality.

Although not intended to do so, Walt Whitman's lines in "By
Blue Ontario's Shore" suggest a full meaning for the word *education:*

> It is to walk rapidly through civilizations, governments, theories,
> Through poems, pageants, shows, to form individuals.

How rapidly the student may walk through human achievements
from the past in order to shape his own intelligence and his own
individuality is determined in great measure by his command over
sensation, feeling, intuition, fact, idea, and language. His ability to
think and to express himself affects his speed, for, as the creative
agent in his encounter with experience, he himself must determine
how fast or how slowly he moves—and not the speed alone but also
the outcome of the encounters.

The student, as a person, stands amid the flow of all experiences,
both the experiences inside him, within his own awareness, and
those external to him, in the world of objects. Any experience may

be a proper subject for inquiry or reflection. Thinking and writing about it become at once a means for the discovery or fuller understanding of both oneself and the world, because thinking about experience and expressing one's thoughts are as natural to man and as capable of development and refinement as the movement of the body in dance or in sports. Thinking and writing are inseparable processes within the privacy of the student's consciousness. What is written may, therefore, be very much a part of one's own inner being, private and personal; but once it has readers, it has also become public. In thinking and in writing, the individual and society meet to confront life's intricacies, trivial or profound. The student's skill in thinking and writing, consequently, is no small factor in the development not only of his private interests but also of his public responsibilities.

Thinking is the questioning and selective process that enables the thinker to isolate from the total flow of his experiences order and design for his own interests and purposes. That order and design is his own creation. And writing is the preservation of that creation in language: privately, to record it for one's own account of oneself; publicly, to communicate it to interested readers.

As one improves one's skill in the dance or in sports by an apprenticeship of observation and practice, so in thinking and in writing. The student's continuing development of his ability to shape his experiences into thoughts and to express himself in language greatly increases when he understands and appreciates all that is happening in the work of intelligent, skillful, and widely recognized writers.

The models for study that follow in Part I of this book provide occasions for students, as apprentices, to observe twenty-five writers structuring and communicating meanings of importance to both them and their readers. How much of oneself may remain in one's ideas and statements, even when a rigidly impersonal objectivity is sought, becomes evident in W. T. Jones's formulation "axes of bias." Photographs accompany the essays by W. T. Jones, Heinrich Zimmer, V. S. Pritchett, and Aldous Huxley for two reasons: first, to emphasize the close tie between the specific and concrete in both perception and expression—the keenness of vision, with both outer and inner eye (D. H. Lawrence's essay on sense-consciousness

is pertinent here); and second, to stress the importance of selectivi-
ty, choice, and judgments of feelings and values in all forms of
artistic expression, in writing, as well as in architecture, sculpture,
and painting.

The significance of fact in any causal analysis of phenomena or
events becomes clear in the essays by Rachel Carson, Morris Ginsberg, and Howard Mumford Jones. That both feeling and intuition are of no less significance to writers than facts becomes at once
evident in the pieces by Aldous Huxley, "Music at Night," and
Alexander Meiklejohn, "Spirit: Ancient and Modern." The vast
reaches and details of history are brought into focus by Henry
Bamford Parkes in his contrast of characteristic European and
American ways and views of life, by Carl Becker's analysis of dominant forces at play during the last three hundred years, and by
Francisco Romero's analysis and contrast of Oriental and Occidental attitudes.

Established writers' interpretations and evaluations of other
writers also supply models: George Santayana on Emerson, E. M.
Forster on Sinclair Lewis, Edmund Wilson on Rimbaud, Isaiah
Berlin on Tolstoy, and Richard Rovere on George Orwell. And
the student, in his apprenticeship, may observe synthesizing interpretations and evaluations, rich in both concrete details and specific ideas, in V. S. Pritchett's "The Escorial"; Georges Duhamel
on American football in "The Modern Temple"; and Leslie
Lipson in "The Criticism of Democracy."

In these and other models the student may observe writers
isolating and dislodging meaning from the flow of experience and
shaping that meaning in hard, clear prose. But beyond models, for
the student's development of his thinking and writing, lie methods. Established principles and procedures in the amplification of
ideas expedite communication. In Part II of this book, consequently, nine methods commonly used in organizing and expressing
thought are examined, with illustrative details. A cross-index
following the Table of Contents suggests correlations between the
two parts of the book.

In the final chapter, all the methods of amplification are to be
observed at work in a single piece, Alfred North Whitehead's
"The Aims of Education." This essay is intended not only to

illustrate the development of ideas but also to return the student
to the questions raised in the first paragraph of this introduction,
"What kind of education am I here to get; and what difference will
my getting it make in my life? Can I tell a really educated person
when I see one?"

WARREN TAYLOR

Part I

Models

OF PLEASANT THINGS

Francis Hackett

When I was a child we lived on the border of the town, and the road that passed our windows went in two ways. One branch ran up the hill under the old city gateway and out through the mean city "lanes." The other branch turned round our corner and ran into the countryside. Day and night many carts lumbered by our windows, in plain hearing. In the day-time I took no pleasure in them, but when I awoke at night and the thick silence was broken by the noise of a single deliberate cart it filled me with vague enchantment. I still feel this enchantment. The steady effort of the wheels, their rattle as they passed over the uneven road, their crunching deliberateness, gives me a sense of acute pleasure. That pleasure is at its highest when a solitary lantern swings underneath the wagon. In the old days the load might be coal, with the colliery-man sitting hunched on the driver's seat, a battered silhouette. Or the load might be from the brewery, making a start at dawn. Or it might be a load of singing harvest-women, hired in the market square by the sweet light of the morning. But not the wagon or the sight of the wagoner pleases me, so much as that honest, steady, homely sound coming through the vacancy of the night. I like it, I find it friendly and companionable, and I hope to like it till I die.

The city sounds improve with distance. Sometimes, in lazy summer evenings, I like the faint rumble, the growing roar, the receding rumble of the elevated, with the suggestion of its open windows and its passengers relaxed and indolent after the exhausting day. Always I like the moaning sounds from the river craft, carried so softly into the town. But New York sounds and Chicago

1

sounds are usually discords. I hate bells—the sharp spinsterish telephone bell, the lugubrious church bell, the clangorous railway bell. Well, perhaps not the sleigh bell or the dinner bell.

I like the element of water. An imagist should write of the waters of Lake Michigan which circle around Mackinac Island: the word crystal is the hackneyed word for those pure lucent depths. When the sun shines on the bottom, every pebble is seen in a radiance of which the jewel is a happy memory. In Maine lakes and along the coast of Maine one has the same visual delight in water as clear as crystal, and on the coast of Ireland I have seen the Atlantic Ocean slumber in a glowing amethyst or thunder in a wall of emerald. On the southern shore of Long Island, who has not seen the sumptuous ultramarine, with a surf as snowy as apple-blossom? After shrill and meager New York, the color of that Atlantic is drenching.

The dancing harbor of New York is a beauty that never fades, but I hate the New York skyline except at night. In the day-time those punctured walls seem imbecile to me. They look out on the river with such a lidless, such an inhuman, stare. Nothing of man clings to them. They are barren as the rocks, empty as the deserted vaults of cliff-dwellers. A little wisp of white steam may suggest humanity, but not these bleak cliffs themselves. At night, however, they become human. They look out on the black moving river with marigold eyes. And Madison Square at nightfall has the same, or even a more aetherial, radiance. From the hurried streets the walls of light seem like a deluge of fairy splendor. This is always a gay transformation to the eye of the citydweller, who is forever oppressed by the ugliness around him.

Flowers are pleasant things to most people. I like flowers, but seldom cut flowers. The gathering of wild flowers seems to me unnecessarily wanton, and is it not hateful to see people coming home with dejected branches of dogwood or broken autumn festoons or apple-blossoms already rusting in the train? I like flowers best in the fullness of the meadow or the solitude of a forsaken garden. Few things are so pleasant as to find oneself all alone in a garden that has, so to speak, drifted out to sea. The life that creeps up between its broken flagstones, the life that trails so impudently across the path, the life that spawns in the forgotten pond—this has a fascination beyond the hand of gardeners. Once I shared a neglected garden with an ancient turtle, ourselves the only living things within sight or sound. When the turtle wearied of sunning himself he shuffled to the artificial pond, and there he lazily paddled through waters laced down with scum. It was pleasant to see him, a not too clean turtle in waters not too clean. Perhaps if the family had been home the gardener would have scoured him.

Yet order is pleasant. If I were a millionaire—which I thank heaven I am not, nor scarcely a millionth part of one—I should take pleasure in the silent orderliness that shadowed me through my home. Those invisible hands that patted out the pillows and shined the shoes and picked up everything, even the Sunday newspapers—those I should enjoy. I should enjoy especially the guardian angel who hid from me the casualties of the laundry and put the surviving laundry away. In heaven there is no laundry, or mending of laundry. For the millionaire the laundry is sent and the laundry is sorted away. Blessed be the name of the millionaire; I envy him little else. Except, perhaps, his linen sheets.

The greatest of all platitudes is the platitude that life is in the striving. Is this altogether true? I think not. Not for those menial offices so necessary to our decent existence, so little decent in their victims or themselves. But one does remember certain striving that brought with it almost instant happiness, like the reward of the child out coasting or the boy who has made good in a hard, grinding game. It is pleasant to think of one's first delicious surrender to fatigue after a long day's haul on a hot road. That surrender, in all one's joints, with all one's driven will, is the ecstasy that even the Puritan allowed himself. It is the nectar of the pioneer. In our civilization we take it away from the workers, as we take the honey from the bees—but I wish to think of things pleasant, not of our civilization. Fatigue of this golden kind is unlike the leaden fatigue of compulsion or of routine. It is the tang that means a man is young. If one gets it from games, even golf, I think it is pleasant. It is the great charm that Englishmen possess and understand.

These are ordinary pleasant things, not the pleasant things of the poet. They barely leave the hall of pleasant things. A true poet, I imagine, is one who captures in the swift net of his imagination the wild pleasantnesses and delights that to me would be flying presences quickly lost to view. But every man must bag what he can in his own net, whether he be rational or poetic. For myself, I have to use my imagination to keep from being snared by too many publicists and professors and persons of political intent. These are invaluable servants of humanity, admirable masters of our mundane institutions. But they fill the mind with *-ations*. They pave the meadows with concrete; they lose the free swing of pleasant things.

Questions for Study

1. Define *mean,* in the phrase "mean city 'lanes' "; *platitudes; decent,* in "decent existence, so little decent"; *compulsion,* in "fatigue of compulsion"; *invaluable; mundane;* and *-ations.*
2. Why *spinsterish* and *lugubrious* bells?
3. How would the substitution of *lazy* for *indolent* affect the meaning of the passage in paragraph 2?
4. Might the words *fascination* or *delight* be substituted effectively for *enchantment* in paragraph 1? Why?
5. What phrase or sentence summarizes the content of the essay?
6. Was the essay written to show that "life is in the striving"? Do any points in the essay run counter to that belief?
7. What is the antecedent of *these* at the beginning of the last paragraph?
8. What was Hackett's motive in writing this essay? What response, presumably, did he want it to evoke in the reader?
9. How many kinds of pleasant things does Hackett here "bag...in his own net"? How many unpleasant? Why does he name both kinds?
10. Why does paragraph 6 begin with *yet?* What images or ideas link paragraphs 1 and 2, 2 and 3, 3 and 4, 4 and 5, 7 and 8?
11. What kinds of flowers grew in the neglected garden which Hackett once shared with the turtle?
12. What is the main point in paragraph 5: "I like flowers" or "I like finding myself all alone in a garden that has drifted out to sea"?
13. What difference in descriptive method appears in these two statements from paragraph 3:

a. "the Atlantic Ocean slumber in a glowing amethyst"
b. "the sumptuous ultramarine, with a surf as snowy as apple-blossom?"
Which of the two methods appears here:
a. "The sea is feline. It licks your feet—its huge flanks purr very pleasant for you; but it will crack your bones and eat you, for all that, and wipe the crimson foam from its jaws as if nothing had happened."—Oliver W. Holmes, *The Autocrat of the Breakfast Table,* 1858
b. "They look out on the river with such a lidless, such an inhuman, stare."

14. State in literal terms the meaning of the metaphor: "They pave the meadows with concrete."

15. A reviewer described Hackett's essays in this remark: "The personal reactions—keen, by turn amusing and subtle, always fluent—of a shrewd observer..." (*The Booklist,* 17:244).
Which of the two following statements is keener?
a. "a solitary lantern swings underneath the wagon."
b. "the walls of light seem like a deluge of fairy splendor."
Which is the more subtle?
a. "I have to use my imagination to keep from being snared by too many publicists and professors and persons of political intent."
b. "If one gets it from games, even golf, I think it is pleasant."
Which is more fluent?
a. "Not for those menial offices so necessary to our decent existence, so little decent in their victims or themselves."
b. "I like it, I find it friendly and companionable, and I hope to like it till I die."
Which shows more shrewdness of observation:
a. "every pebble is seen in a radiance of which the jewel is a happy memory."
b. "A little wisp of white steam may suggest humanity, but not these bleak cliffs themselves."
Cite other details from this essay which show keenness, subtlety, fluency, and shrewdness of observation. Which is the more dominant in the essay: sensuous details or Hackett's personal reaction to those details?

16. What details in the essay stand out most vividly now in your memory?

17. Describe in not more than two or three sentences a sense impression that you either like or hate.

THE PRINTING PRESS

Arthur Koestler

At the dawn of the fifteenth century printing was no longer a novelty in Europe. Printing from wooden blocks on vellum, silk, and cloth apparently started in the twelfth century, and printing on paper was widely practised in the second half of the fourteenth. The blocks were engraved in relief with pictures or text or both, then thoroughly wetted with a brown distemper-like substance; a sheet of damp paper was laid on the block and the back of the paper was rubbed with a so-called *frotton*—a dabber or burnisher —until an impression of the carved relief was transferred to it. Each sheet could be printed on only one side by this method, but the blank backs of the sheets could be pasted together and then gathered into quires and bound in the same manner as manuscript-books. These 'block books' or *xylographs* circulated already in considerable numbers during Gutenberg's youth.

He was born in 1398 at Mainz and was really called Gensfleisch, meaning gooseflesh, but preferred to adopt the name of his mother's birthplace. The story of his life is obscure, highlighted by a succession of lawsuits against money-lenders and other printers; his claim to priority is the subject of a century-old controversy. But there exists a series of letters to a correspondent [in *Histoire de l'-Invention de l' Imprimerie par les Monuments,* ed. Höfer, Paris, 1840], Frère Cordelier, which has an authentic ring and gives a graphic description of the manner in which Gutenberg arrived at his invention. Whether others, such as Costa of Haarlem, made the same invention at the same time or before Gutenberg is, from our point of view, irrelevant.

Oddly enough, the starting point of Gutenberg's invention was not the block-books—he does not seem to have been acquainted with them—but playing-cards. In his first letter to Cordelier he wrote:

For a month my head has been working; a Minerva, fully armed, must issue from my brain. . . . You have seen, as I have, playing-cards and pictures of saints. . . . These cards and pictures are engraved on small pieces of wood, and below the pictures there are words and entire lines also engraved. . . . A thick ink is applied to the engraving; and upon this a leaf of paper, slightly damp, is placed; then this wood, this ink, this paper is rubbed and rubbed until the back of the paper is polished. This paper is then taken off and you see on it the picture just as if the design had been traced upon it, and the words as if they had been written; the ink applied to the engraving has become attached to the paper, attracted by its softness and by its moisture. . . .

Well, what has been done for a few words, for a few lines, I must succeed in doing for large pages of writing, for large leaves covered entirely on both sides, for whole books, for the first of all books, the Bible. . . .

How? It is useless to think of engraving on pieces of wood the whole thirteen hundred pages. . . .

What am I to do? I do not know: but I know what I want to do: I wish to manifold the Bible, I wish to have the copies ready for the pilgrimage to Aix la Chapelle.

Here, then, we have matrix or skill No. I: the printing from wood-blocks by means of rubbing.

In the letters which follow we see him desperately searching for a simpler method to replace the laborious carving of letters in wood:

Every coin begins with a punch. The punch is a little rod of steel, one end of which is engraved with the shape of one letter, several letters, all the signs which are seen in relief on a coin. The punch is moistened and driven into a piece of steel, which becomes the 'hollow' or 'stamp'. It is into these coin-stamps, moistened in their turn, that are placed the little discs of gold, to be converted into coins, by a powerful blow.

This is the first intimation of the method of type-casting. It leads Gutenberg, by way of analogy, to the *seal:* 'When you apply to the vellum or paper the seal of your community, everything has been said, everything is done, everything is there. Do you not see that you can repeat as many times as necessary the seal covered with signs and characters?'

Yet all this is insufficient. He may cast letters in the form of coins, or seals, instead of engraving the wood, yet they will never make a clear print by the clumsy rubbing method; so long as his search remains confined to this one and only traditional method of making an 'imprint', the problem remains blocked. To solve it, an entirely different kind of skill must be brought in. He tries this and that; he thinks of everything under the sun: it is the period of incubation. When the favourable opportunity at last offers itself he is ready for it:

I took part in the wine harvest. I watched the wine flowing, and going back from the effect to the cause, I studied the power of this press which nothing can resist. . . .

At this moment it occurs to him that the same, steady pressure might be applied by a seal or coin—preferably of lead, which is easy to cast—on paper, and that owing to the pressure, the lead would leave a trace on the paper—Eureka!

. . . A simple substitution which is a ray of light. . . . To work then! God has revealed to me the secret that I demanded of Him. . . . I have had a large quantity of lead brought to my house and that is the pen with which I shall write.

'The ray of light' was the bisociation of wine-press and seal—which, added together, become the letter-press. The wine-press has been lifted out of its context, the mushy pulp, the flowing red liquid, the jolly revelry—as Sultan's branch was wrenched out of the context of the tree—and connected with the stamping of vellum with a seal. From now onward these separate skills, which previously had been as different as the butcher's, the baker's, and the candlestick-maker's, will appear integrated in a single, complex matrix:

One must strike, cast, make a form like the seal of your community; a mould such as that used for casting your pewter cups; letters in relief like those on your coins, and the punch for producing them like your foot when it multiplies its print. There is the Bible!

Questions for Study

1. Koestler defines the "bisociative pattern of the creative synthesis" as "the sudden interlocking of two previously unrelated skills or matrices of thought." What two previously unrelated skills did Gutenberg interlock when he invented printing with movable types?
2. What is Gutenberg's own statement of his problem?
3. What analogies appear in Gutenberg's thinking as it is here reported?
4. What, in thinking, is "the period of incubation"?
5. When is creative thought completed?
6. How is the topic, the creative synthesis, here developed?

THE MODERN TEMPLE

Georges Duhamel

From far, far away, through the trumpeting of the autumn wind, through the raucous outcry and wrathful expostulations of ten thousand automobiles quarreling for precedence, you could distinguish the murmur of the stadium, its clamors and its storms.

It was a dirty, cluttered, disorderly sort of place, on the edge of the town. There in a great shapeless patch of ground was the stadium that the crowd held like a captured fortress. It was not the Coliseum, or the proud amphitheater of El Djem in its thirsty plain. It belonged to that sort of architecture which is cynically frank about its utilitarian purpose; an enormous, and, you would say, a fragile shell of concrete, open to the sky, and hidden under a thick, swarming layer of human flesh.

We had passed through the turnstile, for the god of the place exacts a pretty heavy obolus. We had made our way along corridors and up stairways, and had finally come into the open air.

The greatest multitude that I have ever seen was assembled there, ranked and disciplined by a ritual that was almost religious. In comparison with it, what are the crowds of the theater or of the concert, of the political rally, or even of the church—or, better still, even of the cinema? Indeed, I had found one of the temples of modern America.

What high, ennobling thought had gathered there so huge an assemblage? What passions had distorted all those faces, and strained all those throats with cheering; what hopes, what hatreds? For a moment I closed my eyes that I might feel, as if deep within me, that mighty crowd, that I might better perceive its sighs, its bursts of joy or rage; not that I might let myself be intoxicated, but rather that I might be carried away, swept off my feet, perhaps rocked by this wave of humanity. Then I emerged from it.

Scattered over a grassy field checkered with white lines, twenty-two men were playing football. As well as I could judge from where I was, they were young men. Their heads were protected with padded helmets and their shins with something like the Roman greave. On their jerseys were large labels, each bearing a number.

The game was not radiant, gay, airy; rather it was grim, savage, and self-contained. Twenty-two men were on the field, in two opposing rows. For an appreciable time they remained motionless in strange postures. They seemed to watch one another like dogs pointing. Then the ball was thrown. There followed a struggle—very short, very confused, and indescribably brutal. There was nothing in it to suggest the grace of a dance, or of a Greek statue. It had no elegance, no imagination, above all, no beauty, unless it were that repellent beauty you may find at times in a display of savagery. And suddenly a whistle blew, the pack was immobile, tense, and watching its prey again before another tussle.

That is what you see in the field. But for me, the impenitent outsider, the show was not what was happening in the field. It was on the stands with the crowd. How many of them were there? Forty, fifty thousand persons, or perhaps more; I cannot say. The university of the city had challenged the university of a neighboring state. Each of the two tribes, brought face to face, had hoisted its oriflamme. The girl students were on the left, the boys were on the right. The common herd filled the gigantic shell. The plebeian crowd, without distinction and without authority, was there, and knew that it was there, only as ballast, as padding, as the odd change that made up the bill. In it you could recognize and count five hundred times the same masculine hat—gray with a black ribbon—and a thousand times the same feminine hat—the same blue, the same shape, the same trimming—and in fact all the stock articles forced on them by the local shopkeepers. In short, here was the mob in all its colorless horror.

The aristocratic element in such an assembly is, today, the students, with their colors, their glee clubs, their bands with gro-

tesque instruments, their songs, and the organized cheering that
the two tribes use to incite the men on the field. Each group has its
captain, its cheerleader. That is an enviable distinction. The
happy incumbent is provided with a megaphone, like a ballyhoo
man at a fair. For the benefit of the crowd, he comments on all the
phases of the match, announces the scores, or the penalties, lets
loose, or moderates, the enthusiasm, and by his witticisms and his
gestures stimulates the reflexes of the public.

At the game I attended, the powdered and rouged girl students
sat in line on the cement steps of the stadium, like parrakeets on a
perch. From their bosoms, still as immature as apples in July, they
sent forth shrill penetrating cries that seemed to have a tonic
influence on the nerves of the competitors. The leader of these
young girls was decidedly pretty. She bore, they told me, one of the
most honorable names in the country. With a megaphone in her
hand, and with her skirts flying in the wind, she screamed,
flounced about, gave play to leg and haunch, and performed a
suggestive and furious *dance du ventre*, like the dances of the
prostitutes in the Mediterranean ports. From time to time she
reassembled her aviary, and encouraged it to a fresh outburst of
shrill screaming.

I do not know this game of football, famous though it is
throughout the world. What those madmen were doing down
there in the field seemed to me not in the least to warrant all that
indecent vociferation. The greater part of the public knew scarcely
more than I of what was going on, did not see clearly, and did not
understand. Sometimes, the birds took flight at the wrong moment
and made mistakes, hooted when they should have applauded,
approved when they should have protested. Many chattered;
others yawned. Then the glee clubs let themselves go, and with
their shrill piping covered the noisy chatter of the spectators. Next,
the young men, stressing each syllable, shouted in unison the
distinctive cheer, the 'slogan' of the tribe. And meanwhile the
sturdy fellows on the gridiron continued like furious ants hotly to
dispute the big leathern egg.

What did they all want? What did those thousands of men and
women come for? Was it really to watch the dangerous struggle
between two clans of students that all that crowd rushed there,

paid money, sat patiently, and stamped its feet on the cement in the chill of the late afternoon?

Did you not come, O crowd, rather to get drunk on yourselves, on your own voice, on your own noise; to feel yourselves numerous and full of strength, to be charged with one another's emanations, and to taste the mysterious pleasures of the herd, the hive, and the ant-hill?

And, after all, what did that sport amount to in which twenty-two stout fellows struggled breathlessly, while forty thousand persons sat immobile, caught cold, smoked cigarettes, and exercised nothing except their vocal cords? To be sure, they reminded me of the men who are referred to in France as enthusiastic, or distinguished, sportsmen because twice a week they go to see horses gallop, and thereby lose some hundreds of francs, with the complicity of the public authorities. I am not one of those crotchety scholars who never use their muscles, who are either lazy or timid, and whom all physical effort bores and depresses. I have traveled over most of Europe with a knapsack on my back. Like every sensible man, I can swim, ride a bicycle, drive a car, use a racket, and even an oar. For years I have made the floor of a *salle d'armes* echo with my endeavors to give a city man's body some honest fatigue. I fully intend that if circumstances permit, my three sons shall be quick, supple, and robust. No, I do not despise physical exercise; I love it, I recommend it, and I often yearn for it from the depth of a too studious retirement. But I admit that this comedy of sport with which the youth of the world is befooled and fascinated seems to me more than a little idiotic.

In proportion as sport goes hand-in-hand with hygiene and morals, it becomes a personal, modest affair, or even a game of easy-going companions, an occasion of friendly rivalry, and especially a pleasure—in the sense that the word bore before it took on its modern meaning—and an amusement, a matter of gayety and recreation. At the hands of ingenious exploiters, sport has become the most profitable of spectacles. And as a necessary corollary, it has become the most astonishing school of vanity. The joyously acquired habit of performing the least important acts of a game before a crowd of on-lookers has bred in a youth poorly protected against wild extravagances, all the faults that only yesterday were attrib-

uted to the most conceited of second-rate actors. A very odd shift
has occurred in popular interest. What light opera tenor, what
fashionable or notorious novelist, what master of political oratory,
can boast today of being so famous, so flattered, and so caricatured
as the gentlemen of the ring, of the stadium, and of the track. I
am not speaking of the great athletes, those who do some particular
feat exceptionally well, those who invent something new, those
who have elements of inspiration, who create a new manner or
leave a tradition, and those who show themselves great by patience,
by courage, by grace, or by imagination. No, I am speaking of those
worthy lads who keep goal decently, who can run a hundred yards
well enough, or who can pedal a bicycle for a long time—and who
can no longer open a newspaper without hunting for their picture, and the account of their Sunday exploits. I speak of those
fine fellows who from babyhood have been in love with strength,
suppleness, skillful play, the graceful and difficult feat, and who
little by little have been spoiled by pride, led to engage in absurd
competitions, delivered over to the worst of publics, that of the
circus, made drunken with a crude and treacherous glory that soon
becomes more tyrannical than alcohol. I speak of all those boys
who are truly called 'amateurs,' because they love something, and
whom we soon see transformed into vain and greedy professionals,
men whom the least loss of popularity sours and upsets, and who
cease to love their pleasure when it becomes their livelihood.

The ambition, doubtless noble in itself, to shine in the first
rank, pushes a great many young men to exact from their body
efforts for which it is not fit. For many of them, sport is no longer
an amusement that harmonizes with their capacity: it is harassing
labor, a pernicious overexertion that exhausts the organs and
warps the will. Too quickly specialized, the athlete does not develop in happy equilibrium. He shows the stigmata, the deformities,
and the uglinesses that mark all professional excess.

When competitions lose their gracious character of pure play,
they become poisoned either with considerations of gain or with
national hatreds. They become brutal and dangerous; assaults
rather than recreations.

The young men who take from their leisure, or from their
working hours, the time to cultivate one of the exacting sports that

are nursed by business men with their apparatus of publicity, run the risk of compromising a substantial career for the sake of a brilliant illusion. What saint, obliged to choose between an obscure employment in some trade, and the hope of some day becoming a football captain, would keep his serenity? Who would not drop the unattractive substance for the delightful shadow?

QUESTIONS FOR STUDY

1. What words in the opening sentence set an emotional tone?
2. Define *obolus, greave, impenitent, oriflamme,* and *plebeian.* What tone does the use of these words create?
3. Do the details which the writer selects in describing the game strengthen his evaluation of it? Explain.
4. Why *impenitent* in the phrase "the impenitent outsider?" Why plebeian in "the plebeian crowd?"
5. Where are images from herd, hive, and ant-hill woven into this piece?
6. Why *"comedy* of sport" (paragraph 14)?
7. What are the writer's basic objections to football as it is played in the United States?
8. In the last paragraph what is the meaning of "brilliant illusion"?
9. In a short, carefully organized paper, with ample concrete details, state your opinion of a sport or of one kind of popular entertainment.

WATER AND CHAINS OF LIFE

Rachel Carson

Water must be thought of in terms of the chains of life it supports—from the small-as-dust green cells of the drifting plant plankton, through the minute water fleas to the fishes that strain plankton from the water and are in turn eaten by other fishes or by birds, mink, raccoons—in an endless cyclic transfer of materials from life to life. We know that the necessary minerals in the water are so passed from link to link of the food chains. Can we suppose that poisons we introduce into water will not also enter into these cycles of nature?

The answer is to be found in the amazing history of Clear Lake, California. Clear Lake lies in mountainous country some 90 miles north of San Francisco and has long been popular with anglers. The name is inappropriate, for actually it is a rather turbid lake because of the soft black ooze that covers its shallow bottom. Unfortunately for the fishermen and the resort dwellers on its shores, its waters have provided an ideal habitat for a small gnat, *Chaoborus astictopus*. Although closely related to mosquitoes, the gnat is not a bloodsucker and probably does not feed at all as an adult. However, human beings who shared its habitat found it annoying because of its sheer numbers. Efforts were made to control it but they were largely fruitless until, in the late 1940's, the chlorinated hydrocarbon insecticides offered new weapons. The chemical chosen for a fresh attack was DDD, a close relative of DDT but apparently offering fewer threats to fish life.

The new control measures undertaken in 1949 were carefully planned and few people would have supposed any harm could result. The lake was surveyed, its volume determined, and the insecticide applied in such great dilution that for every part of chemical there would be 70 million parts of water. Control of the gnats was at first good, but by 1954 the treatment had to be repeated, this time at the rate of 1 part of insecticide in 50 million parts of water. The destruction of the gnats was thought to be virtually complete.

The following winter months brought the first intimation that other life was affected: the western grebes on the lake began to die, and soon more than a hundred of them were reported dead. At Clear Lake the western grebe is a breeding bird and also a winter visitant, attracted by the abundant fish of the lake. It is a bird of spectacular appearance and beguiling habits, building its floating nests in shallow lakes of western United States and Canada. It is called the "swan grebe" with reason, for it glides with scarcely a ripple across the lake surface, the body riding low, white neck and shining black head held high. The newly hatched chick is clothed in soft gray down; in only a few hours it takes to the water and rides on the back of the father or mother, nestled under the parental wing coverts.

Following a third assault on the ever-resilient gnat population, in 1957, more grebes died. As had been true in 1954, no evidence of infectious disease could be discovered on examination of the dead birds. But when someone thought to analyze the fatty tissues of the grebes, they were found to be loaded with DDD in the extraordinary concentration of 1600 parts per million.

The maximum concentration applied to the water was 1/50 part per million. How could the chemical have built up to such prodigious levels in the grebes? These birds, of course, are fish eaters. When the fish of Clear Lake also were analyzed the picture began to take form—the poison being picked up by the smallest organisms, concentrated and passed on to the larger predators. Plankton organisms were found to contain about 5 parts per million of the insecticide (about 25 times the maximum concentration ever reached in the water itself) ; plant-eating fishes had built up accumulations ranging from 40 to 300 parts per million; carnivorous species had stored the most of all. One, a brown bullhead, had the astounding concentration of 2500 parts per million. It was a house-that-Jack-built sequence, in which the large carnivores had eaten the smaller carnivores, that had eaten the herbivores, that had eaten the plankton, that had absorbed the poison from the water.

Even more extraordinary discoveries were made later. No trace of DDD could be found in the water shortly after the last application of the chemical. But the poison had not really left the lake; it had merely gone into the fabric of the life the lake supports. Twenty-three months after the chemical treatment had ceased, the plankton still contained as much as 5.3 parts per million. In that interval of nearly two years, successive crops of plankton had flowered and faded away, but the poison, although no longer present in the water, had somehow passed from generation to generation. And it lived on in the animal life of the lake as well. All fish, birds, and frogs examined a year after the chemical applications had ceased still contained DDD. The amount found in the flesh always exceeded by many times the original concentration in the water. Among these living carriers were fish that had hatched nine months after the last DDD application, grebes, and California gulls that had built up concentrations of more than 2000 parts per million. Meanwhile, the nesting colonies of the grebes dwindled—from more than 1000 pairs before the first insecticide treatment to about 30 pairs in 1960. And even the thirty seem to have nested in vain, for no young grebes have been observed on the lake since the last DDD application.

This whole chain of poisoning, then, seems to rest on a base of minute plants which must have been the original concentrators. But what of the opposite end of the food chain—the human being who, in probable ignorance of all this sequence of events, has rigged his fishing tackle, caught a string of fish from the waters of Clear Lake, and taken them home to fry for his supper? What could a heavy dose of DDD, or perhaps repeated doses, do to him?

Although the California Department of Public Health professed to see no hazard, nevertheless in 1959 it required that the use of DDD in the lake be stopped. In view of the scientific evidence of the vast biological potency of this chemical, the action seems a minimum safety measure. The physiological effect of DDD is probably unique among insecticides, for it destroys part of the adrenal gland—the cells of the outer layer known as the adrenal cortex, which secretes the hormone cortin. This destructive effect, known since 1948, was at first believed to be confined to dogs, because it was not revealed in such experimental animals as monkeys, rats, or rabbits. It seemed suggestive, however, that DDD produced in dogs a condition very similar to that occurring in man in the presence of Addison's disease. Recent medical research has revealed that DDD does strongly suppress the function of the human adrenal cortex. Its cell-destroying capacity is now clinically utilized in the treatment of a rare type of cancer which develops in the adrenal gland.

The Clear Lake situation brings up a question that the public needs to face: Is it wise or desirable to use substances with such strong effect on physiological processes for the control of insects, especially when the control measures involve introducing the chemical directly into a body of water? The fact that the insecticide was applied in very low concentrations is meaningless, as its explosive progress through the natural food chain in the lake demonstrates. Yet Clear Lake is typical of a large and growing number of situations where solution of an obvious and often trivial problem creates a far more serious but conveniently less tangible one. Here the problem was resolved in favor of those annoyed by gnats, and at the expense of an unstated, and probably not even clearly understood, risk to all who took food or water from the lake.

It is an extraordinary fact that the deliberate introduction of poisons into a reservoir is becoming a fairly common practice. The purpose is usually to promote recreational uses, even though the water must then be treated at some expense to make it fit for its intended use as drinking water. When sportsmen of an area want to "improve" fishing in a reservoir, they prevail on authorities to dump quantities of poison into it to kill the undesired fish, which are then replaced with hatchery fish more suited to the sportsmen's taste. The procedure has a strange, Alice-in-Wonderland quality. The reservoir was created as a public water supply, yet the community, probably unconsulted about the sportsmen's project, is forced either to drink water containing poisonous residues or to pay out tax money for treatment of the water to remove the poisons— treatments that are by no means foolproof.

As ground and surface waters are contaminated with pesticides and other chemicals, there is danger that not only poisonous but also cancer-producing substances are being introduced into public water supplies. Dr. W. C. Hueper of the National Cancer Institute has warned that "the danger of cancer hazards from the consumption of contaminated drinking water will grow considerably within the foreseeable future." And indeed a study made in Holland in the early 1950's provides support for the view that polluted waterways may carry a cancer hazard. Cities receiving their drinking water from rivers had a higher death rate from cancer than did those whose water came from sources presumably less susceptible to pollution such as wells. Arsenic, the environmental substance most clearly established as causing cancer in man, is involved in two historic cases in which polluted water supplies caused widespread occurrence of cancer. In one case the arsenic came from the slag heaps of mining operations, in the other from rock with a high natural content of arsenic. These conditions may easily be duplicated as a result of heavy applications of arsenical insecticides. The soil in such areas becomes poisoned. Rains then carry part of the arsenic into streams, rivers, and reservoirs, as well as into the vast subterranean seas of groundwater.

QUESTIONS FOR STUDY

1. To what consequences does the contamination, by poisons, of ground and surface waters lead?
2. How is the cyclic transfer of materials from life to life illustrated?
3. Trace the interweaving of narrative and descriptive details with statistical facts.
4. What effect does the writer achieve by describing the western grebe?
5. Outline the essay.
6. What methods of developing the main points are used?
7. What "house-that-Jack-built" sequence became evident at Clear Lake?
8. What do the key syllables in *turbid* (Sanskrit: *tur*) and *predators* (Latin: *pre* and *hed,* in *prehendere*) mean? Consult W. W. Skeat, *An Etymological Dictionary of the English Language.*

The Escorial

THE ESCORIAL

V. S. Pritchett

Thirty-one miles north-west of Madrid on a platform of the mountains three thousand feet up, stands the royal monastery, palace, and burial house of the Escorial, the supreme architectural symbol of Castilian ambition and its tragedy. The eye comes suddenly upon the monotonous prison-like façade, and the first pleasure which the sight of gravity and order give us, as they break the wild mountain scene and the grim wilderness of pine and boulder, quickly gives way to awe and melancholy before the cold statement of military power and the governing will. Built from the bluish granite of these mountains, so that it seems to be a projection of them, and coldly slated, the sombre establishment is one of the bare overstatements of the Castilian genius. Its thousands of windows, stare and blink in the mountain light.

The Spanish genius is for excess, for excesses of austerity as well as excesses of sensual decoration. The soldier architect of the Escorial and the King, half-monk, half-bureaucrat, who built it, disdained the sunlight of the Renaissance and built their tomb in the shadow of the wild mountains and in the hard military spirit of the Counter-Reform. The Escorial is the mausoleum of Spanish power.

So it must seem to the foreign traveller, and most have been chilled if they have not been appalled by the sombreness of the place. To go there in the bitter Castilian winter when the snow is piled in the streets of the village and lids every one of the innumerable sills of the palace with white; to go when the wind bites, and when the halls, refectories, and chapels are dark, takes the heart out of the European. In the summer, when one gets out of the heat of the plain, the pine woods are cool and gracious and the palace is then grateful to the eye. The village has indeed become a week-end resort.

Yet calm, repose, or even that resignation which is exquisite to those who have learned obedience, are not suggested by the outward aspect of the Escorial. Outwardly it displays the platitudes of great power, and inside, though there are dignity and beautiful things, we are haunted by the melancholy of the founder, his morbidity, and the tragic quality of his faith and of his defeat. Here Philip II is said to have boasted that he ruled an empire from two inches of paper; here, like some bureaucrat, he tried to do all the work of the state, delegating nothing, devoid of the imagination or the gifts of his father, the Emperor—the prototype of the inadequate son who has been left an estate too large for him.

What were the estates that Philip II inherited from his father, the Emperor Charles V, who had come in with his crowds of Flemings to rule the country? There were the kingdoms of Sicily and Sardinia and Naples. There was Holland under the Spanish jackboot, brutalized by the Duke of Alba, ruled by the Inquisition. There was land in Africa and Northern Italy; and there were the Indies, which Columbus, Cortés, and Pizarro had added a century before. The largest empire on earth since the time of the Romans was the possession of the melancholy, uncertain, and mistrustful King who looked out of the windows of the Escorial and saw in his lifetime the beginnings of the Spanish disaster—the estate too great to manage, the stupendous act of will which cannot, in itself, sustain a nation for very long.

The Escorial is the oppressive monument to the first totalitarian state of Europe, for what distinguishes Spain in its short period of world power is its attempt to impose an idea upon the mind and soul of its own people and the people it conquered completely.

"He saw the deaths of almost all those whom he loved well, parents, children, wives, favourites, ministers, and servants of great importance"; Azorín quotes from Baltasar Porreño in *Una Hora de España*. "Great losses in the matter of his estates, bearing all these blows and trials with an equality of soul which astonished the world." . . .

The Escorial is a monastery, the house of the dead God who hangs on the Cross or lies on the earth beside it. The sense of martyrdom and death can hardly have been more starkly conveyed by any edifice. It is a stone statement of the end. In it is the mausoleum of the Spanish kings, a chamber for the caskets of the monarchs, a chamber for the caskets of the princes, and empty caskets awaiting those yet to die. The new king in the days of the monarchy saw his future resting-place. To the traveller, Philip II has seemed the horrifying personification of a death morbidly longed for. One sees the couch brought down to the corner from which he could gaze every day at the high altar, a shrivelled bald man with all the crimes of a great empire on his head, a man now covered with ulcers, swollen in arms and legs by gout, rotting with gangrene. Few people attended him, for few indeed could stand the stench.

"I had meant to spare you this scene," he said after he had taken the sacrament, "but I wish you to see how the monarchies of the earth end."

One walks out into the peace of the little town of the Escorial and smells the thyme and the lavender of the buzzing wilderness; one meets again the immense Spanish light. One will never be able to take that clarity for granted, for it is a material presence in itself. Light, which in the north is thought of as something relative, as an arrangement of varying degrees of shadow, a changing and filtering of colour, and which has no definition, is here positive and absolute. In the hot weather the tableland is like some lake or sea on fire; in the cold weather the light goes up higher than any light we know and transmits the sight to distances our eyes are not accustomed to. Above all, since it brings so much more of the world to our eyes, it has the effect of a tremendous accession of the sense of life. Here most earthily and most powerfully one feels oneself alive. Yet here one is confronted (and above all at the Escorial) with the Spanish preoccupation with death. No other race in Europe has this consuming preoccupation; where it has appeared in the German culture or in the addicts of the funerary urn and the skull in the English seventeenth century, it has been a passing mood. In Spanish life and art the preoccupation is continuous. *¡Viva la muerte!* was the slogan of the Falangists in the Civil War, and bloody pictures of the death of Manolete, the bullfighter, may be seen in the bars off the Puerta del Sol. The popular signs of the cult of death are as noticeable as the more sumptuous. One recalls the black-plumed horses of the ornate death coaches that move up the Castellana in the Madrid winter, the balconies and doorways hung with black cloths and sashes, the houses that are sombrely decorated for a period of mourning, not for the mere day of the funeral alone. Death, too, is a fiesta. In this cult no doubt some of the Spanish love of state and pomp and spectacle has its part. What contemporary foreigners could not but observe in the *autos de fé* was the solemnity of the occasion; the whole pomp of court and state displayed in person at the burnings. In Spanish painting and sculpture the theme of death is treated again and again by every artist. The gloom of the mortuary, the luxury of a lying-in-state, is their favourite subject. The preoccupation is common in Catholic art, but no Catholic artists in other countries have had so exclusive a passion; it appears also in non-religious painting. Goya's pictures of the terror and madness of war owe their dramatic force not only to the carnal realism, but to the sense of the life-and-death struggle, to the sense of life corroded at the height of its contest by mortal decay. In how many ways (Goya seems to have asked himself) can human beings be shown meeting their death? In Toledo, in the Church of San Tomé, we shall find the supreme expression of this emotion; in El Greco's *The Burial of Count Orgaz*.[1] It is contemporary with Philip II. The body is lowered into the grave, the grandees of Spain stand stiffly by. They are literal portraits of a ruling caste, proud, ascetic in appearance, their minds turned away from this world in a satisfied contemplation of the next; and some have seen in this picture the idea of the living death of a caste, the suggestion of a racial suicide. They will rule in the Kingdom of

[1]This famous picture was painted by El Greco in the last years of the reign of Philip II, and Cossío calls it "one of the truest pictures of the history of Spain" and of what Spanish society was like in body and in soul. The picture commemorates the death of a famous citizen, Don Gonzalo Ruya de Toledo, who was buried in 1323. He had built the Church of San Tomé in Toledo, and at his funeral the mourners at the grave were not astonished to see him carried up to heaven by Saint Stephen. The portraits are all taken from people contemporary with El Greco; the group is a gathering of neurotic gentlemen who have the air of monks. Cassío comments on "the cold and monotonous sobriety of its grey tones, its sharp spiritual note, its energetic expression of the national life."

God; we must neglect this life and hunger for death and the life to come.

Some writers have seen a mystical conjunction of voluptuousness and death in the nature of Spaniards. To Unamuno in *The Tragic Sense of Life,* the human tragedy was a passion: the sensual man of flesh and bone is born and will die, but there is planted in his mind the desire for immortality. In every moment of his life, he is living out this intense and dramatic agony. The sense of death is a continuous presence, as a fact and not as the shadow of a fear, and is therefore as intense as the sense of life. Man—for this Spanish egotist—must live out his life in absolute terms. Once more (one reflects) the preoccupation with death shows us the Spanish desire to see everything and live everything in black and white. Like Tolstoy, the Spanish egotist cries out: "What is Truth if a man dies?" But Tolstoy expected an answer; the Spaniard does not.

The foreigner need not think the strangeness of Spanish life has deceived him on this point. Menéndez Pidal directs us to the writings of Jorge Manrique, a Knight of the Order of Santiago in the fifteenth century, who describes three phases of life: the temporal life of the body, the life of fame, which is more enduring, and then eternal life, which is the crown.

"Now, these two lives after death," Menéndez Pidal says, "are as consciously felt by the Spaniard today as in the past, and so intense is his awareness that it contrasts with the attitude of neighbouring races. . . . The thought of death, which is thirst for immortality, is the profound concern of the Spanish people."

It is the individualist's thirst for a freedom that is absolute.

Questions for Study

Read the entire essay before answering these questions.
1. Why "prison-like façade"?
2. Explain "Castilian ambition" and "Castilian genius."
3. What details define the writer's idea of "Spanish power"?
4. What details throughout the essay reinforce the idea that the

Escorial is a mausoleum?

5. The writer's presentation of those details leads to a climax in what word?

6. How does the writer make that word a means of transition to the following section?

7. The dominant imagery in this piece emphasizes what contrast?

8. What sentences summarize that contrast?

9. Define the Spanish "tragic sense of life."

10. How does that sense of tragedy tie together the contrasts in the piece?

SINCLAIR LEWIS

E. M. Forster

"I would like to see Gopher Prairie," says the heroine of Mr. Sinclair Lewis's *Main Street*, and her husband promptly replies: "Trust me. Here she is. Brought some snapshots down to show you." That, in substance, is what Mr. Lewis has done himself. He has brought down some snapshots to show us and posterity. The collection is as vivid and stimulating as any writer who adopts this particular method can offer. Let us examine it; let us consider the method in general. And let us at once dismiss the notion that any fool can use a camera. Photography is a great gift, whether or no we rank it as an art. If we have not been to Gopher Prairie we cry: "So that's it!" on seeing the snap. If we have been we either cry: "How like it!" or "How perfectly disgraceful, not the least like it!" and in all three cases our vehemence shows that we are in the presence of something alive.

I have never been to Gopher Prairie, Nautilus, Zenith, or any of their big brothers and sisters, and my exclamations throughout are those of a non-American, and worthless as a comment on the facts. Nevertheless, I persist in exclaiming, for what Mr. Lewis has done for myself and thousands of others is to lodge a piece of a continent in our imagination. America, for many of us, used to mean a very large apron, covered with a pattern of lozenges, edged by a frill, and chastely suspended by a boundary tape round the ample waist of Canada. The frill, like the tape, we visualized slightly; on the New York side it puckered up into skyscrapers, on the farther side it was a blend of cinemas and cowboys, and more or less down the middle of the preposterous garment we discerned a pleat associated with the humour of Mark Twain. But the apron proper, the lozenges of pale pink and pale green—they meant nothing at all: they were only something through which railways went and dividends occasionally came from, and which had been arbitrarily spattered with familiar names, like a lunar landscape. As we murmured "Syracuse, Cairo, London even, Macon, Memphis, Rochester, Plymouth," the titles, so charged with meaning in their old settings, cancelled each other out in their new, and helped to make the apron more unreal. And then Sinclair Lewis strode along, developed his films, and stopped our havering. The lozenges lived. We saw that they were composed of mud, dust, grass, crops, shops, clubs, hotels, railway stations, churches, universities, etc., which were sufficiently like their familiar counterparts to be real, and sufficiently unlike them to be extremely exciting. We saw men and women who were not quite ourselves, but ourselves modified by new surroundings, and we heard them talk a language which we could usually, but not always, understand. We enjoyed at once the thrills of intimacy and discovery, and for that and much else we are grateful, and posterity will echo our gratitude. Whether he has "got" the Middle West, only the Middle West can say, but he has made thousands of people all over the globe alive to its existence, and anxious for further news. Ought a statue of him, camera in hand, to be erected in every little town? This, again, is a question for the Middle West.

Let us watch the camera at work:

In the flesh, Mrs. Opal Emerson Mudge fell somewhat short of a prophetic aspect. She was pony-built and plump, with the face of a haughty Pekinese, a button of a nose, and arms so short that, despite her most indignant endeavours, she could not clasp her hands in front of her as she sat on the platform waiting.

Angus Duer came by, disdainful as a greyhound, and pushing on white gloves (which are the whitest and the most superciliously white objects on earth) . . .

At the counter of the Greek Confectionery Parlour, while they [i.e., the local youths] ate dreadful messes of decayed bananas, acid cherries, whipped cream, and gelatinous ice cream, they screamed to one another: "Hey, lemme 'lone," "Quit dog-gone you, looka what you went and done, you almost spilled my glass swater," "Like hell I did," "Hey, gol darn your hide, don't you go sticking your coffin-nail in my i-scream."

She saw that his hands were not in keeping with a Hellenic face. They were thick, roughened with needle and hot iron and plough handle. Even in the shop he persisted in his finery. He wore a silk shirt, a topaz scarf, thin tan shoes.

The drain pipe was dripping, a dulcet and lively song: drippety-drip-drip-dribble; drippety-drip-drip-drip.

The method throughout is the photographic. Click, and the picture's ours. A less spontaneous or more fastidious writer would have tinkered at all of the above extracts, and ruined everything. The freshness and vigour would have gone, and nothing been put in their places. For all his knowingness about life, and commercially-travelled airs, Mr. Lewis is a novelist of the instinctive sort, he goes to his point direct. There is detachment, but not of the panoramic type: we are never lifted above the lozenges, Thomas Hardy fashion, to see the townlets seething beneath, never even given as wide a view as Arnold Bennett accords us of his Five Towns. It is rather the detachment of the close observer, of the man who stands half a dozen yards off his subject, or at any rate within easy speaking distance of it, and the absence of superiority and swank (which so pleasantly characterizes the books) is connected with this. Always in the same house or street as his characters, eating their foodstuffs, breathing their air, Mr. Lewis claims no special advantages; though frequently annoyed with them, he is never contemptuous, and though he can be ironic and even denunciatory, he has nothing of the aseptic awfulness of the seer. Neither for good nor evil is he lifted above his theme; he is neither a poet nor a preacher, but a fellow with a camera a few yards away.

Even a fellow with a camera has his favourite subjects, as we can see by looking through the Kodak-albums of our friends. One amateur prefers the family group, another bathing-scenes, another his own house taken from every possible point of view, another cows upon an alp, or kittens held upside down in the arms of a black-faced child. This tendency to choose one subject rather than another indicates the photographer's temperament. Nevertheless, his passion is for photography rather than for selection, a kitten will serve when no cows are present, and, if I interpret Mr. Lewis correctly, we must not lay too much stress on his attitude to life.

He has an attitude; he is against dullness, heartiness and intolerance, a trinity of evils must closely entwined; he mistrusts Y.M.C.A. helpfulness and rotarian idealism; while as for a positive creed (if we can accept *Martin Arrowsmith* as an unaided confession of faith) he believes in scientific research. "So many men, Martin, have been kind and helpful, so few have added to knowledge," complains the old bacteriologist. One can safely class him with writers termed "advanced," with people who prefer truth to comfort, passion to stability, prevention to cure. But the classification lets what is most vital in him escape; his attitude, though it exists, does not dwell in the depths of his being. His likes and dislikes mean less to him than the quickness of his eye, and though he tends to snapshot muscular Christians when they are attacked with cramp, he would sooner snap them amid clouds of angels than not at all. His commentary on society is constant, coherent, sincere; yet the reader's eye follows the author's eye rather than his voice, and when Main Street is quitted it is not its narrowness, but its existence that remains as a permanent possession.

His method of book-building is unaffected and appropriate. In a sense (a very faint sense) his novels are tales of unrest. He takes a character who is not quite at ease in his or her surroundings, contrives episodes that urge this way or that, and a final issue of revolt or acquiescence. In his earlier work both character and episodes are clear-cut; in his later—but let us postpone for a moment the painful problem of a photographer's old age. Carol Endicott, the heroine of his first important book, is a perfect medium, and also a living being. Her walks down Main Street are overwhelming; we see the houses, we see her against them, and when the dinginess breaks and Erik Valborg arises with his gallant clothes and poet's face, we, too, are seduced, and feel that such a world might well be lost for love. Never again is Mr. Lewis to be so poignant or to arrange his simple impressions so nearly in the order of high tragedy; "I may not have fought the good fight, but I have kept the faith" are Carol's final words, and how completely are they justified by all she has suffered and done! Babbitt follows her—of grosser clay, and a native while she was an exile, but even Babbitt sees that there is something better in life than graft and goodfellowship, though he acquiesces in them at the close. Martin Arrow-smith succeeds where Carol and Babbitt failed, because he is built strongly and prepared to sacrifice a home, but, regarded as a medi-um, he is identical with them, he can register their doubts and difficulties. And the same is true of Elmer Gantry; his heavy feet are turned to acquiescence from the first, but he, too, has moments of uneasiness, and hypocrisy; religious eroticism and superstition can be focussed through him. And so with Samuel Dodsworth in *Dodsworth*. He reacts this way and that among the main streets of Europe, and many pictures of them can be taken before he decides that they will not do.

Now, in the earlier books this method was a complete success, but with *Elmer Gantry* doubts begin; the theme is interesting, but the snapshots less remarkable. And in *Dodsworth* doubt becomes dismay. Dodsworth is a decent citizen of Zenith who retires early and goes to Europe with his wife. She is cultivated and snobby—a *rechauffée* of the second Mrs. Arrowsmith, but served upon an enormous dish. She talks, talks, flirts, patronizes, talks, and he, humble and observant, gradually realizes her inadequacies, but all the time he talks, talks, talks. The talk is rhetoric, the slang tired, the pictures blurred. The English country church, palace at Venice, restaurant at Paris, journey in an aeroplane, Bernese Oberland, back in New York, the right sort of American tourist, the wrong sort, is there a right sort, is it wrong to think there is a right sort? . . . on the story trundles, unprofitably broadminded and with unlucky thematic parallels to Henry James. The method remains, but something has died. The following quotation will show us what:

> He found that in certain French bathrooms one can have hot water without waiting for a geyser. He found that he needn't have brought two dozen tubes of his favourite (and very smelly) toothpaste from America—one actually could buy toothpaste, corn-plaster, New York Sunday papers, Bromo-Seltzer, Lucky Strikes, safety razor blades, and ice cream almost as easily in Paris as in the United States; and a man he met in Luigi's bar insisted that if one quested earnestly enough he could find B.V.D.'s.

What has happened? What has changed the Greek Confection-

ery Parlour at Gopher Prairie, where every decaying banana mat-
tered, to this spiritless general catalogue? The explanation is all
too plain: photography is a pursuit for the young. So long as a
writer has the freshness of youth on him, he can work the snapshot
method, but when it passes he has nothing to fall back upon. It is
here that he differs from the artist. The artist has the power of
retaining and digesting experiences, which, years later, he may
bring forth in a different form; to the end of life he is accompanied
by a secret store.

The artist may not be good. He may be very bad. He generally is.
And it is not to celebrate him and to decry the photographer that I
draw this distinction between them. But it does explain, I think,
why quick spontaneous writers (the kind that give me more pleasure than any) are apt, when they lose their spontaneity, to have
nothing left, and to be condemned by critics as superficial. They
are not superficial, they are merely not artistic; they are members
of a different profession, the photographic, and the historian of our
future will cease to worry over this, will pick up the earlier and
brighter volumes in which their genius is enshrined, and will find
there not only that genius, but a record of our age.

Mr. Lewis is not our sole photographer. There is always Mr.
H. G. Wells. They have just the same gift of hitting off a person or
place in a few quick words; moreover, they share the same
indifference to poetry, and pass much the same judgments on
conduct. Consequently, one might have expected that their literary careers would be similar, that the authors of *Love and Mr.
Lewisham* and *Main Street* would develop in the same way and at
the same rate. They have diverged, and for an instructive reason.
Wells is still kicking because photography was only one of his
resources. When his early freshness wore off, he could bring into
play his restless curiosity about the universe, and thus galvanize his
later novels into life. In Mr. Lewis, curiosity about the universe
has never been very strong. Only occasionally has he thought of the
past, the future, international relationships, science, labour, the
salvation or damnation of the globe. The people in the room and
the houses across the street are what really interest him, and when
the power to reproduce them sharply fails, he has nothing to do
except to reproduce them dimly. If this view of his development is

correct, the later stages of it are bound to be disappointing. However, there the early books are, done, safe, mankind's for ever; also, the longer one lives, the less important does "development" appear.

QUESTIONS FOR STUDY

1. Define *posterity, havering, trundles.*
2. What purpose does the writer set forth in the opening paragraph? Summarize it in a single infinitive phrase.
3. Why does Forster call Sinclair Lewis a gifted photographer?
4. Of what use to non-Americans is his writing?
5. Is the figure of America as an apron appropriate? Explain.
6. List the specific snapshots which the writer gives to support his interpretation of Lewis as photographer.
7. What are "commercially-travelled airs"?
8. Contrast the descriptive methods of Lewis and Hardy.
9. Analyze Lewis's attitude toward people and places.
10. With what group of writers is Lewis here classified?
11. For what reason does the writer call the novels of Lewis "tales of unrest"? How does Forster develop the idea?
12. In Forster's opinion, how does the writer as artist differ from the writer as photographer?
13. What contrast develops in the closing paragraph of the essay?
14. How does the subject matter of Lewis and Wells differ?
15. What is the writer's final judgment of Lewis's achievement?

THE HEDGEHOG AND THE FOX

Isaiah Berlin

There is a line among the fragments of the Greek poet Archilo-
chus [fl. 720–680 B.C.] which says: 'The fox knows many things,
but the hedgehog knows one big thing.' Scholars have differed
about the correct interpretation of these dark words, which may
mean no more than that the fox, for all his cunning, is defeated by
the hedgehog's one defence. But, taken figuratively, the words can
be made to yield a sense in which they mark one of the deepest
differences which divide writers and thinkers, and, it may be,
human beings in general. For there exists a great chasm between
those, on one side, who relate everything to a single central vision,
one system less or more coherent or articulate, in terms of which
they understand, think and feel—a single, universal, organizing
principle in terms of which alone all that they are and say has
significance—and, on the other side, those who pursue many ends,
often unrelated and even contradictory, connected, if at all, only in
some *de facto* way, for some psychological or physiological cause,
related by no moral or aesthetic principle; these last lead lives,
perform acts, and entertain ideas that are centrifugal rather than
centripetal, their thought is scattered or diffused, moving on many
levels, seizing upon the essence of a vast variety of experiences and
objects for what they are in themselves, without, consciously or
unconsciously, seeking to fit them into, or exclude them from, any
one unchanging, all-embracing, sometimes self-contradictory and
incomplete, at times fanatical, unitary inner vision. The first kind
of intellectual and artistic personality belongs to the hedgehogs,
the second to the foxes; and without insisting on a rigid classification, we may, without too much fear of contradiction, say

that, in this sense, Dante belongs to the first category, Shakespeare
to the second; Plato, Lucretius, Pascal, Hegel, Dostoevsky,
Nietzsche, Ibsen, Proust are, in varying degrees, hedgehogs; Herod-
otus, Aristotle, Montaigne, Erasmus, Molière, Goethe, Pushkin,
Balzac, Joyce are foxes.

   Of course, like all over-simple classifications of this type, the
dichotomy becomes, if pressed, artificial, scholastic, and ultimately
absurd. But if it is not an aid to serious criticism, neither should it
be rejected as being merely superficial or frivolous; like all distinctions which embody any degree of truth, it offers a point of view
from which to look and compare, a starting-point for genuine
investigation. Thus we have no doubt about the violence of the
contrast between Pushkin and Dostoevsky; and Dostoevsky's celebrated speech about Pushkin has, for all its eloquence and depth of
feeling, seldom been considered by any perceptive reader to cast
light on the genius of Pushkin, but rather on that of Dostoevsky
himself, precisely because it perversely represents Pushkin—an
arch-fox, the greatest in the nineteenth century—as a being similar
to Dostoevsky who is nothing if not a hedgehog; and thereby
transforms, indeed distorts, Pushkin into a dedicated prophet, a
bearer of a single, universal message which was indeed the centre
of Dostoevsky's own universe, but exceedingly remote from the
many varied provinces of Pushkin's protean genius. Indeed, it
would not be absurd to say that Russian literature is spanned by
these gigantic figures—at one pole Pushkin, at the other Dostoevsky; and that the characteristics of other Russian writers can,
by those who find it useful or enjoyable to ask that kind of question, to some degree be determined in relation to these great
opposites. To ask of Gogol', Turgenev, Chekhov, Blok how they
stand in relation to Pushkin and to Dostoevsky leads—or, at any
rate, has led—to fruitful and illuminating criticism. But when we
come to Count Lev Nikolaevich Tolstoy, and ask this of him—ask
whether he belongs to the first category or the second, whether he
is a monist or a pluralist, whether his vision is of one or of many,
whether he is of a single substance or compounded of heterogeneous elements, there is no clear or immediate answer. The question does not, somehow, seem wholly appropriate; it seems to
breed more darkness than it dispels. Yet it is not lack of informa-

tion that makes us pause: Tolstoy has told us more about himself and his views and attitudes than any other Russian, more, almost, than any other European writer; nor can his art be called obscure in any normal sense: his universe has no dark corners, his stories are luminous with the light of day; he has explained them and himself, and argued about them and the methods by which they are constructed, more articulately and with greater force and sanity and lucidity than any other writer. Is he a fox or a hedgehog? What are we to say? Why is the answer so curiously difficult to find? Does he resemble Shakespeare or Pushkin more than Dante or Dostoevsky? Or is he wholly unlike either, and is the question therefore unanswerable because it is absurd? What is the mysterious obstacle with which our inquiry seems faced?

I do not propose in this essay to formulate a reply to this question, since this would involve nothing less than a critical examination of the art and thought of Tolstoy as a whole. I shall confine myself to suggesting that the difficulty may be, at least in part, due to the fact that Tolstoy was himself not unaware of the problem, and did his best to falsify the answer. The hypothesis I wish to offer is that Tolstoy was by nature a fox, but believed in being a hedgehog; that his gifts and achievement are one thing, and his beliefs, and consequently his interpretation of his own achievement, another; and that consequently his ideals have led him, and those whom his genius for persuasion has taken in, into a systematic misinterpretation of what he and others were doing or should be doing. No one can complain that he has left his readers in any doubt as to what he thought about this topic: his views on this subject permeate all his discursive writings—diaries, recorded *obiter dicta,* autobiographical essays and stories, social and religious tracts, literary criticism, letters to private and public correspondents. . . .

The unresolved conflict between Tolstoy's belief that the attributes of personal life alone were real and his doctrine that analysis of them is insufficient to explain the course of history (i.e. the behaviour of societies) is paralleled, at a profounder and more personal level, by the conflict between, on the one hand, his own gifts both as a writer and as a man and, on the other, his ideals— that which he sometimes believed himself to be, and at all times profoundly believed in, and wished to be.

If we may recall once again our division of artists into foxes and hedgehogs: Tolstoy perceived reality in its multiplicity, as a collection of separate entities round and into which he saw with a clarity and penetration scarcely ever equalled, but he believed only in one vast, unitary whole. No author who has ever lived has shown such powers of insight into the variety of life—the differences, the contrasts, the collisions of persons and things and situations, each apprehended in its absolute uniqueness and conveyed with a degree of directness and a precision of concrete imagery to be found in no other writer. No one has ever excelled Tolstoy in expressing the specific flavour, the exact quality of a feeling—the degree of its 'oscillation,' the ebb and flow, the minute movements (which Turgenev mocked as a mere trick on his part) —the inner and outer texture and 'feel' of a look, a thought, a pang of sentiment, no less than that of the specific pattern of a situation, or an entire period, continuous segments of lives of individuals, families, communities, entire nations. The celebrated life-likeness of every object and every person in his world derives from this astonishing capacity of presenting every ingredient of it in its fullest individual essence, in all its many dimensions, as it were; never as a mere datum, however vivid, within some stream of consciousness, with blurred edges, an outline, a shadow, an impressionistic representation: nor yet calling for, and dependent on, some process of reasoning in the mind of the reader; but always as a solid object, seen simultaneously from near and far, in natural, unaltering daylight, from all possible angles of vision, set in an absolutely specific context in time and space—an event fully present to the senses or the imagination in all its facets, with every nuance sharply and firmly articulated.

Yet what he believed in was the opposite. He advocated a single embracing vision; he preached not variety but simplicity, not many levels of consciousness but reduction to some single level— in *War and Peace* to the standard of the good man, the single, spontaneous, open soul: as later to that of the peasants, or of a simple Christian ethic divorced from any complex theology or metaphysic, some simple, quasi-utilitarian criterion, whereby everything is interrelated directly, and all the items can be assessed in terms of one another by some simple measuring rod. Tolstoy's genius lies in a capacity for marvellously accurate reproduction of the irreproducible, the almost miraculous evocation of the full, untranslatable individuality of the individual, which induces in the reader an acute awareness of the presence of the object itself, and not of a mere description of it, employing for this purpose metaphors which fix the quality of a particular experience as such, and avoiding those general terms which relate it to similar instances by ignoring individual differences—'the oscillations of feeling'—in favour of what is common to them all. But then this same writer pleads for, indeed preaches with great fury, particularly in his last, religious phase, the exact opposite: the necessity of expelling everything that does not submit to some very general, very simple standard: say, what peasants like or dislike, or what the gospels declare to be good.

This violent contradiction between the data of experience from which he could not liberate himself, and which, of course, all his life he knew alone to be real, and his deeply metaphysical belief in the existence of a system to which they *must* belong, whether they appear to do so or not, this conflict between instinctive judgment and theoretical conviction—between his gifts and his opinions— mirrors the unresolved conflict between the reality of the moral life with its sense of responsibility, joys, sorrows, sense of guilt and sense of achievement—all of which is nevertheless illusion; and the laws which govern everything, although we cannot know more than a negligible portion of them—so that all scientists and historians who say that they do know them and are guided by them are lying and deceiving—but which nevertheless alone are real. Beside Tolstoy, Gogol' and Dostoevsky, whose abnormality is so often contrasted with Tolstoy's 'sanity,' are well-integrated personalities, with a coherent outlook and a single vision. Yet out of this violent conflict grew *War and Peace:* its marvellous solidity should not blind us to the deep cleavage which yawns open whenever Tolstoy remembers, or rather reminds himself—fails to forget—what he is doing, and why. . . .

. . . . Tolstoy began with a view of human life and history which contradicted all his knowledge, all his gifts, all his inclinations, and which, in consequence, he could scarcely be said to have embraced in the sense of practising it, either as a writer or as a man. From this, in his old age, he passed into a form of life in which he tried to resolve the glaring contradiction between what he believed about men and events, and what he thought he believed, or ought to believe, by behaving, in the end, as if factual questions of this kind were not the fundamental issues at all, only the trivial preoccupations of an idle, ill-conducted life, while the real questions were quite different. But it was of no use: the Muse cannot be cheated. Tolstoy was the least superficial of men: he could not swim with the tide without being drawn irresistibly beneath the surface to investigate the darker depths below; and he could not avoid seeing what he saw and doubting even that; he could close his eyes but not forget that he was doing so; his appalling, destructive, sense of what was false frustrated this final effort at self-deception as it did all the earlier ones; and he died in agony, oppressed by the burden of his intellectual infallibility and his sense of perpetual moral error, the greatest of those who can neither reconcile, nor leave unreconciled, the conflict of what there is with what there ought to be. Tolstoy's sense of reality was until the end too devastating to be compatible with any moral ideal which he was able to construct out of the fragments into which his intellect shivered the world, and he dedicated all of his vast strength of mind and will to the lifelong denial of this fact. At once insanely proud and filled with self-hatred, omniscient and doubting everything, cold and violently passionate, contemptuous and self-abasing, tormented and detached, surrounded by an adoring family, by devoted followers, by the admiration of the entire civilized world, and yet almost wholly isolated, he is the most tragic of the great writers, a desperate old man, beyond human aid, wandering self-blinded at Colonus.

QUESTIONS FOR STUDY

1. Define each of the following words: *dichotomy, scholastic, protean, monist, pluralist, discursive, heterogeneous, entities, datum,* and *nuance.*

2. Berlin makes the hedgehog stand, figuratively, for one group of writers and thinkers; the fox, for another. Characterize each group. Why are the hedgehog and the fox appropriately chosen images to contrast those characteristics?

3. What characteristics of each of the writers and thinkers Berlin mentions justify his classifying them as he does?

4. What is Berlin's own appraisal of the classification?

5. How does Dostoevsky's criticism of Pushkin transform him into a different person?

6. Dostoevsky is properly classified as a hedgehog; Pushkin, a fox; but Tolstoy—which? Explain Berlin's answer.

7. List contrasts (or opposites, such as variety and simplicity) in Berlin's analysis of Tolstoy's views and attitudes.

8. Does the description of Tolstoy's genius place him as hedgehog or fox? The source, then, of his conflict?

9. From your own knowledge or experience, illustrate the conflict between "instinctive judgment and theoretical conviction," or, put more simply, the conflict between gifts or talents and opinions.

10. What were the final manifestations in Tolstoy of the conflict between what is and what ought to be?

11. Why does the writer compare Tolstoy to Oedipus?

Shiva Natarāja

THE DANCE OF SHIVA

Heinrich Zimmer

Shiva, the lord of the lingam, the consort of [the goddess] Shakti-Devī, also is Natarāja, "king of dancers."

Dancing is an ancient form of magic. The dancer becomes amplified into a being endowed with supra-normal powers. His personality is transformed. Like yoga, the dance induces trance, ecstasy, the experience of the divine, the realization of one's own secret nature, and, finally, mergence into the divine essence. In India consequently the dance has flourished side by side with the terrific austerities of the meditation grove—fasting, breathing exercises, absolute introversion. To work magic, to put enchantments upon others, one has first to put enchantments on oneself. And this is effected as well by the dance as by prayer, fasting and meditation. Shiva, therefore, the arch-yogī of the gods, is necessarily also the master of the dance.

Pantomimic dance is intended to transmute the dancer into whatever demon, god, or earthly existence he impersonates. The war dance, for example, converts the men who execute it into warriors; it arouses their warlike virtues and turns them into fearless heroes. And the hunting-party dance-pantomime, which magically anticipates and assures the successes of the hunting party, makes of the participants unerring huntsmen. To summon from dormancy the nature-powers attendant upon fruitfulness, dancers mimic the gods of vegetation, sexuality, and rain.

The dance is an act of creation. It brings about a new situation and summons into the dancer a new and higher personality. It has a cosmogonic function, in that it arouses dormant energies which then may shape the world. On a universal scale, Shiva is the cosmic dancer; in his "dancing manifestation" *(nritya-mūrti)* he embodies in himself and simultaneously gives manifestation to eternal energy. The forces gathered and projected in his frantic, ever-enduring gyration, are the powers of the evolution, maintenance, and dissolution of the world. Nature and all its creatures are the effects of his eternal dance.

Shiva-Natarāja is represented in a beautiful series of South Indian bronzes dating from the tenth and twelfth centuries A.D. The details of these figures are to be read, according to the Hindu tradition, in terms of a complex pictorial allegory. The upper right hand, it will be observed, carries a little drum, shaped like an hour-glass, for the beating of the rhythm. This connotes sound, the vehicle of speech, the conveyer of revelation, tradition, incantation, magic, and divine truth. Furthermore, sound is associated in India with ether, the first of the five elements. Ether is the primary and most subtly pervasive manifestation of the divine substance. Out of it unfold, in the evolution of the universe, all the other elements, air, fire, water, and earth. Together, therefore, sound and ether signify the first, truth-pregnant moment of creation, the productive energy of the absolute, in its pristine, cosmogenetic strength.

The opposite hand, the upper left, with a half-moon posture of the fingers, bears on its palm a tongue of flame. Fire is the element of the destruction of the world. At the close of the Kali Yuga, [when man and his world are at their worst], fire will annihilate the body of creation, to be itself then quenched by the ocean of the void. Here, then, in the balance of the hands, is illustrated a counterpoise of creation and destruction in the play of the cosmic dance. As a ruthlessness of opposites, the transcendental shows through the mask of the enigmatic master: ceaselessness of production against an insatiate appetite of extermination, sound against flame. And the field of the terrible interplay is the dancing ground of the universe, brilliant and horrific with the dance of the god.

The "fear not" gesture *(abhaya mudrā)*, bestowing protection and peace, is displayed by the second right hand, while the remaining left lifted across the chest, points downward to the uplifted left foot. This foot signifies release and is the refuge and salvation of the devotee. It is to be worshiped for the attainment of union with the absolute. The hand pointing to it is held in a pose imitative of the outstretched trunk or "hand" of the elephant *(gaja-hasta-mudrā)*, reminding us of Ganesha, Shiva's son, the remover of obstacles.

The divinity is represented as dancing on the prostrate body of a dwarfish demon. This is Apasmāra Purusha, "the man or demon *(purusa)* called forgetfulness, or heedlessness" *(aspasmāra)*. It is symbolical of life's blindness, man's ignorance. Conquest of this demon lies in the attainment of true wisdom. Therein is release from the bondages of the world.

A ring of flames and light *(prabhā-mandala)* issues from and encompasses the god. This is said to signify the vital processes of the universe and its creatures, nature's dance as moved by the dancing god within. Simultaneously it is said to signify the energy of wisdom, the transcendental light of the knowledge of truth, dancing forth from the personification of the all. Still another allegorical meaning assigned to the halo of flames is that of the holy syllable AUM or OM. This mystical utterance ("aye," "amen") stemming from the sacred language of Vedic praise and incantation, is understood as an expression and affirmation of the totality of creation. A—is the state of waking consciousness, together with its world of gross experience. U—is the state of dreaming consciousness, together with its experience of the subtle shapes of dream. M—is the state of dreamless sleep, the natural condition of quiescent, undifferentiated consciousness, wherein every experience is dissolved into a blissful non-experience, a mass of potential consciousness. The silence following the pronunciation of the three, A, U, and M, is the ultimate unmanifest, wherein perfected supra-consciousness totally reflects and merges with the pure, transcendental essence of divine reality—Brahman is experienced as Atman, the self. AUM, therefore, together with its surrounding silence, is a sound-symbol of the whole of consciousness-existence, and at the same time its willing affirmation.

The origin of the ring of flames is, probably, in the destructive aspect of Shiva-Rudra [his manifestation as destroyer; *rudra* means howler or roarer]; but Shiva's destruction is finally identical with release.

Shiva as the cosmic dancer is the embodiment and manifestation of eternal energy in its "five activities" *(pañca-hriya)*: (1) creation *(sristi)*, the pouring forth or unfolding, (2) maintenance, *(sthiti)*, the duration, (3) destruction *(samhāra)*, the taking back of reabsorption, (4) concealment *(tiro-bhāva)*, the veiling of true being behind the masks and garbs of apparitions, aloofness, display of Māyā, and (5) favor *(anugraha)* acceptance of the devotee, acknowledgment of the pious endeavor of the yogī, bestowal of peace through a revelatory manifestation. The first three and the last two are matched, as groups of co-operative mutual antagonisms; the god displays them all. And he displays them, not only simultaneously, but in sequence. They are symbolized in the positions of his hands and his feet—the upper three hands being respectively, "creation," "maintenance" and "destruction"; the foot planted in forgetfulness is "concealment," and the foot uplifted, "favor"; the "elephant hand" indicates the linkage of the three to the two, and promises peace to the soul that experiences the relationship. All five activities are made manifest, simultaneously with the pulse of every moment, and in sequence through the changes of time.

. . . As Natarāja, king of dancers, his gestures, wild and full of grace, precipitate the cosmic illusion; his flying arms and legs and the swaying of his torso produce—indeed, they are—the continuous creation-destruction of the universe, death exactly balancing birth, annihilation the end of every coming-forth. The choreography is the whirligig of time. History and its ruins, the explosion of suns, are flashes from the tireless swinging sequence of the gestures. In the medieval bronze figurines, not merely a single phase or movement, but the entirety of this cosmic dance is miraculously rendered. The cyclic rhythm, flowing on and on in the unstayable, irreversible round of the Mahāyugas, or great eons, is marked by the beating and stamping of the master's heels. But the face remains, meanwhile, in sovereign calm.

Steeped in quietude, the enigmatic mask resides above the whirl of the four resilient arms, cares nothing for the superb legs as they beat out the tempo of the world ages. Aloof, in sovereign silence, the mask of the god's eternal essence remains unaffected by the tremendous display of his own energy, the world and its progress, the flow and the changes of time. This head, this face, this mask, abides in transcendental isolation, as a spectator unconcerned. Its smile, bent inward, filled with the bliss of self-absorption, subtly refutes, with a scarcely hidden irony, the meaningful gestures of the feet and hands. A tension exists between the marvel of the dance and the serene tranquility of this expressively inexpressive countenance, the tension, that is to say, of eternity and time, the paradox—the silent, mutual confutation—of the absolute and the phenomenal, the self-immortal and the perishable psyche, Brahman-Atman and Māyā. For neither one is the entirety it would seem, whereas, on the other hand, the two, invisible and visible, are quintessentially the same. Man with all the fibers of his native personality clings to the duality, in anxiety and delight; nevertheless, actually and finally, there is no duality. Ignorance, passion, egotism, disintegrate the experience of the highest essence (crystal clear and beyond time and change, free from suffering and bondage) into the universal illusion of a world of individual existences. This world, for all its fluidity, however, *is*—and it never will end.

The bronze, dancing figures of southern India insist on the paradoxical identity of the personality, carried away by experiences and emotions, with the quiet, all-knowing self. In these figures the contrast of the blissfully dreaming, silent countenance with the passionate agility of the limbs represents, to those ready to understand, the absolute and its Māyā as a single trans-dual form. We and the divine are one and the same, precisely as the vitality of these swaying limbs is one and the same with the utter unconcern of the dancer who flings them into play.

But there is even more to be said about the god of the dance, as represented in the South Indian bronzes.

Shiva's tresses are long and matted, partly streaming, partly stacked in a kind of pyramid. This is the hair of the model yogī of the gods. Supra-normal life-energy, amounting to the power of magic, resides in such a wilderness of hair untouched by the scissors. Similarly, the celebrated strength of Samson, who with naked hands tore asunder the jaws of a lion and shook down the roof of a pagan temple, resided in his uncut hair.—Furthermore, if we may judge by those magicians, genii, and demons of wondrous spells, who work their incantations on the concert stage, the sorcery of music demands a virtuoso lion-maned. No question either, but that much of womanly charm, the sensual appeal of the eternal feminine, *das Ewig-Weibliche, le charm éternel,* is in the fragrance, the flow and luster of beautiful hair. On the other hand, anyone renouncing the generative forces of the vegetable-animal realm, revolting against the procreative principle of life, sex, earth, and nature, to enter upon the spiritual path of absolute asceticism, has first to be shaved. He must simulate the sterility of an old man whose hairs have fallen and who no longer constitutes a link in the chain of generation. He must coldly sacrifice the foliage of the head. . . .

The ascetic hostility to the hair of the human organism is so excessive in the extreme sect of the Jains that they will tolerate no hair whatsoever on the person of an ordained holy-man. Part of their ritual of ordination consists in a thorough weeding out of every single hair growing on the head and body. Here the idea of the tonsure is, so to say, carried to its limit; and correspondingly, the Jaina idea of life-renunciation is drastic beyond bounds. In accordance with their archaic, fundamentalist, and thoroughgoing doctrine, the Jains so schedule their disciplines of bodily mortification, that in old age these ideally culminate in death from an absolute fast. As with the hair so with the last vegetable-requirement of the flesh: the revolt against the principle of life is pressed to the end.

But though the spiritual and even earthly rewards of the ascetic attitude are high, Shiva does not shave or shear his hair, "so sweet with many a pleasant scent." Refusing to take advantage of the symbolical and potent devices of self-curtailment and deprivation, the divine dancer and arch-yogī is forever the unshorn male. The long tresses of his matted hair, usually piled up in a kind of pyramid, loosen during the triumphant, violent frenzy of his untiring dance, and expand, so as to form two wings, to right and to left, a kind of halo—broadcasting, as it were, on their magic waves, the exuberance and sanctity of vegetative life, the charm, the appeal, the solemn command, of the generative forces of procreating Māyā.

Shiva's tresses are commonly represented as filled with little symbolic figures. Those that appear most frequently in his images are the following: (1) a diminutive figure of the goddess Ganges, whom he received on his head when she descended from heaven to earth, (2) flowers of the datura (from which an intoxicating drink is prepared), (3) a skull, symbolic of death—the common crown-jewel or forehead-ornament both of Shiva and of the lesser divinities who constitute part of his retinue and realm (the *memento mori* of the lord of destruction), and (4) a crescent moon, called in Sanskrit *sisu*, "the quickly swelling one, the eagerly growing one," but also, "the newborn babe," which from week to week, clinging to the mother breasts, quickly grows, like the crescent moon.

Shiva is the personification of the absolute, particularly in its dissolution of the universe. He is the embodiment of super-death. He is called Yamāntaka, "the ender of the tamer, he who conquers and exterminates Yama, the god of death, the tamer." Shiva is Mahā-Kāla, great time, eternity, the swallower of time, swallower of all the ages and cycles of ages. He reduces the phenomenal rhythm and whirlpool to nought, dissolving all things, all beings, all divinities, in the crystal pure, motionless ocean of eternity— from the viewpoint of which nothing whatsoever fundamentally comes to pass. But then again as Shishu, the babe, the crescent moon, Shiva is a sheer delight and the most auspicious thing to see, a promise of life and life-strength, gentle but irresistible. The moon, Shishu, is regarded as the cup of the fluid of life immortal, quickening the vegetable realm and whatsoever grows in the sub-lunar sphere, quickening also the immortals on high, so that they may be fit to perform their beneficent cosmic duties. Shiva as Shishu is this cup, this moon.

Shiva is apparently, thus, two opposite things: archetypal ascetic, and archetypal dancer. On the one hand he is total tranquillity— inward calm absorbed in itself, absorbed in the void of the absolute, where all distinctions merge and dissolve, and all tensions are at rest. But on the other hand he is total activity—life's energy, frantic, aimless, and playful. These aspects are the dual manifestations of an absolutely non-dual, ultimate reality. The two are represented side by side in the sanctuaries of Shiva: the reality known to the enlightened ones, to the Buddhas, knowers, and yogīs, side by side with that enjoyed by the children of Māyā, who are still under the spell of the world.

It is extremely interesting to observe that among the few remains surviving to us from the Indus civilization—coming down through a corridor of some six thousand years as echoes of a religiosity antedating the arrival of the Vedic Aryans, an antique religiosity, old as the pyramids of the Nile—the two aspects of the god are already revealed. . . .

. . . . The probability is that we have here [in remaining artifacts] a precious symptom of a continuity of tradition over a period of no less than four thousand years. The episode of the invading Aryans, their establishment of their Olympic pantheon of orthodox Vedic divinities, the gradual resurgence of the earlier Indian forms, and their definitive reassumption of power with the triumph of Vishnu, Shiva, and the Goddess over Indra, Brahmā, and their entourage, we must regard as nothing more than a titanic *incident,* which came to pass in the timeless theater of the Indian soul.

The life strength of symbols and symbolic figures is inexhaustible, especially when carried forward by a highly conservative, traditional civilization, such as that of India. Our conventional histories of the development of mankind, the growth of human institutions, and the progress of religion, virtues, and ideals, not infrequently misrepresent the situation totally, by describing as new departures the returns to power of archaic, archetypal forms. Very often, as during the greater part of the history of India, evidence for the continuity may be woefully lacking; the materials in which the forms were rendered—wood, largely, and clay— were perishable, and have simply disappeared. Oral traditions, furthermore, and the fleeting features of popular festivals, are practically impossible to reconstruct in detail for the centuries and centuries behind us. We have only the living present, and certain accidentally preserved relics—but the latter largely from the upper, official circles of society: how are we to dogmatize for mankind as a whole? Every so often tangible evidence appears—such as that which has suddenly been opened to us with the excavations of Harappa, Mohenjo-Daro and Chanhu-Daro—staggering the imagination with its demonstration of continuities never suspected by the historians. And we are forced to a more humble estimate of all our judgments of the past. We can never be certain but that in one or another of the innumerable undocumented centuries of human history, in one or another of the unexcavated hilltops of the world, there may not lurk some simple fact, which, if disclosed, would refute our least-questioned belief. Evidences of the existence in the third millennium B.C. of forms that were by our scholars thought to have evolved only very much later cannot, and must not, be lightly shrugged away. The vista of *duration* that they open, while it does not precisely refute everything that we are wont to say about progress and change, at least supplies to our accepted view a counter-view—suggesting spiritual continuities persisting through immense reaches of time.

QUESTIONS FOR STUDY

1. Define *magic, transform, yoga, trance, introversion, dormancy, cosmogonic, cosmic, transcendental, absolute, spiritual, trans-dual, Jains, phenomenon, archetypal.* Relate the meaning of each word to the context in which it occurs.
2. What is the topic of the second paragraph?
3. Some dances are for courage and victory in war; others, for the skill to obtain abundant game in hunting. Why the dance of Shiva?
4. What specific meanings are visualized in the bronze representations of the figure of Shiva? List abstractions and the concrete representation of each.
5. In paragraph 5, is use of the phrase "a complex pictorial allegory" justified? Why?
6. What are the significances of the ring of flames?
7. What is "the cosmic illusion"?
8. Where does Zimmer shift from static analysis, detail after detail, to the movement of descriptive synthesis?
9. Where does Zimmer suggest consciousness and feelings within the dancing figure one sees?
10. What contrast on the symbolic significances of hair is here developed? Why? List contrasted meanings and values.
11. What conceptions of time are symbolized in the bronze figure?
12. What opposites, generally felt to be contradictory—dual and non-dual—are here reconciled? How?
13. How old are the earliest artifacts which symbolize these aspects? What great historic events have they survived?

14. What continuity in archetypal forms does Zimmer see?
15. This analysis and interpretation of a work of art leads to what generalization about the cosmos?

MUSIC AT NIGHT

Aldous Huxley

Moonless, this June night is all the more alive with stars. Its
darkness is perfumed with faint gusts from the blossoming lime
trees, with the smell of wetted earth and the invisible greenness of
the vines. There is silence; but a silence that breathes with the soft
breathing of the sea and, in the thin shrill noise of a cricket, insistently, incessantly harps on the fact of its own deep perfection. Far
away, the passage of a train is like a long caress, moving gently,
with an inexorable gentleness, across the warm living body of the
night.

Music, you say; it would be a good night for music. But I have
music here in a box, shut up, like one of those bottled djinns in
the *Arabian Nights,* and ready at a touch to break out of its prison.
I make the necessary mechanical magic, and suddenly, by some
miraculously appropriate coincidence (for I had selected the
record in the dark, without knowing what music the machine
would play), suddenly the introduction to the *Benedictus* in
Beethoven's *Missa Solemnis* begins to trace its patterns on the
moonless sky.

The *Benedictus.* Blessed and blessing, this music is in some sort
the equivalent of the night, of the deep and living darkness, into
which, now in a single jet, now in a fine interweaving of melodies,
now in pulsing and almost solid clots of harmonious sound, it
pours itself, stanchlessly pours itself, like time, like the rising and
falling, falling trajectories of a life. It is the equivalent of the night
in another mode of being, as an essence is the equivalent of the
flowers, from which it is distilled.

There is, at least there sometimes seems to be, a certain blessedness lying at the heart of things, a mysterious blessedness, of whose existence occasional accidents or providences (for me, this night is one of them) make us obscurely, or it may be intensely, but always fleetingly, alas, always only for a few brief moments aware. In the *Benedictus* Beethoven gives expression to this awareness of blessedness. His music is the equivalent of this Mediterranean night, or rather of the blessedness at the heart of the night, of the blessedness as it would be if it could be sifted clear of irrelevance and accident, refined and separated out into its quintessential purity.

'*Benedictus, benedictus . . .*' One after another the voices take up the theme propounded by the orchestra and lovingly meditated through a long and exquisite solo (for the blessedness reveals itself most often to the solitary spirit) by a single violin. '*Benedictus, benedictus . . .*' And then, suddenly, the music dies; the flying djinn has been rebottled. With a stupid insect-like insistence, a steel point rasps and rasps the silence.

At school, when they taught us what was technically known as English, they used to tell us to 'express in our own words' some passage from whatever play of Shakespeare was at the moment being rammed, with all its annotations—particularly the annotations—down our reluctant throats. So there we would sit, a row of inky urchins, laboriously translating 'now silken dalliance in the wardrobe lies' into 'now smart silk clothes lie in the wardrobe,' or 'To be or not to be' into 'I wonder whether I ought to commit suicide or not.' When we had finished, we would hand in our papers, and the presiding pedagogue would give us marks, more or less, according to the accuracy with which 'our own words' had 'expressed' the meaning of the Bard.

He ought, of course, to have given us naught all round with a hundred lines to himself for ever having set us the silly exercise. Nobody's 'own words,' except those of Shakespeare himself, can possibly 'express' what Shakespeare meant. The substance of a work of art is inseparable from its form; its truth and its beauty are two and yet, mysteriously, one. The verbal expression of even a metaphysic or a system of ethics is very nearly as much of a work of art as a love poem. The philosophy of Plato expressed in the 'own words' of Jowett is not the philosophy of Plato; nor in the 'own words' of, say Billy Sunday, is the teaching of St. Paul St. Paul's teaching.

'Our own words' are inadequate even to express the meaning of other words; how much more inadequate, when it is a matter of rendering meanings which have their original expression in terms of music or one of the visual arts! What, for example, does music 'say'? You can buy at almost any concert an analytical programme that will tell you exactly. Much too exactly; that is the trouble. Every analyst has his own version. Imagine Pharaoh's dream interpreted successively by Joseph, by the Egyptian soothsayers, by Freud, by Rivers, by Adler, by Jung, by Wohlgemuth: it would 'say' a great many different things. Not nearly so many, however, as the Fifth Symphony has been made to say in the verbiage of its analysts. Not nearly so many as the Virgin of the Rocks and the Sistine Madonna have no less lyrically said.

Annoyed by the verbiage and this absurd multiplicity of attributed 'meanings,' some critics have protested that music and painting signify nothing but themselves; that the only things they 'say' are things, for example, about modulations and fugues, about colour values and three-dimensional forms. That they say anything about human destiny or the universe at large is a notion which these purists dismiss as merely nonsensical.

If the purists were right, then we should have to regard painters and musicians as monsters. For it is strictly impossible to be a human being and not to have views of some kind about the universe at large, very difficult to be a human being and not to express those views, at any rate by implication. Now, it is a matter of observation that painters and musicians are *not* monsters. Therefore . . . The conclusion follows, unescapably.

It is not only in programme music and problem pictures that composers and painters express their views about the universe. The purest and most abstract artistic creations can be, in their own peculiar language, as eloquent in this respect as the most deliberately tendencious.

Compare, for example, a Virgin by Piero della Francesca with a Virgin by Tura. Two Madonnas—and the current symbolical conventions are observed by both artists. The difference, the

". . . a kind of supernatural substantiality . . ."

Piero della Francesca

Madonna della Misericordia, detail

" . . . a mysterious chaos . . ."

Cosimo Tura

Madonna and Angels Making Music

enormous difference between the two pictures is a purely pictorial difference, a difference in the forms and their arrangement, in the disposition of the lines and planes and masses. To any one in the least sensitive to the eloquence of pure form, the two Madonnas say utterly different things about the world.

Piero's composition is a welding together of smooth and beautifully balanced solidities. Everything in his universe is endowed with a kind of supernatural substantiality, is much more 'there' than any object of the actual world could possibly be. And how sublimely rational, in the noblest, the most humane acceptation of the word, how orderly philosophical is the landscape, are all the inhabitants of this world! It is the creation of a god who 'ever plays the geometer.'

What does she say, this Madonna from San Sepolcro? If I have not wholly mistranslated the eloquence of Piero's forms, she is telling us of the greatness of the human spirit, of its power to rise above circumstance and dominate fate. If you were to ask her, 'How shall I be saved?' 'By Reason,' she would probably answer. And, anticipating Milton, 'Not only, not mainly upon the Cross,' she would say, 'is Paradise regained, but in those deserts of utter solitude where man puts forth the strength of his reason to resist the Fiend.' This particular mother of Christ is probably not a Christian.

Turn now to Tura's picture. It is fashioned out of a substance that is like the living embodiment of flame—flame-flesh, alive and sensitive and suffering. His surfaces writhe away from the eye, as though shrinking, as though in pain. The lines flow intricately with something of that disquieting and, you feel, magical calligraphy, which characterizes certain Tibetan paintings. Look closely; feel your way into the picture, into the painter's thoughts and intuitions and emotions. This man was naked and at the mercy of destiny. To be able to proclaim the spirit's stoical independence, you must be able to raise your head above the flux of things; this man was sunk in it, overwhelmed. He could introduce no order into his world; it remained for him a mysterious chaos, fantastically marbled with patches, now of purest heaven, now of the most excruciating hell. A beautiful and terrifying world, is this Madonna's verdict; a world like the incarnation, the material projection, of Ophelia's madness. There are no certainties in it but suffering and occasional happiness. And as for salvation, who knows the way of salvation? There may perhaps be miracles, and there is always hope.

The limits of criticism are very quickly reached. When he has said 'in his own words' as much, or rather as little, as 'own words' can say, the critic an only refer his readers to the original work of art: let them go and see for themselves. Those who overstep the limit are either rather stupid, vain people, who love their 'own words' and imagine that they can say in them more than 'own words' are able in the nature of things to express. Or else they are intelligent people who happen to be philosophers or literary artists and who find it convenient to make the criticism of other men's work a jumping-off place for their own creativity.

What is true of painting is equally true of music. Music 'says' things about the world, but in specifically musical terms. Any attempt to reproduce these musical statements 'in our own words' is necessarily doomed to failure. We cannot isolate the truth contained in a piece of music; for it is a beauty-truth and inseparable from its partner. The best we can do is to indicate in the most general terms the nature of the musical beauty-truth under consideration and to refer curious truth-seekers to the original. Thus, the introduction to the *Benedictus* in the *Missa Solemnis* is a statement about the blessedness that is at the heart of things. But this is about as far as 'own words' will take us. If we were to start describing in our 'own words' exactly what Beethoven felt about this blessedness, how he conceived it, what he thought its nature to be, we should very soon find ourselves writing lyrical nonsense in the style of the analytical programme makers. Only music, and only Beethoven's music, and only this particular music of Beethoven, can tell us with any precision what Beethoven's conception of the blessedness at the heart of things actually was. If we want to know, we must listen—on a still June night, by preference, with the breathing of the invisible sea for background to the music and the scent of lime trees drifting through the darkness, like some exquisite soft harmony apprehended by another sense.

QUESTIONS FOR STUDY

1. What sounds and images set the tone of the first paragraph?
2. What image links the first three paragraphs?
3. Sight and sound evoke Huxley's experience of what quality?
4. What point in common do "the presiding pedagogue" and the musical analyst have?
5. On what point do critics of music disagree? What are the arguments for each side?
6. What "conclusion follows, unescapably"?
7. How are the paintings by Piero della Francesca and Tura alike? Unlike?
8. How does Huxley tie the contrast of the two painters in with his comments on music?
9. What is the limit of criticism?
10. What other kinds of truths may be contrasted with "beauty-truth"?
11. What are Huxley's "own words" about the *Benedictus?*
12. Huxley builds this essay around sense impressions. List them, in sequence.
13. Explain the etymology of each of the following words: *inexorable, quintessential, reluctant, harmony, metaphysic, analyst, verbiage, stoical.*

D. H. Lawrence

It is childish. What we have now to admit is that the beginning of the new era (our own) coincided with the dying of the old era of the true pagans or, in the Greek sense, barbarians. As our present civilisation was showing the first sparks of life, say in 1000 B.C., the great and ancient civilisation of the older was waning: the great river civilisation of the Euphrates, the Nile, and the Indus, with the lesser sea-civilisation of the Aegean. It is puerile to deny the age and the greatness of the three river civilisations, with their intermediary cultures in Persia or Iran, and in the Aegean, Crete or Mycenae. That any of these civilisations could do a sum in long division we do not pretend. They may not even have invented the wheel-barrow. A modern child of ten could lick them hollow in arithmetic, geometry, or even, maybe, astronomy. And what of it?

What of it? Because they lacked our modern mental and mechanical attainments, were they any less "civilised" or "cultured," the Egyptians and the Chaldeans, the Cretans and the Persians and the Hindus of the Indus, than we are? Let us look at a great seated statue of Rameses, or at Etruscan tombs; let us read of Assiburnipal or Darius, and then say: How do our modern factory-workers show beside the delicate Egyptian friezes of the common people of Egypt? or our khaki soldiers, beside the Assyrian friezes? or our Trafalgar Square lions beside these of Mycenae? Civilisation? it is revealed rather in sensitive life than in inventions: and have we anything as good as the Egyptians of two or three thousand years before Christ as a people? Culture and civilisation are tested by vital consciousness. Are we more vitally conscious than an Egyptian 3000 years B.C. was? Are we? Probably we are less. Our

conscious range is wide, but shallow as a sheet of paper. We have
no depth to our consciousness.

A rising thing is a passing thing, says Buddha. A rising civilisation is a passing civilisation. Greece rose upon the passing of the
Aegean: and the Aegean was the link between Egypt and Babylon.
Greece rose as the passing of the Aegean civilisation, and Rome
rose as the same, for the Etruscan civilisation was a last strong wave
from the Aegean, and Rome rose, truly, from the Etruscans. Persia
arose from between the cultures of the Euphrates and the Indus,
and no doubt, in the passing of these.

Perhaps every rising civilisation must fiercely repudiate the
passing civilisation. It is a fight within the self. The Greeks fiercely
repudiated the barbarians. But we know now, the barbarians of
the east Mediterranean were as much Greeks as most of the Greeks
themselves. They were only Greeks, or autochthonous Hellenes
who adhered to the old way of culture instead of taking on the
new. The Aegean must always have been, in the primitive sense,
Hellenic. But the old Aegean culture is different from what we call
Greek, especially in its religious basis. Every old civilisation, we
may be certain of it, had a definitely religious basis. The nation
was, in a very old sense, a church, or a vast cult-unit. From cult to
culture is only a step, but it took a lot of making. Cult-lore was the
wisdom of the old races. We now have culture.

It is fairly difficult for one culture to understand another. But
for culture to understand cult-lore is extremely difficult, and, for
rather stupid people, impossible. Because culture is chiefly an
activity of the mind, and cult-lore is an activity of the senses. The
pre-Greek ancient world had not the faintest inkling of the lengths
to which mental activity could be carried. Even Pythagoras, whoever he was, had no inkling: nor Herakleitos nor even Empedokles
or Anaxagoras. Socrates and Aristotle were the first to *perceive* the
dawn.

But on the other hand, we have not the faintest conception of
the vast range that was covered by the ancient sense-consciousness.
We have lost almost entirely the great and intricately developed
sensual awareness, or sense-awareness, and sense-knowledge, of the
ancients. It was a great depth of knowledge, arrived at direct, by
instinct and intuition, as we say, not by reason. It was a knowledge

based not on words but on images. The abstraction was not into generalisations or into qualities, but into symbols. And the connection was not logical but emotional. The word "therefore" did not exist. Images or symbols succeeded one another in a procession of instinctive and arbitrary physical connection—some of the Psalms give us examples—and they "get nowhere" because there was nowhere to get to, the desire was to achieve a consummation of a certain state of consciousness, to fulfil a certain state of feeling-awareness. Perhaps all that remains to us today of the ancient way of "thought-process" are games like chess and cards. Chess-men and card-figures are symbols: their "values" are fixed in each case: their "movements" are non-logical, arbitrary; and based on the power-instinct.

Not until we can grasp a little of the working of the ancient mind can we appreciate the "magic" of the world they lived in. Take even the sphinx conundrum: *What is it that goes first on four legs, then on two, and then on three?*—The answer is: Man.— To us it is rather silly, the great question of the sphinx. But in the uncritical ancient who *felt* his images, there would spring up a great complex of emotions and fears. The thing that goes on four legs is the animal, in all its animal difference and potency, its hinterland consciousness which circles round the isolated consciousness of man. And when, in the answer, it is shown that the baby goes on four legs, instantly there springs up another emotional complex, half fear, half amusement, as man realises himself as an animal, especially in the infantile state, going on all fours with face to the ground and belly or navel polarised to the earth's centre, like a true animal, instead of navel polarised to the sun, as in the true man, according to primitive conception. The second clause, of the two-legged creature, would bring up complex images of men, monkeys, birds, and frogs, and the weird falling into relationship of these four would be an instant imaginative act, such as is very hard for us to achieve, but which children still make. The last clause, of the three-legged creature, would bring wonder, faint terror, and a searching of the great hinterlands beyond the deserts and the sea for some still-unrevealed beast.

So we see that the emotional reaction to such a conundrum was enormous. And even kings and heroes like Hector or Menelaus would make the same reaction, as a child now does, but a thousand-fold stronger and wider. Men were not fools for so doing. Men are far more fools today, for stripping themselves of their emotional and imaginative reactions, and feeling nothing. The price we pay is boredom and deadness. Our bald processes of thought no longer are life to us. For the sphinx-riddle of man is as terrifying today as it was before Oedipus, and more so. For now it is the riddle of the dead-alive man, which it never was before.

Man thought and still thinks in images. But now our images have hardly any emotional value. We always want a "conclusion," an end, we always want to come, in our mental processes, to a decision, a finality, a full stop. This gives us a sense of satisfaction. All our mental consciousness is a movement onwards, a movement in stages, like our sentences, and every full-stop is a mile-stone that marks our "progress" and our arrival somewhere. On and on we go, for the mental consciousness. Whereas of course there is no goal. Consciousness is an end in itself. We torture ourselves getting somewhere, and when we get there it is nowhere, for there is nowhere to get to.

While men still thought of the heart or the liver as the seat of consciousness, they had no idea of this on-and-on process of thought. To them a thought was a completed state of feeling-aware-ness, a cumulative thing, a deepening thing, in which feeling deepened into feeling in consciousness till there was a sense of fulness. A completed thought was the plumbing of a depth like a whirlpool, of emotional awareness, and at the depth of this whirl-pool of emotion the resolve formed. But it was no stage in a jour-ney. There was no logical chain to be dragged further.

This should help us to appreciate that the oracles were not supposed to say something that fitted plainly in the whole chain of circumstance. They were supposed to deliver a set of images or symbols of the real dynamic value, which should set the emotional consciousness of the enquirer, as he pondered them, revolving more and more rapidly, till out of a state of intense emotional absorption the resolve at last formed; or, as we say, the decision was arrived at. As a matter of fact, we do very much the same in a crisis. When anything very important is to be decided we withdraw and ponder and ponder until the deep emotions are set working and revolving together, revolving, revolving, till a centre is formed and we "know what to do." And the fact that no politician today has the courage to follow this intensive method of "thought" is the reason of the absolute paucity of the political mind today.

QUESTIONS FOR STUDY

1. Explain the etymological meanings of the following words: *barbarism, autochthonous, conundrum, perceive, puerile,* and *paucity.*
2. What civilizations does Lawrence include in "the new era" and "the old era"? List them.
3. What meaning does Lawrence give the word *civilization?*
4. To Lawrence, in what ways do the old and the new eras differ?
5. How do cult-lore and culture differ? Symbols and ideas?
6. What illustration of "feeling-awareness" does Lawrence develop?
7. Why, to Lawrence, is the riddle of the sphinx more terrifying today than it was in antiquity?
8. Contrast mental consciousness and sense-consciousness.

THE GRAY BEGINNINGS

Rachel Carson

As soon as the earth's crust cooled enough, the rains began to fall. Never have there been such rains since that time. They fell continuously, day and night, days passing into months, into years, into centuries. They poured into the waiting ocean basins, or, falling upon the continental masses, drained away to become sea.

That primeval ocean, growing in bulk as the rains slowly filled its basins, must have been only faintly salt. But the falling rains were the symbol of the dissolution of the continents. From the moment the rains began to fall, the lands began to be worn away and carried to the sea. It is an endless, inexorable process that has never stopped—the dissolving of the rocks, the leaching out of their contained minerals, the carrying of the rock fragments and dissolved minerals to the ocean. And over the eons of time, the sea has grown even more bitter with the salt of the continents.

In what manner the sea produced the mysterious and wonderful stuff called protoplasm we cannot say. In its warm, dimly lit waters the unknown conditions of temperature and pressure and saltiness must have been the critical ones for the creation of life from non-life. At any rate they produced the result that neither the alchemists with their crucibles nor modern scientists in their laboratories have been able to achieve.

Before the first living cell was created, there may have been many trials and failures. It seems probable that, within the warm saltiness of the primeval sea, certain organic substances were fashioned from carbon dioxide, sulphur, phosphorus, potassium, and calcium. Perhaps these were transition steps from which the complex molecules of protoplasm arose—molecules that somehow acquired the ability to reproduce themselves and begin the endless stream of life. But at present no one is wise enough to be sure.

Those first living things may have been simple microorganisms rather like some of the bacteria we know today—mysterious borderline forms that were not quite plants, not quite animals, barely over the intangible line that separates the non-living from the living. It is doubtful that this first life possessed the substance chlorophyll, with which plants in sunlight transform lifeless chemicals into the living stuff of their tissues. Little sunshine could enter their dim world, penetrating the cloud banks from which fell the endless rains. Probably the sea's first children lived on the organic substances then present in the ocean waters, or, like the iron and sulphur bacteria that exist today, lived directly on inorganic food.

All the while the cloud cover was thinning, the darkness of the nights alternated with palely illumined days, and finally the sun for the first time shone through upon the sea. By this time some of the living things that floated in the sea must have developed the magic of chlorophyll. Now they were able to take the carbon dioxide of the air and the water of the sea and of these elements, in sunlight, build the organic substances they needed for life. So the first true plants came into being.

Another group of organisms, lacking the chlorophyll but needing organic food, found they could make a way of life for themselves by devouring the plants. So the first animals arose, and from that day to this, every animal in the world has followed the habit it learned in the ancient seas and depends, directly or through complex food chains, on the plants for food and life.

As the years passed, and the centuries, and the millions of years, the stream of life grew more and more complex. From simple, one-celled creatures, others that were aggregations of specialized cells arose, and then creatures with organs for feeding, digesting, breathing, reproducing. Sponges grew on the rocky bottom of the sea's edge and coral animals built their habitations in warm, clear waters. Jellyfish swam and drifted in the sea. Worms evolved, and starfish, and hard-shelled creatures with many-jointed legs. The plants, too, progressed, from the microscopic algae to branched and curiously fruiting seaweeds that swayed with the tides and were plucked from the coastal rocks by the surf and cast adrift.

During all this time the continents had no life. There was little to induce living things to come ashore, forsaking their all-providing, all-embracing mother sea. The lands must have been bleak and hostile beyond the power of words to describe. Imagine a whole continent of naked rock, across which no covering mantle of green had been drawn—a continent without soil, for there were no land plants to aid in its formation and bind it to the rocks with their roots. Imagine a land of stone, a silent land, except for the sound of the rains and winds that swept across it. For there was no living voice, and nothing moved over its surface except the shadows of the clouds.

Meanwhile, the gradual cooling of the planet, which had first given the earth its hard granite crust, was progressing into its deeper layers; and as the interior slowly cooled and contracted, it drew away from the outer shell. This shell, accommodating itself to the shrinking sphere within it, fell into folds and wrinkles—the earth's first mountain ranges.

Geologists tell us that there must have been at least two periods of mountain building (often called "revolutions") in that dim period, so long ago that the rocks have no record of it, so long ago that the mountains themselves have long since been worn away. Then there came a third great period of upheaval and readjustment of the earth's crust, about a billion years ago, but of all its majestic mountains the only reminders today are the Laurentian hills of eastern Canada, and a great shield of granite over the flat country around Hudson Bay.

The epochs of mountain building only served to speed up the processes of erosion by which the continents were worn down and their crumbling rock and contained minerals returned to the sea. The uplifted masses of the mountains were prey to the bitter cold of the upper atmosphere and under the attacks of frost and snow and ice the rocks cracked and crumbled away. The rains beat with greater violence upon the slopes of the hills and carried away the substance of the mountains in torrential streams. There was still no plant covering to modify and resist the power of the rains.

And in the sea, life continued to evolve. The earliest forms have left no fossils by which we can identify them. Probably they were soft-bodied, with no hard parts that could be preserved. Then, too, the rock layers formed in those early days have since been so al-tered by enormous heat and pressure, under the foldings of the earth's crust, that any fossils they might have contained would have been destroyed.

For the past 500 million years, however, the rocks have pre-served the fossil record. By the dawn of the Cambrian period, when the history of living things was first inscribed on rock pages, life in the sea had progressed so far that all the main groups of backboneless or invertebrate animals had been developed. But there were no animals with backbones, no insects or spiders, and still no plant or animal had been evolved that was capable of venturing onto the forbidding land. So for more than three-fourths of geologic time the continents were desolate and uninhabited, while the sea prepared the life that was later to invade them and make them habitable. Meanwhile, with violent tremblings of the earth and with the fire and smoke of roaring volcanoes, mountains rose and wore away, glaciers moved to and fro over the earth, and the sea crept over the continents and again receded.

It was not until Silurian time, some 350 million years ago, that the first pioneer of land life crept out on the shore. It was an ar-thropod, one of the great tribe that later produced crabs and lobsters and insects. It must have been something like a modern scorpion, but, unlike its descendants, it never wholly severed the ties that united it to the sea. It lived a strange life, half-terrestrial, half-aquatic, something like that of the ghost crabs that speed along the beaches today, now and then dashing into the surf to moisten their gills.

Fish, tapered of body and stream-molded by the press of running waters, were evolving in Silurian rivers. In times of drought, in the drying pools and lagoons, the shortage of oxygen forced them to develop swim bladders for the storage of air. One form developed an air-breathing lung and by its aid could live buried in the mud for long periods.

It is very doubtful that the animals alone would have succeeded in colonizing the land, for only the plants had the power to bring about the first amelioration of its harsh conditions. They helped make soil of the crumbling rocks, they held back the soil from the rains that would have swept it away, and little by little they sof-tened and subdued the bare rock, the lifeless desert. We know very little about the first land plants, but they must have been closely related to some of the larger seaweeds that had learned to live in the coastal shallows, developing strengthened stems and grasping, rootlike holdfasts to resist the drag and pull of the waves. Perhaps it was in some coastal lowlands, periodically drained and flooded, that some such plants found it possible to survive, though separated from the sea. This also seems to have taken place in the Silurian period.

The mountains that had been thrown up by the Laurentian revolution gradually wore away, and as the sediments were washed from their summits and deposited on the lowlands, great areas of the continents sank under the load. The seas crept out of their basins and spread over the lands. Life fared well and was exceedingly abundant in those shallow, sunlit seas. But with the later retreat of the ocean water into the deeper basins, many creatures must have been left stranded in shallow, landlocked bays. Some of these animals found means to survive on land. The lakes, the shores of the rivers, and the coastal swamps of those days were the testing grounds in which plants and animals either became adapted to the new conditions or perished.

As the lands rose and the seas receded, a strange fishlike creature emerged on the land, and over the thousands of years its fins became legs, and instead of gills it developed lungs. In the Devonian sandstone this first amphibian left its footprint.

On land and sea the stream of life poured on. New forms evolved; some old ones declined and disappeared. On land the mosses and the ferns and the seed plants developed. The reptiles for a time dominated the earth, gigantic, grotesque, and terrifying. Birds learned to live and move in the ocean of air. The first small mammals lurked inconspicuously in hidden crannies of the earth as though in fear of the reptiles.

When they went ashore the animals that took up a land life carried with them a part of the sea in their bodies, a heritage which they passed on to their children and which even today links each land animal with its origin in the ancient sea. Fish, amphibian, and reptile, warm-blooded bird and mammal—each of us carries in our veins a salty stream in which the elements sodium, potassium, and calcium are combined in almost the same proportions as in sea water. This is our inheritance from the day, untold millions of years ago, when a remote ancestor, having progressed from the one-celled to the many-celled stage, first developed a circulatory system in which the fluid was merely the water of the sea. In the same way, our lime-hardened skeletons are a heritage from the calcium-rich ocean of Cambrian time. Even the protoplasm that streams within each cell of our bodies has the chemical structure impressed upon all living matter when the first simple creatures were brought forth in the ancient sea. And as life itself began in the sea, so each of us begins his individual life in a miniature ocean within his mother's womb, and in the stages of his embryonic development repeats the steps by which his race evolved, from gill-breathing inhabitants of a water world to creatures able to live on land.

Some of the land animals later returned to the ocean. After perhaps 50 million years of land life, a number of reptiles entered the sea in Mesozoic time. They were huge and formidable creatures. Some had oarlike limbs by which they rowed through the water; some were web-footd, with long, serpentine necks. These grotesque monsters disappeared millions of years ago, but we remember them when we come upon a large sea turtle swimming many miles at sea, its barnacle-encrusted shell eloquent of its marine life. Much later, perhaps no more than 50 million years ago, some of the mammals, too, abandoned a land life for the ocean. Their descendants are the sea lions, seals, sea elephants, and whales of today.

Among the land mammals there was a race of creatures that took to an arboreal existence. Their hands underwent remarkable development, becoming skilled in manipulating and examining objects, and along with this skill came a superior brain power that compensated for what these comparatively small mammals lacked in strength. At last, perhaps somewhere in the vast interior of Asia, they descended from the trees and became again terrestrial. The past million years have seen their transformation into beings with the body and brain and the mystical spirit of man.

Eventually man, too, found his way back to the sea. Standing on its shores, he must have looked out upon it with wonder and curiosity, compounded with an unconscious recognition of his lineage. He could not physically re-enter the ocean as the seals and whales had done. But over the centuries, with all the skill and ingenuity and reasoning powers of his mind, he has sought to explore and investigate even its most remote parts, so that he might re-enter it mentally and imaginatively.

He fashioned boats to venture out on its surface. Later he found ways to descend to the shallow parts of its floor, carrying with him the air that, as a land mammal long unaccustomed to aquatic life, he needed to breathe. Moving in fascination over the deep sea he could not enter, he found ways to probe its depths, he let down nets to capture its life, he invented mechanical eyes and ears that could re-create for his senses a world long lost, but a world that, in the deepest part of his subconscious mind, he had never wholly forgotten.

And yet he has returned to his mother sea only on her own terms. He cannot control or change the ocean as, in his brief tenancy of earth, he has subdued and plundered the continents. In the artificial world of his cities and towns, he often forgets the true nature of his planet and the long vistas of its history, in which the existence of the race of men has occupied a mere moment of time. The sense of all these things comes to him most clearly in the course of a long ocean voyage, when he watches day after day the receding rim of the horizon, ridged and furrowed by waves; when at night be becomes aware of the earth's rotation as the stars pass overhead; or when, alone in this world of water and sky, he feels the loneliness of his earth in space. And then, as never on land, he knows the truth that his world is a water world, a planet dominated by its covering mantle of ocean, in which the continents are but transient intrusions of land above the surface of the all-encircling sea.

QUESTIONS FOR STUDY

1. List words from the essay which emphasize movement, like *poured, drained, drifted,* and *floated.*
2. List other words which accent change in the ocean and on land, as do *dissolving, leaching, devouring.*
3. List words which emphasize time, such as *eons, centuries, epochs.*
4. Cite phrases rich in imagery, like "the receding rim of the horizon, ridged and furrowed by waves."

5. Contrast the phrasing in each of the three paired statements:
a. the warm waters of the ocean
the warm saltiness of the primeval sea
b. Sponges grew on the rocky bottom of the sea's edge and coral animals built their habitations in warm, clear waters.
Sponges and coral animals grew in the sea.
c. Our skeletons are a heritage from Cambrian time.
Our lime-hardened skeletons are a heritage from the calcium-rich ocean of Cambrian time.

6. Give the etymology of each of the following words: *intangible, protoplasm, chlorophyll, arthropod, amelioration, torrential, arboreal, terrestrial, amphibian.*

7. What images develop the bleak hostility of early land?

8. Contrast the choice of imagery and words in these two statements:
Frost, snow, and ice wore the mountains down.
The uplifted masses of the mountains were prey to the bitter cold of the upper atmosphere and under the attacks of frost and snow and ice the rocks cracked and crumbled away.

9. Outline progressions in this essay which are centered (a) in time and (b) in increasing complexity. How are the two principles interwoven? Cite links.

SPIRIT: ANCIENT AND MODERN

Alexander Meiklejohn

The three centuries of our history are also the centuries in which the Western civilization to which we belong has passed from an ancient into a modern form. Three hundred years ago Europe was a society which had found its expression chiefly in the ideas and aspirations of the Greeks and the Jews. Into that society have now come two vast and powerful alien influences. In the field of knowledge "the sciences" have appeared. Into the activities of practical living, mechanized industry has entered with immense transforming influence. In the social revolution which has ensued from these two forces our American experience has been unique only in the fact that we, as a new nation building itself afresh in a new continent, have been more easily torn away from the old moorings. In us the new tendencies have found a more crude, a less sophisticated, a more radical and unhindered expression than in the older countries in which, by sheer inertia, the ancient culture keeps something of its power. What is this larger transformation of which our own development is only a special, extreme phase?

It seems to me that the most striking feature of the modern mind, as against the ancient, is its loss of use of the term "Spirit." For the Greeks and the Jews who most powerfully influenced our forefathers, the separation of spirit and matter was primary and fundamental. For them the human world was two worlds. And their problem, both in thought and in action, was that of keeping these two realms in right relations one to another. To make the body of man the servant of his soul, to keep the outer world subservient to the inner life—that was the dominant aspiration of the

cultures from which our own has sprung. But with the coming of
the modern sciences, the modern industries, that dualism has by
the loss of one of its members diminished to the very point of
vanishing. For both of these enormous waves of human activity,
externalization is the dominant motive. Both of them are frankly
and inevitably on the side of matter. The sciences think in, and
only in, external relations. The industries, following their scientific leaders, deal with human beings more and more in merely
material terms. Together they have driven the words of the spirit
out of our calculations. With every passing year the human mind
becomes more clear, more accurate, more explicit in its expressions
of material fact. And at the same time, by the same process, what
was formerly known as the life of the spirit becomes more vague,
more inarticulate, less able to keep a reputable place in clear,
objective thinking. We have fallen—or risen—into ways of thinking and acting for which appeals to the spirit of man, demands that
the outer world shall serve the purposes of the inner life are nonsense—the sentimental dreamings of idealists who cannot face the
facts, who forever seek escape from an actual world in the realms of
fancy where solace and comfort for weakness may be found.

Now the question here involved can be very simply stated. It is
this: Did Socrates and Jesus, the Greek and the Jew, talk nonsense?
Are the words of Ecclesiasticus, of Isaiah, of Buddha, of Francis of
Assisi, of Roger Williams, of Thomas Jefferson, now meaningless?
And on this point my own conviction is deep and passionate. I am
convinced that to speak of America, in terms of its spirit, as against
the terms of material welfare, is to use that form of speech which,
among all our ways of speaking, is most significant. To see American life in terms of aspiration and of disappointment, to measure it
as admirable or contemptible, to think of it as meeting or failing to
meet its obligations—that is the one really important approach to
an understanding of the nation. Other ways of thinking may serve
our partial, superficial purposes. But no one of these finds its real
meaning except as it leads down to the spiritual life of which
admiration and comtempt are the defining terms. How well—or
how ill—are we doing the thing which, in duty, in honor, in conscience, we are bound to do? That is the question of the Spirit of
America. So long as that question is not asked, all our knowledge is
nonsense. To try to answer it is to venture upon the way of wisdom.

"But which of the sciences," I shall be asked, "gives answer to this question which you urge upon us? By what intellectual method do you gather your material? How do you verify or reject conclusions? What are your tests of validity?" And the suggestion underlying these queries is very clear. It is that in the field of what I am calling the "spiritual" there is no verifiable knowledge. Here men think with their emotions. And each man's thinking varies with the yearnings and passions, the hates and loves, the joy or bitterness by which his own personal attitude is for the moment dominated. Now, in the face of this challenge, we ought, I think, to study such men as Socrates and Jesus. These two men had genius in the examination of the spiritual life. Each was a thinker of the highest order. Just as Galileo, Newton, Darwin, Loeb, excel in intellectual mastery of the world of outer fact, so do these two surpass their fellows in the search for human wisdom. In the same way, then, that we discover what is "scientific" method by examining the work of Galileo or Darwin, so we may discover how spiritual study should be done by observing the ways of Socrates and Jesus. They, in their own field, can show us what good thinking is. We can learn about good method by watching them.

It is recorded of the great Greek and of the great Jew that they went about among their fellows, talking with them of the values which they had found in human experience, and then pondering, meditating upon what they had seen and heard. Of Socrates, we are told that in his youth he was strongly attracted by the physical studies of his day but that soon he saw that these had little significance for his own chosen line of investigation. He therefore put them aside. Daily he was to be found in the market-place, on the athletic field, in the banqueting-hall, among artists, politicians, soldiers, wherever he could get men to tell him about their own inner interests and activities, to consider with him the validity of their own attitudes and beliefs. And when he was alone he reflected, meditated upon what had been said to him. And apparently the method of Jesus was essentially the same. Both of them sought acquaintance with men and their intentions. Both tried to weave this information into a scheme of meaning, to understand, to interpret human purposes in ways of which they found those purposes to be sorely in need.

Out of these two studies there came what are, I think, the two

most fruitful insights which Western civilization has known. For
men who are forever asking, "What shall I be and do?" Socrates
summed up his wisdom in the phrase, "Be intelligent; act critically." And Jesus, likewise pondering on human action, said to his
fellows, "Be kind." And in terms of sheer domination over the
mind of the Western world no other pair of intellectual achievements can equal these two. I do not mean that we have in any full
measure conformed to them. But in our more clear, more sensitive
moments, we have recognized them as the basic principles of the
human living which we are all trying to do. Out of them came the
two great practical tests which we apply to any proposal of action,
any social institution, any individual attitude. First we demand,
with Socrates, "Is it intelligent or is it stupid?" Second we ask with
Jesus, "Does it spring from hate and indifference, or does it come
from love?" What would one not give to see these two great teachers at work in America to-day as centuries ago they labored in
Athens and Palestine! They would be searching to the very bottom of our hearts and minds. They would reveal us to ourselves.
And always they would be flashing through the darkness and
confusion of our purposes the two fundamental demands of intelligence and humanity. In the light of these we might see ourselves as
wisdom would see us. They would display before our eyes the part
which America has played, the part she should play, in the age-long
struggle of understanding and generosity against stupidity and
hate for the domination of the Western world. Such self-interpreta-
tion is, I am sure, the greatest need not only of America but of all
our "modern" society. Spiritually we are lost in externalized confusion. The time has come when we must try to find again "ourselves."

But I shall again be asked, "Which of the sciences carries on this
work on acquaintance and meditation?" And to this I must answer
that, in our modern use of the term, Socrates and Jesus were not
scientific, nor was their problem one with which any science or all
of them taken together may deal. These two students did not work
in laboratories. Not for them were exact quantitative measurements and crucial experiments and decisive verifications. In the
scientific sense, their results remain, and must forever remain,
"unverified" and "unvalidated." And yet they were thinkers.

Their intellectual achievements seem to me to have the quality of genius of the highest order. But to this statement there will come, I am sure, a quick and sharp retort. "Are you," it will be asked, "recommending for an Age of Science forms and methods of thinking which men used in the ancient days before Science had been created?" And to this, if my courage will sustain me, I must answer with a plain "Yes." In my opinion, the devising of the new scientific methods has in no essential way affected our dealing with the problems which Socrates and Jesus faced. And those are still in changing forms our most fundamental, our most urgent intellectual problems. When faced with them the results and methods of the sciences and technologies are relatively superficial and subsidiary. It is true that the new techniques have brought to us a vast enrichment in the discovery of fact, the amassing of information. It is not true that they have changed either the nature of our inquiry or the method of our dealing with it. To interpret the quality of the human spirit means to-day essentially what it meant for Socrates and for Jesus, what it meant in the days before the sciences had been born.

In support of the negative statement just made, may I call upon evidence from our own time and country? We have had, and still have in America, interpreters of human living. William James—especially in his later, philosophic years—Veblen, Dewey, Royce, Whitehead, Otto, Holmes, Hamilton, Cohen—these are all engaged in the same activity as that which Socrates and Jesus followed. In each of them one finds the same demand for excellence in human living. Each of them has offered significant suggestions as to how that excellence may be achieved. And yet all that I have said about the methods of their ancient colleagues applies to them. They have worked in their studies, at their desks, in discussion with fellow-workers near and far. In quiet and seclusion they have pondered on the activities of men. No one of them has been a discoverer of new information. I doubt if any one of them has added a single important fact to our stock of knowledge. Certainly it is not for such additions that we do them honor. And with respect to "verification," the situation is the same. In the scientific sense, they have never dreamed of "validating" their conclusions. It is true that they have welcomed eagerly every bit of new information which the sciences have made available. But, in the main, their search has been within themselves, within the group of people whom they have known as like themselves. Here they have sought to understand the living which men do. And, in doing this, they have risen above their fellows, not by the breadth and accuracy of their information, but by the shrewdness of their insight, the keenness of their analysis, the depth and richness of the spiritual passion which has inspired their learning.

Two other remarks, more positive in character, must be added as bearing upon the method of Socrates and of Jesus. For both of them the interpretation of life included a criticism, a method of accepting or rejecting men's opinions about human living. In their hands, judgments about human nature are, in ways of clear, incisive reasoning, changed, corrected, discarded, enriched. And in the practice of this art they are both masters. I know nothing in literature more exciting, more illuminating than the conversations in which these two teachers reveal to their pupils the falsity of the opinions which they have been holding. "Let him that is without sin among you cast the first stone," says Jesus. And at the touch of that piercing insight conventional moral judgments go clattering into silly ruins. "Does not your omniscient brother seem to you to have made a mistake?" asks Socrates in the *Euthydemus*. And the demonstration that his opponent has been talking nonsense is so devastating that the whole argument disappears. In its own non-scientific way, meditation includes a keen dialectical process by which truth and falsity are separated from one another.

And, second, the great interpreters of life seem to possess an unusual capacity for weaving together into one single pattern the vast collection of human attitudes and judgments. The formulas of Socrates and Jesus send flashing through our experience principles of interpretation by which every human action is offered a place in an ordered, illumined scheme. Under the saying "Know thyself," Socrates endeavors to gather up all our virtues, all our modes of admirable living. Each is seen to be a special form of wisdom, of self-understanding. And, in like manner, "Thou shalt love thy neighbor as thyself," brings intelligibility into the social order. Every right social attitude, Jesus tells us, is a form of friendliness. In all good human behavior, human sympathy appears as a common basis. Such insights as these are not, of course, in any complete sense the interpretation of life, but they are principles upon which an interpretation may be built and rebuilt, fashioned and refashioned as wisdom grows among us. They are the intellectual tools which the human spirit uses in the neverending attempt to create and to understand its own meaning.

QUESTIONS FOR STUDY

1. By giving the root meaning of each word, define *spirit, spiritual, principle, quantity, quality, matter.* Contrast the meanings of *science* and *scientism.*
2. What does the phrase "old moorings" denote?
3. What forces have torn the modern world away from those moorings during the last three hundred years?
4. What evidences of a loss of spirit in the modern world does Meiklejohn give?
5. What other contrasts in this essay parallel the contrast of body and soul, the material and the spiritual?
6. In paragraph 2, why the alternative in "We have fallen—or risen —into ways of thinking . . ."?
7. Can the outer, material world serve the purposes of the inner spiritual life? Explain.
8. To Meiklejohn, what questions concerning "the Spirit of America" must be raised in order to understand and criticize the nation?
9. Contrast Meiklejohn's conceptions of the spiritual and the scientific.
10. What principles give spiritual value to the "good thinking" of Socrates and Jesus?
11. What bearing do those principles have on both the personal and the social life of the individual?
12. Has the new scientific emphasis of the past three hundred years affected the wisdom of Socrates and Jesus? Explain.
13. How does a speculative quest for standards and values differ from scientific inquiry?
14. What standards for accepting or rejecting attitudes and judgments in one's life appear in the insights of Socrates and Jesus?
15. What bearing may those standards have in evaluating "the Spirit of America"?

THE IMPORTANCE OF GEORGE ORWELL

Richard Rovere

It took Orwell to uncover the living roots of totalitarianism in contemporary thought and speech, in the puritanism of civic virtue, in our slackening of ties with the usable past, in cravenness before the gods of security, in mass entertainment's deadening of impulses. He put Newspeak and Doublethink into the language, and our habits of speech and thought are the better for this. If we and our offspring never have to endure *Nineteen Eighty-Four* [first published in 1949], we and they will have Orwell partly to thank.

Nineteen Eighty-Four was a dazzling illumination, and I suppose that for most people it will always be the first thing to spring to mind whenever Orwell's name is mentioned—just as most of us, in free association, would respond to "Swift" with *"Gulliver's Travels."* Yet it was not Orwell's first illumination but his last. Years earlier, even before *Animal Farm* [1946] had won him his first really wide circle of readers, he had exerted a liberating and strengthening influence on a whole generation of writers and intellectuals. That generation, of which I am a member, knew him first as a journalist. In my own case, I did not even know that he had written any fiction until some time after I read his political and literary criticism. . . . I think my own awareness of him must date from late 1939 or more probably early 1940; in any case, I knew enough about him by 1941 to go to some lengths to get hold of a copy of *The Lion and the Unicorn*, a wartime study of English life and ideals that has never been published here. Orwell was a socialist when he wrote it, as he was to the day of his death, and the book may justly be regarded as a piece of socialist literature, though it spends less time telling how socialism might improve England than how England might improve socialism.

I followed *The Lion and the Unicorn* [1941] with *Homage to Catalonia* [1938] and all the fugitive pieces, in English periodicals and in *Partisan Review*, that I could lay hands on. It was not Orwell's view of any particular question that made his work as a journalist so exciting and his example as a writer so bracing to his colleagues. Nor was it merely the verve and acuity of his writing, though this was indeed part of it: quite apart from any special tendencies of his thinking, he was a magnificent performer. But the important and stirring thing was the way he coupled contempt for all the "smelly little orthodoxies" of his time with a continuing interest in ideas and a decent respect for the opinions of mankind. He was free, on the one hand, of pieties of any sort and, on the other, of flippancy. He was at once responsible and absolutely independent, and this in a day when responsibility and independence were customarily disjoined. He fused a moral commitment with a fiercely critical mind and spirit, and if today there are more writers who approach this ideal than there were twenty years ago, it is largely because they have profited by his precepts and have been moved by the magnificent gesture of his career.

Orwell was a writer of great force and distinction. He would be remembered today if he had been only a journalist and critic. But he was far more; he was—among other things, though certainly first among them—an artist, and a many-sided one. The thrust of his moral imagination has been felt by all those who read *Nineteen Eighty-Four*, but that was by no means the end of it, nor was it the beginning. Though *Nineteen Eighty-Four* was no doubt his most important book, that work of apocalyptic fury did not provide the most impressive display of his gifts. The reader of *Burmese Days* [1934] and *Coming Up for Air* [1939], which seem to me the two most successful of his early novels, will discover that his imagination was more than moral. He could deal superbly with the individual consciousness and with the intercourse of character. He could be wonderfully evocative of moods and times and scenes and conditions of life. No one who has seen anything of England or encountered any members of the British lower middle class can miss the verisimilitude of *Coming Up for Air*. We have it on excellent authority that *Burmese Days* is as sensitive a rendering of Indian and Anglo-Saxon life; in any case, it could scarcely be more memorable. I would rank *Down and Out in Paris and London* [1933] with these two novels if I did not think it too directly autobiographical and reportorial a work to be described as a novel at all; whatever its category, it is a matchlessly vivid description of the life of poverty and unemployment and squalor. It is impossible to read the *plongeur* passages without having the sensation of gray soapy water sloshing about the arms up to the elbow. Though Orwell's bent was for such description and for a manner that is ironical, astringent, and detached, he could on occasion be lyrical and quite astonishingly tender, as one may learn from the sections on Tubby Bowling's boyhood in *Coming Up for Air* or from the haunting and pathetic scenes between Julia and Winston in *Nineteen Eighty-Four*.

In all of his novels, including those that might, on balance, be described as failures, one feels oneself always in the presence of a writer who is fully alive and has eyes and an intellect and a vibrant character of his own. The conventions of criticism demand, I suppose, that he be placed as a "minor" novelist. He was not in any crucial sense an innovator, and he did not penetrate the mysteries to the depths reached by Dostoevski or Conrad. He did not people a world as Balzac did—though one has the feeling that something like this would have been within his powers if he had devoted himself entirely to fiction or if he had lived and written longer. He was of the second rank, but he was never second-rate, and to my mind and taste the distinction is anything but invidious. All of us, I think, get major satisfactions from certain minor novelists, and minor satisfactions from certain major novelists. Stendhal, for example, means less to me than Samuel Butler, and Orwell more than Joyce. I believe that Orwell is, as Irving Howe has said, "one of the few contemporary writers who really matter."

John Atkins, the author of a useful critical study of Orwell, has said that "his uniqueness lay in his having the mind of an intellectual and the feelings of a common man." I cannot quite accept this, for I recognize no sentient state that can be described as "the feelings of a common man." As for "the mind of an intellectual," that is what every intellectual has. Still, I think Atkins is reaching for a central truth about Orwell and one that is not easy to grasp. Perhaps one could say that his uniqueness lay to some degree in his almost studied avoidance of the unique. The experience he chose to deal with was the kind of experience known to large numbers of people, to whole social classes, to entire nations. He did not often concern himself with the single instance. As a novelist, he was rather old-fashioned in the sense that he did not explore the extremes of behavior. The merely anomalous, the merely phenomenal, the exotic, the bizarre—none of these attracted his interest very much. In fact, the most obvious and persistent of his faults was an intolerance of eccentricity and neurosis. As a critic, he was rather old-fashioned in the sense that he paid the most attention to books that have been read by millions and left to other critics those works of genius that are admired chiefly in genius circles. It was Dickens and Kipling, staples in a national culture, rather than, say, Henry James or Gerard Manley Hopkins, who drew forth his greatest critical efforts. He pioneered in the serious analysis of popular culture, writing brilliantly of "good bad" books, boys' magazines, patriotic verse and marching songs, penny dreadfuls, and even the bawdy postcards on sale at seaside resorts. In a striking essay on Henry Miller, which was, I think, one of his few appreciations of what some people would call a "coterie" writer, he found it necessary to convince himself that the lives of the odd fish of whom Miller wrote "overlap fairly widely with those of more normal people." Had he been unable to say this, he would have been unable to admire Miller.

He set great store by normality. This is not to say that he despised the extraordinary or placed no value on the uncommon or superior. He was an extraordinary person himself, he detested conformity, and he never celebrated mediocrity. "The average sensual man is out of fashion," he wrote, and he proposed to restore him, giving him "the power of speech, like Balaam's ass" and uncovering his genius. Because we know that he believed there was a great deal in a name, we can assume that in *Nineteen Eighty-Four* he did not settle lightly on one for the central character, Winston Smith, who linked the memory of a most uncommon Englishman with the commonest of English patronymics. What Orwell cared about most deeply was the general quality of human

experience in his time. The virtues he honored were the universally accessible ones—candor, courage, love, common sense, integrity,
decency, charity. The tyrannies he anatomized were those that
could hurt us all.

QUESTIONS FOR STUDY

1. What do the following phrases mean in context: "the puritanism of
   civic virtue," "the usable past," and "apocalyptic fury"?
2. What characteristics distinguish Orwell's writing as a journalist?
   As a novelist?
3. With what writers and on what points is Orwell contrasted.
4. What does Rovere believe Orwell's uniqueness to be? What illustrations of that interpretation are given?
5. What were the tyrannies that Orwell "anatomized"? List antonyms
   for the virtues Orwell honored, "candor, courage, love, common
   sense, integrity, decency, charity." Illustrate each antonym by naming a specific manifestation of it during this century.

THE CAUSES OF MODERN WARS

Morris Ginsberg

I may perhaps bring together the main trends of my argument by setting out the principal factors which interwoven with one another appear to me to be responsible for modern wars. It is useful to distinguish between the fundamental predisposing conditions and the immediate or inciting conditions and I will mention chiefly the former.

First, there are imperialist rivalries due to differences in economic and political power between different nations and particularly to the existence of relatively undeveloped parts of the world offering opportunities for expansion and exploitation. This tendency to expansion is encouraged by the capitalist form of economic organization which necessitates the search for new markets and thus generates animosities which tend to express themselves in political conflicts. Whether these imperialistic rivalries would disappear under a Socialist organization may be doubted. It must be remembered that under a Socialist regime the linking up of the political with the economic is carried to its extreme point, since all foreign trade is politically controlled. In the case of those countries which have or believe themselves to have an insufficient supply of raw materials in their own domain or which have developed their production beyond what is necessary for internal consumption, occasions of friction might well arise quite as difficult to resolve as those which exist between capitalist states. Nevertheless, it is arguable that the profit motive once eliminated there might be a greater chance than there is now of an amicable solution of the problems of raw materials, immigration, and export.

Secondly, I should put the fear that nations have of each other due to a large extent to the resentment left behind by former wars and the treaties of peace which concluded them.

Thirdly, the existence of armaments which heighten this fear and keep it alive.

Fourthly, and as a consequence in part of the foregoing, the unwillingness of nations to give up their right of self-defence and the resulting absence of any effective international organization for dealing with disturbances of equilibrium.

Fifthly, the psychological factors making for anxiety, fear, and hate, partly the result of economic and political factors, and partly having their roots deeper in the forces discussed by the psychoanalysts.

Sixthly, another factor is to be found in the nature of public opinion in complex societies. It is sometimes held that there is now a general will for peace, but a general will is just what there is not. Here, as in so many other phases of public life, what is will is not general and what is general is not will. The truth is that the mass of people do not feel either individually responsible or competent to deal with the complex issues that arise, and realizing that they cannot control policy they leave events to take their course. Hence it frequently happens that statesmen having blundered into catastrophe console themselves with the reflection that owing to public opinion they could not have acted otherwise, while it is quite likely that had they given a lead public opinion might well have welcomed a generous and peaceful policy. Thus as Lowes Dickinson has said: "Governments do not lead and nations do not follow. There is a general slithering into the pit, into which, nevertheless, everybody would say they do not wish to fall."

The discussion of the origins of war and the conditions of peace abounds in overdrawn antitheses. Thus the political is contrasted with and even separated from the economic and, what is even stranger, both are contrasted with the psychological. In fact the causation is extremely complex and the attempt to control the factors involved frequently results in vicious circles. You cannot get a reorganization of the economic life within a country without raising international problems, and international troubles cannot be got rid of without raising problems of internal organization.

You will never get peace until you get Socialism, say some. To which the reply is made: You will never get Socialism until you get peace. You must first reeducate mankind, it is maintained, and the political and economic reconstruction will follow. You must first revolutionize society and human nature will be transformed in consequence, say others in return. The essence of the matter is the recognition that the circles *are* vicious and that to break them a simultaneous and concerted attack at different points is necessary.

Assignment

In a single paragraph, develop one of the six causes of war by giving specific historical details.

Henry Bamford Parkes

That this movement of the European races into the New World should be regarded as the essential substance of American history is not difficult to understand. The explorer, the conquistador, the pioneer, and the liberator are the primary symbols of the American cultures. But the full implications, political and psychological, of this migration are not so easy to define. Establishing himself in the New World, the American repudiated a part of his European inheritance. In certain respects, though not in all, he ceased to be a European and became a new subspecies of humanity. It is only by understanding the qualities of this new man, the American, that we can interpret much that may otherwise seem puzzling or disturbing in his achievements and his behavior. We must, above all, avoid the error of regarding the civilization of America as a mere extension, without essential changes, of that of Europe. The differences between them should, in fact, be emphasized, since otherwise the American peoples will be unable either to form a sound evaluation of their own institutions or to avoid misunderstandings with those European nations with whom they must be associated.

This volume is concerned with the evolution of civilization in the United States, and here the divergence from European traditions was sharper than in the Spanish-speaking countries. Both the North and the South Americans have displayed certain common American characteristics, but these developed more fully in the north. The imprint of European institutions, of monarchy, aristocracy, and clericalism, and of the view of life and habits of thought

95

associated with them, was much deeper and more lasting in the southern countries than it was in the United States. This was owing partly to the authoritarian policies of Spanish imperialism and partly to the presence of large Indian populations who could be reduced to a servitude resembling that of the peasants of feudal Europe. To a large degree Latin America became an extension of Latin Europe. The migration to the United States, on the other hand, created a new way of life that quickly acquired certain unique qualities.

The impulse of migration may be described, negatively, as an impulse of escape. The American fled from a Europe where he could find no satisfying fulfillment of his energies and was confronted by conflicts and dilemmas that had no easy solution. The groups who came to all parts of the New World were, in general, those who were most acutely discontented with their status in European society and who had the least hope of being able to improve it. The Hispanic colonies were settled mainly by impoverished members of the lower nobility and by adventurers from the lower classes. Unable to achieve aristocratic status at home, they hoped to win riches, land, and glory for themselves in America. Most of the early immigrants to the United States came from the petty bourgeoisie in the English cities or from the yeoman farmers; a few were motivated primarily by the desire to put into practice novel religious or political ideas, but the majority expected to improve their economic condition. The later migration from the other European countries into both North and South America was similar in character, including some religious and political refugees, but consisting mainly of ambitious younger sons of the bourgeoisie and of oppressed and land-hungry peasants from Ireland, Germany, Scandinavia, Italy, and the Austrian and Russian empires. All sought in the New World an environment where they could act more freely, without being restricted by traditional forms of authority and discipline or by a scarcity of land and natural resources.

Of the various factors that caused men to come to America, the economic was no doubt the most important. Throughout the period of the migrations, there was no free land in Europe; natural resources were limited; and the population was always in danger of increasing faster than the means of subsistence. Migration always occurred chiefly from areas of Europe where agriculture was still the chief occupation and where (owing to the growth of big estates or to genuine overcrowding) the demand for land was in excess of the supply. This was true of Spain in the sixteenth century, of England in the early seventeenth, and of Ireland, Germany, Scandinavia, Italy, and the Slavic countries of the east in the nineteenth.

An almost equally influential stimulus to migration was the European class system. This was, in fact, perhaps the chief cause of European economic privation, since the big estates of the aristocracy diminished the supply of land available for the peasants. Before the discovery of America, European society had been molded by feudalism into a tightly knit organic structure in which every individual, from the king at the top to the humblest peasant at the bottom, was expected to know his place and to perform the duties appropriate to it. These class differences had originated with the barbarian invasions during the fall of the Roman Empire, or even earlier, and for a thousand years they had been a deeply rooted part of the European consciousness. Ambitious and enterprising members of the middle and lower classes could sometimes improve their position, either individually or in groups, but the battle against aristocratic privilege was always difficult, and never reached a conclusion. For such persons the opening of the New World beyond the Atlantic promised an easier escape from frustration and the sense of inferiority.

Privation and inequality weighed upon all underprivileged persons in Europe, but did not cause all of them to come to America. Human behavior is conditioned by economic and social factors in the sense that these establish the problems to be solved, but it is not determined by them: how particular individuals choose to act in a given situation depends upon deeper, more intangible, and more mysterious forces. Confronted by the same difficulties, some individuals preferred to submit to them or to continue struggling with them, while others, generally the more restless and adventurous, decided to come to the New World. Thus the settlement of America was a selective process that attracted those members of the European middle and lower classes who had the appropriate bent and disposition; it appealed not necessarily to the ablest or the strongest, but usually to the most enterprising. In a sense it may be said that America was from the beginning a state of mind and not merely a place.

In the New World, at least during the earlier period of colonization, this selective process continued. Those who had the requisite energy, adaptability, and capacity for endurance survived and prospered; others died of starvation or in battle with the Indians. In the course of centuries certain qualities became established as suitable to the new environment and as characteristically American. Men born in the New World were disposed, both by inheritance and by conditioning, to develop them, and later immigrant groups found it necessary to acquire them. Thus the civilizations of the New World promoted certain special psychic configurations that differentiated the American from the European.

In the Hispanic countries the presence of Indian labor and the importation of Negro slaves enabled many of the early immigrants to achieve the aristocratic status to which they aspired. But in the United States there were no Indian peoples who could be made to work for white overlords; and though the institution of Negro slavery was adopted during the colonial period, its influence was restricted to one section of the country. There were in the United States, on the other hand, enormous stretches of fertile land and vast mineral resources of all kinds. Immigrants could find, in this undeveloped and almost empty country, opportunities for self-advancement that have never been equaled in the whole of human history. The individual had to display industry, courage, and resourcefulness; but if he possessed these qualities, then security, independence, and prosperity were within his reach. This unexampled abundance of land and resources was the cardinal factor in the development of American civilization. It molded the character of the American people, and was the chief reason for the unique qualities of their way of life. It facilitated the growth of individual freedom and social equality, and it promoted attitudes of optimism and self-assurance.

The society that developed under these conditions differed from that of Europe not only in its political and economic characteristics but also in its animating beliefs and view of life. The American acquired new attitudes and learned to see the world in a new way. And the nationality he created became a vast experiment in new social principles and new modes of living.

The European mind had been dominated by a hierarchical sense of order. This sense was embodied most completely in the philosophical and political theory of the Middle Ages; but even after the breakdown of feudalism and the repudiation of the scholastic philosophy, it continued, in one form or another, to permeate the consciousness of most Europeans. Human society was regarded as the reflection of an ideal order derived from the will of God and fully embodied in the cosmos. And the life of the individual acquired meaning and value insofar as he conformed with the order of the society to which he belonged. Yet the Europeans believed also that the attempt to realize this ideal order in concrete forms must always be incomplete. Evil was an inherent element in human experience, and both in nature and in the human spirit there were anarchical and rebellious forces that conflicted with the ideal order and that could never be wholly controlled. This belief in the reality of evil led to the European doctrine of original sin and was the basis of the European sense of tragedy.

The first immigrants to America brought with them this sense of order, but in the American world it gradually grew weaker; it did not remain a permanent part of the American consciousness. Coming to a country where there was no elaborate social organization, and where the individual must constantly do battle with the forces of nature, the American came to see life not as an attempt to realize an ideal order, but as a struggle between the human will and the environment. And he believed that if men were victorious in this struggle, they could hope that evil might gradually be conquered and eliminated. What appeared as evil was not a fundamental and permanent element in the nature of things, but should be regarded merely as a problem to which the correct solution would one day be discovered. The American was therefore a voluntarist and an optimist. He did not believe in the devil, nor did he accept the dogma of original sin.

The most obvious result of this American attitude was the fostering of an extraordinary energy and confidence of will. The American came to believe that nothing was beyond his power to accomplish, provided that he could muster the necessary moral and material resources, and that any obstacle could be mastered by means of the appropriate methods and technology. A failure was the result either of weakness or of an incorrect technique. By contrast with the European, the American was more extroverted, quicker and more spontaneous in action, more self-confident, and psychologically simpler. His character was molded not by the complex moral and social obligations of an ordered hierarchical system, but by the struggle to achieve victory over nature.

Rejecting both the belief in a fixed social order and the belief in the depravity of human beings, the American created a society whose special characteristic was the freedom enjoyed by its individual members. Respect for the freedom of every individual and confidence that he would use his freedom wisely and constructively became the formative principles of the new American nationality. By crossing the Atlantic, the American has asserted a demand to be himself; he had repudiated the disciplines of the class hierarchy, of long-established tradition, and of authoritarian religion. And in the society that took shape in the New World it was by his natural and inherent quality that the individual was measured, rather than by rank or status or conformity to convention. To a much greater degree than elsewhere, society in America was based on the natural man rather than on man as molded by social rituals and restraints. The mores of America were less rigid and less formalized than those of any earlier community, and the individual was less inhibited. The American did not believe that men needed to be coerced, intimidated, or indoctrinated into good behavior.

By European standards this American attitude often seemed unrealistic, Utopian, and naive. The American appeared to be deficient in the recognition of evil and in the sense of tragedy. Yet as long as he was engaged primarily in the conquest of the wilderness, he had good reasons for his optimism. His naiveté was, in fact, an expression of a genuine innocence. He was simpler than the European because his life was freer, more spontaneous, and less frustrated. In Europe, with its economic privation, its hierarchy of classes, and its traditional disciplines and rituals, emotional drives were more inhibited; and it is when aggressive energies are thrown back upon themselves and can find no satisfying outlet in action that they become evil. The European was psychologically much more complex than the American, and therefore capable of deeper and more subtle insights and of profounder spiritual and aesthetic achievements; but he was also more corrupt, with a greater propensity toward the negative emotions of fear and avarice and hatred. He believed in the depravity of human nature because he knew it in his own experience.

In social organization and in practical activity the American confidence in human nature was abundantly justified by its results. The tone of American society was more generous and hospitable, more warmhearted and more genuinely kindly, than that of other peoples. And by encouraging individuals to develop latent talents and to prefer versatility and adaptability to professional specialization, it promoted an astonishing activity and ingenuity. The genius of American life lay in its unprecedented capacity to release for constructive purposes the energies and abilities of common men and women. In consequence, the material achievements of the Americans were stupendous. And though they hated the authoritarian discipline of warfare, they displayed when they went to war an inventiveness and a resourcefulness that no other people could equal.

Yet though the civilization of the Americans had remarkable virtues, it also had grave deficiencies. The conditions that produced their material achievements did not result in any corresponding intellectual efflorescence. Their bent was toward the conquest of nature rather than toward metaphysical speculation or aesthetic creation. And though their suspicion of professional pretensions and their trust in the abilities of the common man had astonishing results in politics, technology, and warfare, the effect upon intellectual life was less desirable; for the common man has usually valued material progress above the difficult and apparently useless disciplines of abstract thought. In consequence, the more formal intellectual activities of the Americans often appeared to be timid, conventional, and derivative. They frequently used ideas that had been borrowed from Europe, and that had little relevance or vital connection with their own society. Their practice was usually bolder and more original than their theory. Outside the fields of practical activity, America developed no living system of general ideas and no continuing intellectual tradition, so that each generation of writers and thinkers had a tendency to start afresh, with little guidance or encouragement from the past.

Questions for Study

1. Define *conquistador, clericalism, configurations, original sin, natural man, mores, inhibited,* and *tone.*
2. Name historical persons who were explorers, conquistadors, pioneers, and liberators.
3. Which sentence in the first paragraph states the theme of the entire essay?
4. Contrast the effects of migration in reshaping ways of life in North America and in South America.
5. List causes of the migration to America.
6. Name some characteristics of an American "state of mind."
7. What are the unique qualities of the American way of life?
8. List the major differences between characteristic European and American attitudes and points of view.
9. What, to Parkes, is the genius of American life?
10. Outline the essay.
11. What methods of development does Parkes use most frequently?

THE OBLIGATIONS OF A TEACHER

Harold Laski

Every teacher, I believe, has three great obligations. He must continually research, he must keep a fresh mind, and he must know his students not as a shapeless mass seen from a dais, but as individuals whom, if he can, he will cultivate as friends. These are grim conditions, physically exacting and intellectually wearing. By continuous research I do not mean constant publication. The modern tendency to judge men by their volume of published output is, I believe, responsible for not a little of inadequate teaching standards. It is a facile test of promotion naturally welcome to busy administrators; it is not the slightest proof of intellectual inadequacy. A man should be asked to publish only when he feels that what he has to say requires the test of criticism by other scholars because, thereby, it is likely to add significantly to the sum of knowledge. By research I mean in part a devotion to the reëxamination of the ultimate principles of a subject, and also an endeavor to extend their boundaries by solution of the problems to which they give rise. Some of the greatest scholars of the last half-century, Lord Acton, for instance, and F. J. Turner, published comparatively little; but their knowledge was so wide and deep, their power, born of that knowledge, to ask creative questions so fundamental, that they were able to fertilize all other work in their generation by reason of it. In this sense, the teacher's real task is himself to embark upon the investigation of a really big theme, and use the new insight that research conveys to illuminate the whole subject he expounds. And, almost invariably, the earlier he finds the big theme with which to grapple, the better work as a teacher he is likely to do.

He must, in the second place, keep a fresh mind. His lectures, his criticism, his discussion must never become a system of formulas that he regurgitates year by year to students whom the academic tradition has already taught what they are to expect. This involves, I think, a number of important decisions. Certainly, in the first place, some such institution as the sabbatical year is imperative. A man who goes on teaching year in and year out, without the opportunity of leisured self-examination, is bound to go stale. His teaching begins to lose vitality; he lacks the power to develop that intellectual second wind of which William James wrote so wisely. The sabbatical year may mean travel, or research, or a happy browsing amid books. Whatever it means, it involves a substantial period in which the teacher does not teach in order to remain an effective teacher. There is no substitute for this experience. I believe, too, that the fresh mind involves consistent exploration by the teacher of the confines of his subject. He must be at constant pains to avoid the dangers of undue specialism. He must learn to see his universe in perspective as well as under a microscope. There is no single way of attaining this end, for the simple reason that intellectual habits are as various as men. Morris Cohen makes his philosophy more profound by a constant study of the law. Graham Wallas has quickened his insight into political science by experience of practical administration on the London County Council. Leonard Hobhouse has laid the foundations of English sociology by the practice of political journalism and industrial negotiation. Freshness of mind, in a word, is born of the cultivation of diverse disciplines; there may be learned teaching without it, but there will never be wise teaching.

A third condition of the fresh mind is more difficult to state. It is important that the teacher change from time to time not only the subject-matter he expounds, but also the period of time he devotes to it. It is a bad thing for any man to go on lecturing year in and year out, upon the same theme. The texture of his mind thereby becomes inelastic. His approach to what he has to say becomes formulistic, and his categories of explanation become tyrants to which he is a slave. One of my first colleagues had lectured upon the same subject (a period of English history) for fifteen years; and year by year, as the session ended, his notes went back to his box in the Safe Deposit Company, so that next year's work would leave him with no problems. The result was the inevitable one that, at least for the purposes of teaching, he had ceased to think upon his subject. His mind was utterly closed to the new view or the new material, simply because the effort of absorption they would have involved was too great. He had ceased to see his theme as a body of principles and problems; it had become a theological creed not open to reëxamination. Something of the same holds, too, about the period of time. Our division of the university year into terms or semesters tempts us, only too often, to spread our treatment of subjects so as to coincide with those periods. Nothing is more urgent in university technique than experiment in this realm. We are handicapped here by the almost universal tradition of compulsory lectures, and the belief that a certain number of credits, taken together, add up to a university degree. These are evil dogmas which betray us at every turn. Oxford and Cambridge have had the wisdom to have no compulsory lectures; Harvard and Swarthmore have taken steps of importance in this direction. We need to go much further. We need to preach insistently to the student that, granted accessible counsel, the responsibility of what lectures he may attend is on his shoulders as a part of the discipline he is to acquire; and we need to free the teacher from the need to think out his lectures in terms of the units convenient for university administration. A teacher who comes back from a long vacation full of ideas about Rousseau will serve his students better by a short course about something that has excited him than by a long course on which he feels he has nothing new to say. We know from his pupils how admirable a vehicle of instruction was Ranke's habit of discoursing at large in the lecture-room upon some new book that had interested him. We need far more of such practice simply because the book that excites the teacher is a natural source of illumination to the student.

The third great obligation in the teacher, I have said, is the need to make his pupils his friends. No teaching work is really successful which remains on a purely official plane. The teacher who disappears from his lecture-room as soon as the lecture is over; the teacher who will see students only within stated office-hours, as though he were a manufacturer receiving commercial travelers;

the teacher who lays it down, as I have heard it too often laid down, that his connection with the university ends as soon as he leaves its buildings—all these are depriving the student of much that makes for the best in university instruction. For upon that official plane the student's mind can never be intimately known. His real thoughts, his profoundest ambitions, are never revealed in casual intercourse of that kind. The teacher who gets the best out of his students makes his home an annex to the university. He is not prepared to divide off his life into compartments, into some of which the student cannot enter. He entertains them, talks with them, gives them the sense that he is eager to proffer counsel. It is, of course, exacting labor; and it may mean a heavy call on his time. But I think that men like Copeland of Harvard, who have devoted their lives to their students, would say that they have been repaid a hundred times by the affection and insight they have gained through their devotion; and I know that there are innumerable students all over America to whom Harvard will always mean certain Monday nights in "Copey's" room, where two dozen undergraduates on the floor have been led by his genius for friend-ship into those high regions of the mind where the mystery of education begins to be revealed.

QUESTIONS FOR STUDY

1. Which sentence summarizes the essay?
2. Give the etymology of *obligation, facile, ultimate, illuminate, regurgitate, tradition, decision, sabbatical, vitality, expound, theme, casual.*
3. List words built on the following stems: *lig-, fac-, lum-, vita-, cad-.*
4. How does Laski define research?
5. What illustrations of ways of keeping a fresh mind does the writer include?
6. What conditions keep the mind of the teacher fresh?
7. What methods of development appear in the last paragraph?
8. Write a paragraph on a teacher or a method of teaching that you have known directly in your schooling.

George Santayana

If we ask ourselves what was Emerson's relation to the scientific and religious movements of his time, and what place he may claim in the history of opinion, we must answer that he belonged very little to the past, very little to the present, and almost wholly to that abstract sphere into which mystical or philosophic aspiration has carried a few men in all ages. The religious tradition in which he was reared was that of Puritanism, but of a Puritanism which, retaining its moral intensity and metaphysical abstraction, had minimized its doctrinal expression and become Unitarian. Emerson was indeed the Psyche of Puritanism, "the latest-born and fairest vision far" of all that "faded hierarchy." A Puritan whose religion was all poetry, a poet whose only pleasure was thought, he showed in his life and personality the meagreness, the constraint, the frigid and conscious consecration which belonged to his clerical ancestors, while his inmost impersonal spirit ranged abroad over the fields of history and nature, gathering what ideas it might, and singing its little snatches of inspired song.

The traditional element was thus rather an external and inessential contribution to Emerson's mind; he had the professional tinge, the decorum, the distinction of an old-fashioned divine; he had also the habit of writing sermons, and he had the national pride and hope of a religious people that felt itself providentially chosen to establish a free and godly commonwealth in a new world. For the rest, he separated himself from the ancient creed of the community with a sense rather of relief than of regret. A literal belief in Christian doctrines repelled him as unspiritual, as manifesting no understanding of the meaning which, as allegories, those doctrines might have to a philosophic and poetical spirit. Although, being a clergyman, he was at first in the habit of referring to the Bible and its lessons as to a supreme authority, he had no instinctive sympathy with the inspiration of either the Old or the New Testament; in Hafiz or Plutarch, in Plato or Shakespeare, he found more congenial stuff.

While he thus preferred to withdraw, without rancour and without contempt, from the ancient fellowship of the church, he assumed an attitude hardly less cool and deprecatory toward the enthusiasms of the new era. The national ideal of democracy and freedom had his entire sympathy; he allowed himself to be drawn into the movement against slavery; he took a curious and smiling interest in the discoveries of natural science and in the material progress of the age. But he could go no further. His contemplative nature, his religious training, his dispersed reading, made him stand aside from the life of the world, even while he studied it with benevolent attention. His heart was fixed on eternal things, and he was in no sense a prophet for his age or country. He belonged by nature to that mystical company of devout souls that recognize no particular home and are dispersed throughout history, although not without intercommunication. He felt his affinity to the Hindoos and the Persians, to the Platonists and the Stoics. Yet he was a shrewd Yankee, by instinct on the winning side; he was a cheery, child-like soul, impervious to the evidence of evil, as of everything that it did not suit his transcendental individuality to appreciate or to notice. More, perhaps, than anybody that has ever lived, he practised the transcendental method in all its purity. He had no system. He opened his eyes on the world every morning with a fresh sincerity, marking how things seemed to him then, or what they suggested to his spontaneous fancy. This fancy, for being spontaneous, was not always novel; it was guided by the habits and training of his mind, which were those of a preacher. Yet he never insisted on his notions so as to turn them into settled dogmas; he felt in his bones that they were myths. Sometimes, indeed, the bad example of other transcendentalists, less true than he to their method, or the pressing questions of unintelligent people, or the instinct we all have to think our ideas final, led him to the very verge of system-making; but he stopped short. Had he made a system out of his notion of compensation, or the over-soul, or spiritual laws, the result would have been as thin and forced as it is in other transcendental systems. But he coveted truth; and he returned to experience, to history, to poetry, to the natural science of his day, for new starting-points and hints toward fresh transcendental musings.

To covet truth is a very distinguished passion. Every philosopher says he is pursuing the truth, but this is seldom the case. As a philosopher has observed, one reason why philosophers often fail to reach the truth is that often they do not desire to reach it. Those who are genuinely concerned in discovering what happens to be true are rather the men of science, the naturalists, the historians; and ordinarily they discover it, according to their lights. The truths they find are never complete, and are not always important; but they are integral parts of the truth, facts and circumstances that help to fill in the picture, and that no later interpretation can invalidate or afford to contradict. But professional philosophers are usually only apologists: that is, they are absorbed in defending some vested illusion or some eloquent idea. Like lawyers or detectives, they study the case for which they are retained, to see how much evidence or semblance of evidence they can gather for the defence, and how much prejudice they can raise against the witnesses for the prosecution; for they know they are defending prisoners suspected by the world, and perhaps by their own good sense, of falsification. They do not covet truth, but victory and the dispelling of their own doubts. What they defend is some system, that is, some view about the totality of things, of which men are actually ignorant. No system would have ever been framed if people had been simply interested in knowing what is true, whatever it may be. What produces systems is the interest in maintaining against all comers that some favourite or inherited idea of ours is sufficient and right. A system may contain an account of many things which, in detail, are true enough; but as a system, covering infinite possibilities that neither our experience nor our logic can prejudge, it must be a work of imagination and a piece of human soliloquy. It may be expressive of human experience, it may be poetical; but how should any one who really coveted truth suppose that it was true?

Emerson has no system; and his coveting truth had another exceptional consequence; he was detached, unworldly, contemplative. When he came out of the conventicle or the reform meeting, or out of the rapturous close atmosphere of the lecture-room, he heard nature whispering to him: "Why so hot, little sir?" No doubt the spirit or energy of the world is what is acting in us, as the sea is what rises in every little wave; but it passes through us, and cry out as we may, it will move on. Our privilege is to have perceived it as it moves. Our dignity is not in what we do, but in what we understand. The whole world is doing things. We are turning in that vortex; yet within us is silent observation, the speculative eye before which all passes, which bridges the distances and compares the combatants. On this side of his genius Emerson broke away from all conditions of age or country and represented nothing except intelligence itself.

There was another element in Emerson, curiously combined with transcendentalism, namely, his love and respect for nature. Nature, for the transcendentalist, is precious because it is his own work, a mirror in which he looks at himself and says (like a poet relishing his own verses), "What a genius I am! Who would have thought there was such stuff in me?" And the philosophical egotist finds in his doctrine a ready explanation of whatever beauty and commodity nature actually has. No wonder, he says to himself, that nature is sympathetic, since I made it. And such a view, one-sided and even fatuous as it may be, undoubtedly sharpens the vision of a poet and a moralist to all that is inspiriting and symbolic in the natural world. Emerson was particularly ingenious and clear-sighted in feeling the spiritual uses of fellowship with the elements. This is something in which all Teutonic poetry is rich and which forms, I think, the most genuine and spontaneous part of modern taste, and especially of American taste. Just as some people are naturally enthralled and refreshed by music, so others are by landscape. Music and landscape make up the spiritual resources of those who cannot or dare not express their unfulfilled ideals in words. Serious poetry, profound religion (Calvinism, for instance), are the joys of an unhappiness that confesses itself; but when a genteel tradition forbids people to confess that they are unhappy, serious poetry and profound religion are closed to them by that;

and since human life, in its depths, cannot then express itself openly, imagination is driven for comfort into abstract arts, where human circumstances are lost sight of, and human problems dissolve in a purer medium. The pressure of care is thus relieved, without its quietus being found in intelligence. To understand oneself is the classic form of consolation; to elude oneself is the romantic. In the presence of music or landscape human experience eludes itself; and thus romanticism is the bond between transcendental and naturalistic sentiment. The winds and clouds come to minister to the solitary ego.

QUESTIONS FOR STUDY

1. Define *vortex, fatuous, quietus, clerical, traditional, rancour, deprecatory, affinity,* and *shrewd.*
2. Explain "the Psyche of Puritanism" and "faded hierarchy."
3. What, to Santayana, are the characteristics of Emerson's transcendentalism?
4. Give an example of a "vested illusion."
5. Was Emerson a professional philosopher in Santayana's sense of the term?
6. What analogy links the spirit of the world and the sea?
7. In what sentence or sentences does Santayana summarize Emerson's view of life?
8. Is Emerson's view of life harmonious with the "national ideal of democracy and freedom"? Explain.

ARTHUR RIMBAUD

Edmund Wilson

One of the principal causes, of course, for [the] withdrawal of the *fin de siècle* poets from the general life of their time, was the fact that in the utilitarian society which had been produced by the industrial revolution and the rise of the middle class, the poet seemed to have no place. For Gautier's generation, the bourgeois had already become the enemy; but one took a lively satisfaction in fighting him. By the end of the century, however, the bourgeois's world was going so strong that, from the point of view of the poet, it had come to seem hopeless to oppose it. The artistic heroes of Thomas Mann with their abject "inferiority complex" in the presence of the good German burgher are typical of the end of the century; but certain writers with a strong Romantic strain like H. G. Wells and Bernard Shaw tried to promote through the new social sciences, in the teeth of the bourgeois world, the realization of those visions of universal happiness which had been cherished by some of the most individualistic of the Romantics, such as Shelley and Rousseau. But if one had no sociological interest and no satirical bent and so no way of turning society to account, one did not try to struggle with it or to attract attention by publishing one's grievances against it: one simply did one's best to ignore it, to keep one's imagination free of it altogether.

The poets of the end of the century, when they happened to be incapable of Naturalism or of social idealism like William Morris's, were thus peculiarly maladjusted persons. We are less conscious of this in the case of the early Symbolist writers . . . because they were men who either, not possessing particularly vigorous personalities,

113

resigned themselves easily to their special situation or, from illness
or for some other reason, were not able to rebel against it long.
Pater and Mallarmé were professors, living quietly and modestly
among their books; Verlaine drifted with every wind; Corbière
and Laforgue were dying of tuberculosis in their twenties; Ducasse
was dead at twenty-four, perhaps murdered for his alliance with
the Socialists; and for Villiers de l'Isle-Adam, a man of distinguished family who had plumbed the depths of poverty and misery
in Paris to emerge finally, with health and disposition ruined, as a
reputation of the literary cafés, it was easy to reject, in the rôle of
the haughty Axel,[1] imaginary treasures and honors. Yet both the
characteristic tendency of the Symbolists to intimate rather than
speak plainly and their cult of the unique personal point of view
are symptomatic of the extent to which they found themselves out
of touch with their fellows and thrown in upon their own private
imaginations. Another hero and pioneer of Symbolism, however,
was both to struggle with the world and survive—though to survive as something other than a poet; and his career reveals the
whole situation in a dramatic burst of light.

Arthur Rimbaud [1854–1891] was born in the north of France,
the son of a pious and strong-willed countrywoman and of an army
officer who, during the years of his campaigning, paid little attention to his family and finally abandoned them altogether. A prize
scholar at his provincial school, Rimbaud had run, by the time he
was nineteen, through the whole repertoire of modern ideas: he
had reacted against a strict religious training into romantic
atheism and paganism; had flamed up, at the fall of the Second
Empire, with social-revolutionary idealism; and had finally de-
voured Darwin and the other evolutionary writers—as, in poems
written between sixteen and nineteen (1870–73), he had, as one of
his biographers has said, "lived in three years the literary evolution
of modern times." Rimbaud's earliest poetry was in a familiar
Romantic vein, to which, however, he soon brought fresh strong
colors and new elements of irony and invective. He had already, at
seventeen, attempted, in a letter to a friend, an original reëstimate
of the Romantics, of whom he asserted that they had never proper-

[1The fastidious young man in Villiers de l'Isle-Adam's *Axel* (1890) who lives less
in action than in his own private imagination.]

ly been judged, and proposed at the same time a new theory of poetry which, though more violent and apocalyptic than most expressions of Symbolist doctrine, prophesied the advent of Symbolism:

I say that one must be a *visionary*—that one must make oneself a VISIONARY.

The poet makes himself a *visionary* through a long, immense and reasoned *derangement of all the senses*. All forms of love, of suffering, of madness; he seeks himself, he exhausts all poisons in himself to keep only their quintessences. An indescribable torture in which he has need of all faith, all superhuman force, in which he becomes, among all, the great sick man, the great criminal, the great accursed—and the supreme Scholar!—for he arrives at the *unknown*—Because he has cultivated his soul, already rich, more than anyone else! He arrives at the unknown; and even if, driven insane, he should end by losing his grasp on his visions, he has seen them! Let him perish, in his plunging, by unheard-of unnamable things: other horrible workers will come; they will begin at those horizons where their predecessors sank! . . .

The poet is a true Stealer of Fire.

He is charged with humanity, with the animals themselves; he must make his inventions felt, handled, heard. If what he brings back from *beyond* has form, he gives form; if it is formless, he gives the formless. To find a language;

—All speech, furthermore, being idea, the time of a universal language will come! One has to be an academician—deader than a fossil —to make a dictionary of any language at all. The weak-minded would begin *thinking* about the first letter of the alphabet and might quickly end by going mad!—

This language will be of the soul for the soul, summing up all, perfumes, sounds, colors, catching hold of thought with thought and drawing it out. The poet would define the quantity of unknown awakening in his time in the universal soul: he would give more than the formula of his thought, more than the annotation of his march to *Progress!* An enormity becoming a norm absorbed by all, he would be a true *multiplier of progress!*. . .

I habituated myself [he wrote later] to simple hallucination: I would see quite honestly a mosque instead of a factory, a school of drummers composed of angels, calashes on the roads of the sky, a drawing-room at the bottom of a lake: monsters, mysteries; the announcement of a musical comedy would cause horrors to rise before me.

Then I explained my magical sophistries by the hallucination of words!

I ended by finding sacred the disorder of my intelligence. . . .

Rimbaud had apparently arrived at the point of view set forth in his letter independently of the influence of any other French poet; and, in the productions described in the later passage, had merely been giving expression to a unique personal way of seeing— though he was to know something of English literature and had probably read Poe's poetry as early as 1872. A few months after writing this letter, however, he had made the acquaintance of Paul Verlaine. Verlaine, though he published his poems in the collections of the Parnassians, was already tending toward pure musical effects and taking unauthorized metrical liberties; and he had a special predisposition toward the sort of poetry with which Rimbaud was beginning to experiment boldly. He helped and encouraged the boy; took him into his house in Paris and tried to put him in touch with the Parisian literary world.

And Rimbaud in his turn was not only profoundly to influence Verlaine's poetry, but to play havoc with his life. Verlaine, then twenty-seven, had just been married and his wife was expecting a baby; but his impressionable feminine nature, at once rakish and sentimental, was delighted and infatuated by Rimbaud. Rimbaud, who, for all the boy's blue eyes and apple-cheeks which were combined with his ungainly figure and his large bumpkin's hands and feet, for all his unsteady adolescent's voice with its northern country accent, had already his hard core and his harsh will; and he now brought to the rôle of outlaw the moral force which he had inherited from his mother, even though her narrowness and rigor, her merciless domination of his childhood, had been driving him to take the part of Satan. A provincial in Paris without a penny, as well as a man of genius at an age when most boys are only just beginning to indulge their first doubts and to hazard their first original phrases, Rimbaud's position would by no means have been easy even if his nature had not been intractable. He ran amuck in the literary circles to which Verlaine introduced him, and, after disrupting Verlaine's household, carried him off on a vagabondage of adventure through Belgium and England. Verlaine had already, presumably, become rather discontented with his bourgeois domestic life—he was obliged to live with his wife's family—and Rimbaud had quickly infected him with his own ambition to become a supreme Visionary and a supreme outlaw against bourgeois society: "I had, indeed, in all sincerity of spirit," Rimbaud writes in one of his prose poems, "undertaken to restore him to his primitive condition of child of the Sun—and we wandered, fed with the wine of thieves' dens and the hardtack of the road, I eager to find the place and the formula." But this programme was too much for Verlaine, whom Rimbaud ridiculed and bedevilled and who was made uneasy by memories of his wife: her child had been born in the meantime and she was now bringing an action for divorce. Rimbaud himself, in the abrupt ruthless confrontation of the realities of his situation which followed this hallucinated period, was aware of the extent to which he had made Verlaine a victim of his own special maladjustment—and of the extent to which he himself, in regard to that maladjustment, had been taking a line of least resistance: "Beside his dear sleeping body," he makes Verlaine say in "Une Saison en Enfer," "how many hours of the night I have watched, seeking why he should desire so furiously to escape from reality. Never before had man such an ambition. I recognized—without fearing for him—that he might be a serious danger to society. Has he perhaps secrets to change life?" Rimbaud had always been given to seeing himself in the rôle of a criminal: "Even as a child," he writes, "I used to admire the incorrigible convict on whom the jail is always closing again. . . . He had for me more strength than a saint, more good sense than a traveller—and himself, himself alone! for witness of his glory and his reason." And now he makes Verlaine play at this game with him: on one occasion, they both get arrested for discussing imaginary robberies and murders in the railway station at Arras.

The literary results of this expedition were Verlaine's "Romances sans Paroles" and Rimbaud's "Illuminations." Their titles indicate the wide difference between the temperaments and geniuses of the two men; yet the poems represent a sort of collaboration which was to be as important as Mallarmé's cénacle in making the new poetry self-conscious and in giving it the courage of its convictions.

At last, after several quarrels and separations, Verlaine and Rimbaud parted definitively—though not until Verlaine had been sentenced to two years in prison at Brussels for shooting Rimbaud in the wrist, and Rimbaud, meeting Verlaine at Stuttgart after the latter's release and finding that he had while in jail repented of his former errors and found repose in the bosom of the Church, had first proceeded to get Verlaine drunk and make him blaspheme his faith, "cause" as Rimbaud wrote in a letter, "the ninety-eight wounds of Our Lord to bleed," and then—according, at least, to the legend—as they were walking through the Black Forest and another altercation arose, knocked him down with a club and left him unconscious.

In the meantime, while Verlaine was in jail, Rimbaud had returned to his mother's house in the Ardennes, where, during the spring and summer of 1873, he composed that extraordinary masterpiece "Une Saison en Enfer," in which the hysteria of the late nineteenth century in France, not very different from that of our own time—an age recently deprived of religious faith, demoralized and embittered by war and already becoming dissatisfied with social utopianism, science and the cult of art as an end in itself— was crystallized in the sharp and dazzling fragments of what Verlaine called a "diamond prose." But now, not merely unreconciled to the bourgeois world and at the centre of the conflict of its intellectual currents, but disillusioned at last with all these, disgusted with his own incoherence and even with the brilliant literature which he had created to give it expression, he had planned an escape from the European reality by a more effective means than self-hallucination. Rimbaud had always thought of himself as a peasant, as a member of "the inferior race," the blue-eyed Gauls whom the Romans had conquered—and he had always longed for some life that would take the place of the lost brutality and innocence of Europe, for the non-Christian, non-middle-class life of the Orient, of Africa:

Priests, professors, masters, [he now writes] you are wrong to give me up to justice. I have never belonged to these people; I have never been a Christian; I am of the race who sang in torture; I do not understand the laws; I haven't the moral sense, I am a brute; you are doing wrong. Yes, my eyes are closed to your light. I am a nigger, a beast. But I may be saved. You yourselves are false niggers, savage and grasping madmen. Tradesman, you are a nigger; magistrate, you are a nigger; general, you are a nigger; emperor, old itching palm, you are a nigger: you have drunk of a contraband liquor from Satan's distillery. This people is inspired by fever and cancer. Invalids and old men are so respectable that they ought to be boiled. The wisest course is to quit this continent, where madness prowls to provide these wretches with hostages. I am entering into the true kingdom of Shem.

Do I know Nature? do I know myself?—*No more words.* I bury the dead in my belly. Shouts, drums, dance, dance, dance! I do not even foresee the hour when the white men will land among us and when I shall be nothing again.

Hunger, thirst, shouts, dance, dance, dance, dance!

Having finished his "pagan book, nigger book," as he called it before he gave it its final name, "A Season in Hell," he went down in the autumn to Paris, where the literary men in the cafés, who had heard of his escapades with Verlaine, received him with insulting coldness. He returned to his mother's house and burnt up all the copies of "Une Saison en Enfer" which he had just received from his publisher, as well as all the other manuscripts he had.

And now he proceeded to carry out the resolution which he had announced in the work he had burnt. Shutting himself up and studying continuously, sometimes for twenty-four hours at a time, he applies himself to learning the modern languages—he had always had a linguistic gift—which are most useful for travel and trade: English, German, Spanish, Italian, Russian, Arabic and Greek. And as a few years before, just out of school, without money and almost without friends, he had kept obstinately running away to Paris—so now, determined to turn his back on Europe, as moneyless and more friendless than before, he tries repeatedly to reach the East. First, after teaching for a year in Germany, he sells his trunk and makes his way to Italy, with the intention of joining a friend who has a soap-factory in the Cyclades; but, undertaking to travel to Brindisi on foot, he gets a sunstroke and is repatriated by the French consul. At Marseilles, he manages to live by unloading cargo and helping truck-drivers, and then enlists in the Carlist army, but finally returns to his mother's house. Next, in order to get passage to Java, he enlists for six years in the Dutch army—lands at Batavia, deserts, joins the crew of an English sailing-vessel, goes back to France and home again. The next year, under the pretext of wanting to go to Austria for the purpose of learning German, he succeeds in getting some money out of his mother; but immediately upon arriving in Vienna, he takes his cabman out for a drink and in return is robbed of his coat with all his money, and finds himself obliged to sell key-rings and shoe-laces in the street till he gets into a row with the Austrian police and is sent back again to France. Soon, however, he sets out on foot for Hamburg, whence he hopes to find some way of getting to the East, but where, instead, he falls in with a circus, with which he travels as interpreter and barker on a tour of the Scandinavian countries, finally getting himself sent back by the consul from Stockholm to Charleville again. On his next attempt, after earning a little money unloading cargo at Marseilles, he buys passage to Alexandria, but on the ship develops gastric fever from a rubbing of his ribs against his abdomen, caused by too much walking—and goes back to Charleville.

Three months afterwards, however—in the spring of 1878—by way of Switzerland, Italy and Egypt, he succeeds in reaching the island of Cyprus and gets a job as foreman in one of the quarries. But he catches typhoid and by the spring of the next year is at home with his family once more. When a friend asks him whether he is writing nowadays, he replies with annoyance and scorn: "I don't do anything with that any more"; and when, on the eve of his departure the next spring, he hears one of his friends congratulate another on having just bought some Lemerre editions—Lemerre had been the publisher of the Parnassians—he bursts out: "That's a lot of money wasted. It's absolutely idiotic to buy books —and especially books like that. You've got a ball between your shoulders that ought to take the place of books. When you put books on your shelves, the only thing they do is cover up the leprosies of the old walls." He looks for work in Cyprus, in Egypt, in Abyssinia, in all the ports of the Red Sea, and finally finds a job at Aden working at twelve francs a day for a firm of French coffee importers. This company presently sends him to Harrar, where it is starting a new branch, and later makes Rimbaud the director of all its expeditions into Galla and Somaliland. Rimbaud was the first European to penetrate into the country of Ogadain; and on his return from an extremely dangerous expedition to one of the native potentates, he traced for the first time the itinerary afterwards taken by the Ethiopian railway. At last, however, he quarrels with his employers and, after adventures of various kinds, sets up at Harrar a trading-post of his own, where he traffics in sugar, rice, silk, cotton-goods and arms, sending out his own caravans, intriguing with the local kings, entertaining European travellers with enchanting and cynical conversation and maintaining a harem of native women carefully selected as coming from different parts of the country so that they may teach him their different languages. During this period, he wrote to a friend on *Le Temps* asking to be sent as war correspondent to cover the Italo-Abyssinian campaign. This poposal was declined, but in answering his letter the friend informed him that his poems, preserved by Verlaine, were being published and read in Paris, and that, in the circles of the new Symbolist school, he had become a legendary figure, an attempt having even been made to found a new literary system on a sonnet in which he had assigned different colors to the vowels. But at this period, Rimbaud's only literary concern was to supply reports to the Geographical Society, and, when he refers to his poetry at all, it is to dismiss it as "absurd" or "disgusting." "I couldn't go on with it," he told his sister later. "I should have gone mad—and besides it was bad stuff." The only ambition he now admits is to make enough money to marry a French girl and retire from his present business—"to have at least one son whom I could spend the rest of my life bringing up according to my own ideas, cultivating and arming him with the completest education that one can get in this age, and whom I could see become a famous engineer, powerful and rich through science."

One winter, however, after Rimbaud had been twelve years in the East, he found himself suffering from what he took at first to be varicose veins; but he refused to go to a doctor, kept on walking and riding, as if he could dominate even disease by his stubborn and brutal will—and presently found that his leg was so swollen that he was obliged to direct his business from bed. At last the pain had become so severe that he was compelled to give up altogether and have himself carried on a litter to Aden, a terrible journey of twelve days, on the second of which he spent sixteen hours without shelter under pouring rain.

The English doctor at Aden told Rimbaud that he would be unable to treat him properly, and shipped him back to France, where, in the hospital at Marseilles, they amputated his leg. For the last time Rimbaud returned to his mother's: he tried to get about on a crutch, but the infection had spread through his whole system. He spent an agonizing summer of pain and fever, and then, with a fixed idea of returning to the East, had himself sent back to Marseilles. There he died, attended only by his sister. It was harvest-time on the family farm, and the daughter's absence was bitterly resented by her mother, who when Arthur had been away, had refused to get for him instruments and books which he had sent her the money to buy. Isabelle, Rimbaud's sister, had never known till after her brother's death, when she read about it in the papers, that Arthur had been a poet, but she heard him "end his life in a sort of continual dream, saying strange things very gently in a voice that would have charmed me if it had not pierced my heart. What he was saying was all dreams, yet it was not the same thing at all as when he had had the fever. It was as if he did it on purpose.... He mixed all sorts of things up, and with art." But Rimbaud, in his final delirium, was still obsessed by the idea of the East: on his death-bed, he insisted upon dictating a letter to a steamship company, asking how much the passage would cost and when he should have himself carried aboard.

One is likely to be guilty of over-simplification in using people's personal careers to point the morals of general social situations. Rimbaud, in his rôle of African trader, had obviously succeeded at last in emulating his father and his mother both at once—repeating the career of the former, who had campaigned in Italy, Algiers and the Crimea, by his wanderings and his intolerant independence at the same time that, by his sound character as a trader and his concentration upon making money, he was achieving the only sort of success which his mother could understand. Yet Rimbaud's life has a typical significance: it moves us, it seems to put before us an acute phase of the human predicament, as if it were a great play. The other poets of whom I have been writing were as little at home in their nineteenth-century world as Rimbaud, and they were mostly as disillusioned with its enthusiasms; but they had remained in it and managed to hold their places in it by excreting, like patient molluscs, iridescent shells of literature— whereas Rimbaud, with genius equal to any's, with genius perhaps superior to any's, had rejected Europe altogether—not merely its

society and ideas, but even the kind of sensibility which one cultivated when one tried to live at odds with it and the kind of literature this sensibility supplied—getting away to a life of pure action
and a more primitive civilization.

And if actions can be compared with writings, Rimbaud's life
seems more satisfactory than the works of his Symbolist contemporaries, than those even of most of his Symbolist successors, who
stayed at home and stuck to literature. Rimbaud was far from
finding in the East that ideal barbarous state he was seeking; even
at Harrar during the days of his prosperity he was always steaming
with anxieties and angers—but his career, with its violence, its
moral interest and its tragic completeness, leaves us feeling that we
have watched the human spirit, strained to its most resolute sincerity and in possession of its highest faculties, breaking itself in the
effort to escape, first from humiliating compromise, and then from
chaos equally humiliating. And when we turn back to consider
even the masterpieces of that literature which Rimbaud had
helped to found and which he had repudiated, we are oppressed by
a sullenness, a lethargy, a sense of energies ingrown and sometimes
festering. Even the poetry of the noble Yeats, still repining
through middle age over the emotional miscarriages of youth, is
dully weighted, for all its purity and candor, by a leaden acquiescence in defeat.

Questions for Study

1. Define *utilitarian, apocalyptic, quintessence, sophistry, intractable,
   incorrigible, cénacle.*
2. What is the romantic strain as it is here defined?
3. What contrasted ideas were current when Rimbaud became twenty?
4. Summarize, in a few sentences, Rimbaud's idea of a poet.
5. What illustrations of "the hallucinated period" of Verlaine and
   Rimbaud does Wilson give?
6. What attitudes, actions, and ideas characterized the France Rimbaud left?

7. What principle of progression from paragraph to paragraph does the writer use?
8. To what point does Wilson's account of Rimbaud's odyssey converge? What did Rimbaud seek in the East?
9. How does Rimbaud's life put before us "an acute phase of the human predicament"?
10. What may stand between humiliating compromise and equally humiliating chaos?
11. How does Rimbaud's life contrast with that of his contemporaries?
12. Explain "tragic completeness."

GENIUS

Loren Eiseley

Directly stated, the evolution of the entire universe—stars, elements, life, man—is a process of drawing something out of nothing, out of the utter void of non-being. The creative element in the mind of man—that latency which can conceive gods, carve statues, move the heart with the symbols of great poetry, or devise the formulas of modern physics—emerges in as mysterious a fashion as those elementary particles which leap into momentary existence in great cyclotrons, only to vanish again like infinitesimal ghosts. The reality we know in our limited lifetimes is dwarfed by the unseen potential of the abyss where science stops. In a similar way the smaller universe of the individual human brain has its lonely cometary passages, or flares suddenly like a super nova, only to subside in death while the waves of energy it has released roll on through unnumbered generations.

As the astrophysicist gazes upon the rare releases of power capable of devastating an entire solar system, so does the student of the behavioral sciences wonder at the manifestations of creative genius and consider whether the dark mechanisms that control the doorways of the human mind might be tripped open at more frequent intervals. Does genius emerge from the genes alone? Does the largely unknown chemistry of the brain contain at least part of the secret? Or is the number of potential cell connections involved? Or do we ordinary men carry it irretrievably locked within our subconscious minds?

That the *manifestations* of genius are culturally controlled we are well aware. The urban world, in all its diversity, provides a background, a cultural base, without which—whatever may be hidden in great minds—creativity would have had to seek other and more ephemeral expression or remain mute. Yet no development in art or scientific theory from the upper Stone Age onward seems to have demanded any further development in the brain of man. Mathematical theory, science, the glories of art lurked hidden as the potential seeds of the universe itself, in the minds of children rocked to sleep by cave fires in Ice Age Europe.

If genius is a purely biological phenomenon one must assume that the chances of its appearance should increase with the size of populations. Yet it is plain that, like toadstools, which spring up in the night in fairy rings and then vanish, there is some delicate soil which nurtures genius—the cultural circumstance and the play of minds must meet. It is not a matter of population statistics alone, else there would not have been so surprising an efflorescence of genius in fourth- and fifth-century Greece—a thing we still marvel at in our vastly expanded world. Darwin, committed to biological explanations alone, was left fumbling uncertainly with a problem that was essentially not reducible to a simplistic biological explanation. Without ignoring the importance of biology as one aspect of an infinitely complicated subject, therefore, the modern researcher favors the view that the intensive examination of the creative mind and its environment may offer some hope of stimulating the source from which it springs, or, at the very least, of nurturing it more carefully.

. . . We have touched upon loneliness, the dweller in the forest as represented by Thoreau, the isolated man in the room who was Hawthorne, and those wandering recluse scientists such as Darwin and Wallace. This loneliness, in the case of literary men, frequently leads to an intense self-examination. "Who placed us with eyes between a microscopic and telescopic world?" questions Thoreau. "I have the habit of attention to such excess that my senses get no rest, but suffer from a constant strain."

Thoreau here expresses the intense self-awareness which is both the burden and delight of the true artist. It is not the mere matter that such men create their universe as surely as shipwrecked bits of life run riot and transform themselves on oceanic islands. It is that in this supremely heightened consciousness of genius the mind *demands* expression. The spirit literally cannot remain within itself. It will talk if it talks on paper only to itself, as in the case of Thoreau.

Anxiety, the disease which many psychiatrists seek to excise completely from the human psyche, is here carried up to painful but enormously creative heights. The freedom of genius, its passage beyond the bonds of culture which controls the behavior of the average man, in itself demands the creation of new modes of being. Says Yeats:

> Man's life is thought and he despite his terror cannot cease
> Ravening through century after century...
> That he may come
> Into the desolation of reality.

Within that desolation, whether he be scientist or poet, man—for this is the nature of his inmost being—will build ever anew. It is not in his nature to do otherwise.

Thoreau, however, presents in his writing an interesting paradox. In his reference to the excessive strain of heightened attention, one might get the impression that creativity was to him a highly conscious exercise that had wriggled into his very fingertips. That he was an intensely perceptive observer there can be no question. Yet, he wrote, in those pre-Freudian, pre-Jungian days of 1852:

> I catch myself philosophizing most abstractly when first returning to consciousness in the night or morning. I make the truest observations and distinctions then, when the will is yet wholly asleep and the mind works like a machine without friction. I am conscious of having, in my sleep, transcended the limits of the individual, and made observations and carried on conversations which in my waking hours I can neither recall nor appreciate. As if in sleep our individual fell into the infinite mind, and at the moment of awakening we found ourselves on the confines of the latter.

"It is," he confides in another place, "the material of all things loose and set afloat that makes my sea."

Psychiatrist Lawrence Kubie has speculated that "the creative person is one who in some manner, which today is still accidental, has retained his capacity to use his pre-conscious functions more freely than is true of others who may potentially be equally gifted." While I do not believe that the time will ever come when each man can release his own Shakespeare, I do not doubt that the freedom to create is somehow linked with facility of access to those obscure regions below the conscious mind.

There is, perhaps, a wonderful analogy here between the potential fecundity of life in the universe and those novelties which natural selection in a given era permits to break through the living screen, the biosphere, into reality. Organic opportunity has thus placed sharp limits upon a far greater life potential than is ever permitted to enter the actual world. Yet this other hidden world, a world of possible but nonexistent futures, is a constant accompaniment, a real but wholly latent twin, of the nature in which we have our being. In a strangely similar manner the mental Censor of a too rigidly blocked or distorted unconscious may interfere, not alone with genius, but even with what might be called ordinary productivity.

Just as, in a given situation, the living biological screen may prevent the emergence of a higher form of life, or precipitate its destruction, so in that dark, soundless area of the brain, which parallels the similarly pregnant void of space, much may be barred from creation that exists only as a potentiality. Here again, culturally imposed forms and individual experiences may open or keep permanently closed the doorways of life. The role of purely genetic expression becomes frightfully obscured by the environmental complexities which surround the birth and development of the individual. There is no doubt that clinical studies devoted to creativity, including private interviews with cooperating and contemporary men of genius, offer the prospect of gaining greater insight into those dark alleys and byways out of which stumble at infrequent intervals the Shelleys, the Shakespeares, the Newtons, and the Darwins of our world.

Sometimes they are starved by poverty, self-schooled, sometimes they have known wealth, sometimes they have appeared like comets across an age of violence. Or they have been selfless, they have been beautiful or unlovely of body, they have been rake and puritan. One thing alone they have had in common: thought, music, art, transmissible but unique.

Questions for Study

1. What parallels between the natural universe and the mind of man does the writer mention?
2. Which of the two following versions of the same idea is more effective? Why?
   a. The student of the behavioral sciences wonders if the states of mind which evidence genius might more frequently appear.
   b. The student of the behavioral sciences asks whether the dark mechanisms that control the doorways of the human mind might be tripped open at more frequent intervals.
3. What possible explanations of the origin of genius does Eiseley mention?
4. What difficulties beset the biological, psychological, and environmental explanations of genius?
5. What is the analogy between the obscure regions of conscious mind and the biological universe?
6. How may geniuses differ? What trait do all have in common?

EDUCATION AND WORLD TRAGEDY

Howard Mumford Jones

If any human being brought up in the tradition of western civilization could, by some miracle, step outside the familiar patterns of that culture; if history could come to him with the same shock of surprise that a new and stimulating novel brings him; if, in sum, retaining the moral idealism of western civilization as a standard of measurement, he could yet discover for the first time what has happened to mankind in the last fifty years, such a person would, I think, be overwhelmed by a single tragic conviction; namely, that the history of mankind for the last half century has been a history of deepening horror.

Since 1896 the earth has scarcely known a year without warfare, armed revolt, massacre, pogrom or other ingenious form of slaughter. During the first thirty years of the present century, according to Quincy Wright's authoritative study of war, European powers alone fought seventy-four wars, which lasted a total of 297 years; roughly, the average war was four years long. One has to go back to the twelfth century to find a comparable record. In that unenlightened century the average war lasted only three years and a half.

These fifty years include two infernal conflicts—World War I and World War II. They include such disastrous struggles as the Boer War of 1899–1902, the Russo-Japanese War of 1904–05, the two bloody Balkan Wars of 1912–13, the innumerable wars, revolts, "interventions," and massacres in Finland, the Caucasus, the Ukraine, Poland, Hungary, Manchuria, Siberia, and other "border" areas, which followed the Bolshevik Revolution of 1917. They include the long drawn out agony of China, which, beginning with the massacre of garrison troops in 1917, continues to this hour. They include the intermittent civil war in Spain. These are the major events.

But there were other episodes, tragic in their time. Who now vividly remembers the Formosa rebellion of 1896? The Cretan massacre of 1897, when Christians slaughtered the Moslem peasantry? The Boxer rebellion of 1900? The Philippine insurrection and the "water cure"? The massacre of a million Armenians between 1896 and 1919? Yet all these are soberly chronicled in any encyclopedia.

The year 1922 is as representative as any. The Irish civil war was raging, and there were Black and Tan outrages. The year opened with the slaughter of 300 Greek civilians in Samsun. By August about 100,000 Greeks had been killed or captured (I do not know the figures for the Turkish dead), some tens of thousands of civilians having been slain. The bloody climax of 1922 was reached at the taking of Smyrna, when an estimated 200,000 Christians were rendered homeless and the city was given over to pillage, rapine, massacre and fire.

Even at the risk of monotony one must chronicle other wars in this unhappy half century. There was an earlier Graeco-Turkish war in 1897–98, and an Italo-Turkish war in 1911. Between 1928 and 1935 Bolivia and Paraguay fought to exhaustion over the possession of a tropical jungle. Indeed, during many, if not most, of these fifty years there have been rebellions in Latin America; and though it is sometimes said that armed revolt is the standard form of presidential election in that distressed area, a man dead of a bullet in Caracas or Asunción will no more come to life again than a man dead of a bullet at Vimy Ridge or Bataan.

The half century has seen armed rebellion sweep through such famous capitals as Paris, Berlin, Madrid, Athens, and Rome. It has seen more or less protracted revolutionary struggles in Russia, Mexico, Spain, France, Germany, India, Egypt, Palestine, the other Arabian states, Mongolia, China, Hungary, Austria, Greece, Iran, and various other countries, besides what uncounted minor uprisings—Nicaragua, Haiti, Albania, Thailand and the like—only the *World Almanac* now tells us. Ours is a sick age.

How many human beings have been killed directly or indirectly in the course of this terrible history? It is almost impossible to find out. One man's guess is as good as another's. Statistics about death by warfare are not kept in some continents, and, moreover, by its very nature modern warfare sometimes destroys both record and statistician. For example, we do not know and probably shall never know how many hundreds of thousands have died of violence in Asia and Africa during these fifty years. How many perished during the obscure struggle for the control of Tannu-Tuwa, a country twice as large as Scotland, lying between Mongolia and Siberia? How many Koreans were slaughtered by their Japanese overlords? How many natives died during the struggle for the control of the Belgium Congo? We do not know, just as we do not know how many hundreds of thousands died in Russia, on its borders, or in neighboring states during the terrible convulsions that swept over the future Soviet Union between 1914 and the adoption of the constitution of 1925. We do not know how many millions Hitler and his agents killed. But what we know with rough accuracy is sufficiently appalling.

Before 1900 about 25 per cent of all battle casualties died; in World War I this increased 33-1/3 per cent. In the seventeenth century it is estimated that, out of every thousand Frenchmen, 11 died in military service; in the twentieth century, up to World War II, 63 thus perished, an increase of almost 600 per cent. Out of every thousand Europeans alive in the twelfth century it is thought that two died as battle casualties; in the first twenty-five years of the twentieth century 54 out of every thousand so died, an increase of 1700 per cent. Professor Pitirim Sorokin estimates that during the first third of this century Europe suffered 24 million war casualties. If we slaughtered or wounded every man, woman, and child in Maine, New Hampshire, Vermont, Massachusetts, Rhode Island, Connecticut, New York, and New Jersey tomorrow, we should about equal this number. . . .

Our technological skills are not used solely for warfare, but in view of the increasing length, ferocity, and destruction of modern war this is not now the point, especially since, in time of war, technological skill devoted to destruction has the highest possible priority. Certain it is, moreover, that the latest destroyers of humanity—the torpedo, the submarine, the airplane, the tank, poison gas, the rocket, and the A-bomb—are products of highly educated, or at least highly trained, personnel. All but one or two of these are principally or wholly the products of American technological ingenuity. We missed out on poison gas, but we made it up on the atom bomb.

However, the connection between warfare and education goes deeper than the simple but impressive connection between destruction and technical training. The training of soldiers, sailors, and airmen grows increasingly complex. If Hitler and Mussolini were men of no particularized education, their rise to military power was abnormal rather than typical, and for the most part, in modern times, the men who launch wars and who manage them are products of professional education at least as exhaustive and specialized as the education of a doctor, a physicist or a lawyer. Members of a modern general staff devote their lives to study, so that a traditional military leader like General Forrest or Mad Anthony Wayne would not know what to make of these studious and intellectual careers.

Indeed, during World War I, William Jennings Bryan was quaintly out of date when he said that in case of invasion the American people would spring to arms—something that the technological advance of the nineteenth century rendered ineffective and impossible. Nowadays it is impossible for a nation to spring to arms in the old-fashioned sense; and if minute men leaving the plow for the musket sufficed for Lexington and Concord, not even the Home Guard would have sufficed for the Battle of Britain if the German invasion had come. The *lévee en masse* of the French Revolution is antiquated in a world in which the elementary education of a private or of a common sailor takes three months, and a year is considered essential for lasting training—a year filled with educational exercises of such rigor that the colleges cannot compete in intensity. If anarchy should settle over the globe, it is of course possible that a new and illiterate Attila or Genghis Khan might raise, equip and lead popular armies, but in the contemporary world warfare like industry depends primarily upon the continuation and advance of highly complex engineering and scientific studies.

This dependence comes by and by to affect not merely the

training of the fighting man, it affects in time the life of the civilian. The difference between a war fought by the professional army of Frederick the Great and total warfare in the twentieth century is that the entire population participates in modern warfare, not merely in the sense that it may reasonably expect to get killed or wounded, but also in the sense that it shares to greater or less degree this professional training, even if it is no more than civilian street patrolling, the care of children in deep underground shelters, or assignment to an "essential" factory. One has to look back at the relative indifference of most of the population in the American Revolution, the War of 1812, or the Mexican War to see how far we have come. Even during the Civil War life in the North went on as usual, and civilian energies were so little controlled by warfare that the settlement of the West went forward, mining was developed, and shipping, agriculture, and industry increased, partly, to be sure, as a function of warfare, but mainly in a normal mode of progression which the war stimulated but which the fighting did not bend to its own purpose. Contrast the control of civilian life by Washington in World War II. Contrast the even more rigid control of national existence in the British Isles during the same period and since.

Education, then, becomes more and more involved with warfare as warfare develops. . . .

A final fact to be observed in this strange, eventful history is to note how nationalism increasingly invades education. The eighteenth century was perhaps the last period when a truly international culture was the common object of study, at least among cultivated classes in the western world. But the schools of the eighteenth century were still characteristically under the control of the church, of princes who prided themselves on participating in the Enlightenment, or of private persons and corporations. As yet education was not customarily created or paid for by the state.

Throughout the nineteenth century, however, and increasingly in the twentieth, the doctrine that education is a proper charge against the public purse has meant that the state, in greater and greater degree, has made education the instrument of its own support. Thus a leading element in the Chinese Revolution was the demand for state-supported schools, schools that would in fact teach doctrines acceptable to Dr. Sun Yat Sen or, latterly, doctrines acceptable to the ministry of education of Generalissimo Chiang Kai-Shek. Thus the Bolshevik revolution destroyed every vestige of Czarist or Greek Orthodox schools and created a system of education which is as much an arm of the state as the Russian air force or the Russian infantry. Even in a small and unmilitaristic country like Norway, government has in fact forced the abolition of private schools. In Italy, in Germany, in Japan, in Spain, the educational system has been integrated with the state to such a degree that in taking over conquered countries the Allies had to begin by abolishing the remnants of existing schools, destroying textbooks and substituting new systems of education that would mirror and support their own political doctrine. And in France it is a nice question whether the church or the state shall control the schools. Again, in a self-conscious state like Eire one finds government through the schools forcing Gaelic, a cumbersome and artificial language, upon the people as essential to a "national" culture. . . .

War, technology in preparation for war, and nationalism—these are, then, three great forces warping the healthy development of education in what we quaintly call the civilized world. The problems they raise are deeper and darker than those polite fictions discussed in most educational meetings, especially at the college level. In truth, one sometimes fears that our concern for the nature of education, notably at higher levels, seldom rises above the plane of the genteel tradition. Certain it is, however, that an uneasy sense of something wrong, of some radical error, haunts our schools and colleges, troubles philosophers, and leads even the common man to endless speculation about the future of his own civilization. The sense that western culture is wildly astray, western civilization in its decline, is everywhere about us as men turn once again to examine the fundamentals of what they believe.

QUESTIONS FOR STUDY

1. How many instances of the major wars since 1896 are given?

2. What phrase or phrases summarize the opening paragraphs?
3. Is the number of human beings killed in wars fought by European powers known?
4. What observation enables the writer to move from warfare to education?
5. What contrast is developed in the paragraph beginning "This dependence comes . . ."?
6. Outline the entire passage.
7. What sentence or sentences best summarize the main point?

GOVERNMENT AND HIGHER EDUCATION

Alfred Cobban

To find an important cause of the trend towards dictatorship in
the existing concentration on specialization in higher education
may at first sight seem an exaggeration. Yet is there anything far-
fetched in attributing to an educational system a leading, even a
decisive influence, on the progress of a civilization? Again, in
England, at least, it might be asked whether we are not over-esti-
mating the importance of formal education and exaggerating its
place in the national life. In the past this would have been a valid
criticism; but at present in all countries social custom among the
wealthier classes, together with a system of scholarships for the
poorer, is directing a large proportion of the intelligent youth of
the country into the universities. There, educational convention
or economic interest concentrate their attention on a single field of
learning, in which they receive a specialist training. As this tendency progresses, it is not unreasonable to assume that in future the
ablest minds from all ranks will be drawn into the service of society as scientists, or technicians, or specialists in some form or other.
In many ways this is an admirable development; but it has the
result that education can no longer be regarded as a preparation
for government. And if it be argued—though to my mind the
argument is false—that it never was this, it still remains true that
the older educational system at least did not call for the whole-
hearted devotion that modern specialization demands, and often
obtains. The absence in most countries of the most highly trained
sections of the population from political life is a necessary consequence, and in itself a sign of their inability to contribute, except
as experts, to the commonweal.

When the tradition of a class brought up to the task of government has died out, can the experts take its place? In so far as the expert is a scientist it is not to be expected that he should. The statesman must have a scale of values: the scientist must know no such thing. One scientific fact may be more significant than another, it cannot be better. The scientist must be, like Adam and Eve, innocent of the knowledge of good and evil, philosophically naked and unashamed. What of the economist, the psychologist, the sociologist, the administrative expert? All these can give essential advice and information; they can provide studies of technique and show how to obtain one objective or another: they cannot explain why one is to be preferred to another. On the ends of the state, in so far as they are pure experts, they can say nothing. As for the methods of ruling the state—the technique of politics is a technique they do not learn. In that field, compared with the authors of *Mein Kampf* or of *Leninism,* who have devoted their lives to learning it in the hard school of experience, they are babes in arms. On the whole, is it not true to say that we have created an educated class, to which we are giving a monopoly of future education, which has little philosophy, lacks any profound social or political principles, and has small knowledge of or perhaps even interest in the ends of the state? Science has bestowed unprecedented power upon society at the very time when it is taking away from education its value as a preparation for exercising control over that power. One of our experts can do more to control the material universe than the tens of thousands of slaves who toiled at the building of the pyramids; but he may have a little understanding of ultimate social purposes, and as little control over social ends, as they.

Is it false, then, to say that the type of education which was a preparation for government is disappearing? Is it paradoxical to suggest that it is the very progress of education which is threatening to rob this country, as it is already robbing others, of a politically educated class of rulers? The strength of aristocracy in a country like England in the past was that it gave to a selected class a training in the art of government and an education appropriate thereto. The class was chosen, of course, by heredity, and therefore naturally a large proportion of it would be quite unfitted to profit by the opportunities it received; but there remained a sufficiently large residue capable of learning its lesson and taking over the government of the country. True, even without adequate training a genius in politics may appear. But if a nation is to rely only on the chance appearance of a political genius then it will have no choice but between anarchy and dictatorship.

There is the further consideration, too, that government is not merely a technique; it is also a psychological attitude. The latter is not easily taught; it is more likely to be transmitted by birth, though there is no doubt that it can be acquired. The aristocracies of the past were selfish, of course, but it was only where they were excluded from government, as in the France of the Bourbons, that they lost their governing capacity. At the worst they continued to believe in themselves and the social order for which they stood. The new aristocracy of experts has no such easy self-confidence or acceptance of things as they are. Its ideals are far higher: it demands progress, social improvement. Yet what criterion has it for knowing these when it sees them, or what capacity for securing them?

QUESTIONS FOR STUDY

1. How does specialization in higher education contribute to a trend toward dictatorship?
2. How does the older educational system differ from that of the present?
3. In what ways do scientists and statesmen differ?
4. What has been the impact of science on higher education?
5. Contrast the abilities and goals of governing aristocracies of the past with the abilities and goals of the new aristocracy of experts.
6. Write a summarizing paragraph which states ways in which higher education may contribute to good government.

Francisco Romero

The fact that, out of the many cultures which have appeared in history, only three survive—the Indian, the Chinese, and the Occidental—seems to suggest that these three possess some particular advantage over the others. In my judgment, this superiority consists in the fact that the three, in contrast to all others, contain an answer (each a radically different one, of course) to the most profound and permanent questions and needs of man. Man is not only the one being that objectifies, he is also a being that objectifies endlessly and untiringly, and he needs the goal and lodestar of a supreme and absolute object to set his mind at rest. Every culture is likely to have aspired to satisfying this need. But while others were unable to supply more than myths, which in the course of time wear out and lose their charm, or halfway goals that proved unsatisfactory, the three mentioned above have each found a great clue or goal which has determined their organization. The clue of Indian culture is the *whole,* the cosmic infinity into which the individual yearns to dissolve, divesting his separate personal existence of all value. In traditional Chinese culture, the clue is the *social reality,* that vast community in which the ancestors live together with their descendants and rule over them, an immense family, held in religious reverence, of which the State is only a political continuation, and which interlaces, through the ties of magic, with the supernatural powers. Occidental tradition has always regarded as the last goal and supreme reality the "I" *qua* soul or person, that is, *qua* absolute entity, deviser of perfect order, and carrier of supreme dignity.

In Indian culture, and likewise in Chinese, the individual achieves reality by giving himself up and merging in a reality he regards as infinitely superior and as the one valid goal or end. This premature resignation and abandonment of the principle of individuality cannot but slow down and weaken the process of the objectification of the "I," whereas the realization of the ultimate goal of the Occident—the "I" as person or absolute subject, as soul or spiritual "I"—requires constant progress in self-objectification and persistence in that objectifying exertion which, as we have seen, constitutes man as such.

From the standpoint here taken, it becomes clear that the success of Occidental man is not an ephemeral historical accident but a consequence of the fact that the course of his culture coincides sufficiently well—at any rate, much better than that of any other culture, dead or living—with the general trend assigned to man by his inmost essence. Despite its limitations and its frequent aberrations, the Occident holds the keys of the future. To those who reproach it with lacking the cosmic sense of India or the social sense of China, one might reply that Occidental culture is not unlikely to accept in due time the holiness of cosmic mystery and to realize the ideal of the solidarity of humanity. For the person taken in his plenitude is a complex of disinterested and reverent intentions toward all that exists. Recognition of the equality of persons and realization of the ideal community of persons is by no means alien to him. Such a cosmic and social union, however, Occidental man will try to accomplish not through annihilation and surrender of his own "I" but, on the contrary, through an ascent from his intentional individual "I" to the spiritual "I." In the course of this ascent, the "I," growing in strength and depth, evolves within himself the person in the image of the personal God who is exclusively characteristic of Occidental culture.

These hypotheses—more they could not be—are borne out by many conspiring signs. Only the Occident is concerned with the concept of time; only the Occident really has history. The individual's flinging himself into the cosmic or social whole—characteristic of the other two great living cultures—is instantaneous; moreover, it is already implied in the central attitude of those cultures, whereas the empirical "I"—the imperfect subject, chained to nature in many ways—is aware, and conceives, of the person as an object to be realized, a duty or task. The process of history has been defined by the greatest Occidental thinkers as a march toward "humanity" (I should prefer to say "humanization") or toward freedom, or again as a progressive realization of the most exalted values. All this signifies nothing if not the gradual triumph of the personal or spiritual principle over concrete individual man who lives immersed in his particular aims and interests. Occidental man believes in time, in history, in progress because his being is given to him as something latent and potential. He endeavors to realize it in time and in history, valiantly taking upon himself the long task of giving existence to what ought to be, of implanting the ideal in the real.

India has worked out a grandiose metaphysics, while the other disciplines into which we are wont to divide philosophy are sporadically developed. The reason is that logic, ethics, and esthetics are meditations on the faculties that shape and consolidate the person in his intercourse with reality. But Indian culture holds such intercourse to be nothing but dream and vanity, for the one thing needed is the integration of the subject into the whole. Metaphysics is concerned with this integration. Metaphysics is conceived, however, not only as knowledge but also, and above all, as practice, as a way to salvation, the gate through which one enters infinite totality. In China formalism and ritual are predominant and all-pervading; they assume a thousand shapes, all very surprising to Europeans. The innumerable threads of an intricate social web knotted in the course of many centuries imprison the individual on all sides and reduce him to a coordinated link within a community which only as an interknit totality possesses value, nay sanctity.

The objectifying will of the Occident, its zest to obtain distinct and exact visions of things, its resolve to maintain intact, in the face of all such visions, the power of the subject have no equal in the Orient. Only Occidental man defines, that is, only he arrives—or believes he arrives, or is in need of arriving—at clear-cut concepts, identical with themselves and hierarchically distributed into rigorous systems of thought. Indian metaphysical systems are mainly interpretations, that is, versions, of traditional wisdom;

they give expression to a truth which may be set forth in various and always fragmentary manners. China's greatest metaphysical work, the *Tao,* eludes any exact determination and any attempt at definition or clear characterization, whereas Western philosophy has, since its beginnings, advanced theses each of which claims to be the only truthful one. The being of things, we have been told, consists of water, air, the *apeiron,* Ideas, matter with its forms. . . . Occidentals are uncompromising and intolerant because they do not for a moment doubt that there exists one true doctrine and many wrong ones. The Orient, save for transitory exceptions, has been tolerant. The faithful of Oriental creeds, for example, are partial to "religious congresses," an idea impossible to occur to Europeans, although they may consent to attend such congresses.

Good or bad, right or wrong, Occidental man goes on objectifying indefatigably. He never tires of coining concepts, of making things. His objectifying urge tends to lead him astray. At times he thinks he was born to fabricate countless things. But he continues, often inadvertently, in his self-objectification. He continues to forge in the dark smithy of his soul "the one thing needed."

Questions for Study

1. Define *objectify, magic, absolute,* and *Occidental.*
2. What stresses differentiate Indian, Chinese, and Occidental cultures?
3. What contrasted trends may man, from his "inmost essence," assign to himself?
4. Explain the meaning of the phrases "the holiness of cosmic mystery" and "the solidarity of humanity."
5. Differentiate (a) the empirical, the individual, and the spiritual "I" and (b) time and history.
6. What is "the process of history"?
7. How is self-realization here described?
8. Contrast the meanings of *logic, ethics,* and *esthetics.*
9. Define *metaphysics* and *salvation.*
10. By adding and stressing illustrative details, describe Occidental man.

SEVEN AXES OF BIAS

W. T. Jones

At the basis of every personality, I assume as a working hypothesis, there is a set of temperamental biases. These are dispositional tendencies, drives, or value attitudes that dispose an individual to prefer (for instance) the static to the dynamic, or the continuous to the discrete. A man's temperamental biases, in a word, provide the basic pattern of orientation by which he unconsciously structures his experience, the categories of explanation to which he appeals, and the final values in the light of which his choices are made. I call the drives about which I am talking "temperamental" because I think they are deep-seated in the personality, rather than expressions of passing environmental changes; I call them "biases" to emphasize that they are prerational—they are not attitudes reached as a result of a reasoning process; it is they, rather, that determine what seems to the individual inevitable, self-evident, "natural," and "reasonable."

Temperamental biases show up not only in overt behavior, but in theoretical work of all kinds (for instance, in metaphysics, philosophy of science, and theology), and also in esthetic production (for instance, the novel, painting, sculpture). They set the underlying framework within which a philosophical or scientific theory is constructed, by defining the kinds of problems that are regarded as important and the kinds of explanation that are felt to be satisfactory; in the arts they influence the choice of esthetic form, the organization of the medium, and the use of metaphor and symbolism. . . .

THE ORDER/DISORDER AXIS

Some individuals prefer system, clarity and structure—what we may call the "neat package." Others, like Marcel's grandmother in the *Recherche du Temps Perdu,* enjoy complexity, fluidity and disorder:

> You would see my grandmother pacing the deserted garden, lashed by the storm, pushing back her grey hair in disorder so that her brows might be more free to imbibe the lifegiving draughts of wind and rain. She would say, "At last one can breathe!" and would run up and down the soaking paths—too straight and symmetrical for her liking. . . .
>
> And in fine weather, she was
>
> always happy to find an excuse for an additional turn in the garden, which she would utilize to remove surreptitiously, as she passed, the stakes of a rosetree or two, so as to make the roses look a little more natural. . . .
> [*Remembrance of Things Past,* trans. C. K. Scott Moncrieff, Random House, New York, 1934, i, 9, 11.]

Those who prize order usually put a high premium on conceptual analysis; those who prize disorder minimize or distrust analysis. Where the former aim at a systematic pigeon-holing and classifying of experience, the latter exclaim with Wordsworth, "We murder to dissect," and condemn reason—the instrument par excellence, of organization—as "that false secondary power by which we multiply distinctions." What the former reject as "hopelessly chaotic," the latter will describe as a "fruitful mess." On the other hand, explanations that satisfy the former are likely to be criticized by the latter as "oversimplified" or "false to the facts."

Consider, for example, this remark by Anatole France about Montaigne:

> What I most admire in Montaigne is his talent for contradicting everything he says. This is the mark of a happy and beneficent spirit.

The richest, most fertile minds are also those which most abound in contradictions.

What France admires, and what he finds in Montaigne, is what we are calling a preference for disorder. We find this same preference expressed in this observation by William James:

All neat schematisms with permanent and absolute distinctions, classifications with absolute pretensions, systems with pigeonholes, . . . all 'classic,' clean, cut and dried, 'noble,' fixed, 'eternal,' *Weltanschauungen* seem to me to violate the character with which life concretely comes and the expression which it bears of being, or at least of involving, a muddle and a struggle, with an 'ever not quite' to all our formulas, and novelty and possibility forever leaking in.
[Ralph Barton Percy, *The Thought and Character of William James*, 1948, pp. 385–6.]

James, it is worth noting, explicitly recognized that the attitude expressed here is a bias. He started out, it is true, by asking himself, "How can I . . . justify the strong antithesis I constantly feel . . . that certain philosophical constructions . . . are subjective caprices, . . . while other constructions, those which work with concrete elements, with change, with indeterminism, are more objective and cling closer to the temperament of nature itself?" But as he wrote he came to see that the distinction he wanted to make was not justified and that the type of "construction" he preferred is no more objective than the type he disliked. Thus the note concludes: "I want a world of anarchy, Münsterberg one of bureaucracy, and each of us appeals to 'nature' to back him up. Nature partly helps and partly resists each of us." Following James, we might call this the "Anarchy/Bureaucracy Axis," or we might call it the "Regularity/Irregularity Axis," or the "Form/Formlessness Axis." It is easy to think of terms to describe the order-end of the axis, but most of the terms that designate the other end— "chaos," "confusion," "muddle," "mess," "fumble," for instance— have pejorative connotations. This suggests that these terms have been introduced by those whose bias is strongly toward order and who dislike disordered, unstructured, unorganized situations.

We conceive, then, of a linear range of value-attitudes with respect to "order" and "disorder," extending all the way from those who are strongly biased in favor of order to those who are as strongly biased in favor of disorder—from those who demand system at all cost and are intolerant of "anarchy" to those who, like James, intensely dislike all forms of "bureaucracy" and prize "muddle," "struggle," "novelty," and "possibility forever leaking in."

It is easy to think of philosophers besides James whose biases are out toward the anarchy end of this particular axis. Bergson, Schopenhauer and Rousseau, to mention three thinkers who differ markedly in other respects, all prefer chance, indeterminacy, novelty and fluidity. And there are many whose biases on this axis are toward the other extreme—for whom system, clarity, and conceptual analysis are prized values—Descartes, Hegel, Hume, and the contemporary Positivists may stand as examples.

Observe that this axis crosses (i.e., is independent of) the traditional dichotomy between rationalism and empiricism. While James and Hume, for instance, are both empiricists, they stand at opposite ends of the Order/Disorder Axis.

THE STATIC/DYNAMIC AXIS

We have already referred to this important pair of contrasting preferences. Plato is an example (I am thinking not only of the eternal, changeless archetypes but also of his fear of political change) of a philosopher whose bias is strongly for the static. As an example of a philosopher (within the same school) whose bias is considerably farther along this axis in the dynamic direction, there is Aristotle. Consider, for instance, the altered emphases that Aristotle gives to the theory of forms and his relatively greater willingness to face up to the facts of constitutional change and of constitutional variation from state to state. Aristotle's bias is certainly not as strongly toward the dynamic end of that of many thinkers, but his feeling for growth and development and his preference for genetic types of explanation show how much his position on this axis differs from his teacher's.

It is worth nothing that this axis crosses the Order/Disorder Axis. Thus Comte, Hegel, Marx, Whitehead and Bergson all prefer the dynamic to the static, but in the first four of these thinkers this bias is coupled with a bias toward order, while in Bergson it is coupled with a bias toward disorder. When a dynamic bias is combined with a bias for disorder, the superior value of cognitive states like "perception" or "intuition" is asserted, and "reason" and "science" are condemned on the grounds that they distort reality by freezing into rigid compartments what is fluid and moving. Bergson, for instance, writes:

Concepts . . . have the disadvantage that each of them . . . retains only that part of the object which is common to it and to others. . . . Concepts, laid side by side, never actually give us more than an artificial reconstruction of the object. . . . The different concepts that we form of the properties of a thing inscribe round it so many circles, each much too large and none of them fitting it exactly. . . . Metaphysics . . . must transcend concepts . . . it is only true to itself when it . . . frees itself from rigid and ready-made concepts in order to create . . . supple, mobile, and almost fluid representations always ready to mould themselves on the fleeting forms of intuition.

[H. Bergson, *Introduction to Metaphysics*, 1912, pp. 17–19, 21.]

On the other hand, when (as with Comte, Hegel, Marx and Whitehead) a dynamic bias is combined with a bureaucratic bias, the thinker in question must struggle with the problem of making a conceptual analysis of "process." Hegel's philosophical system is perhaps the best example of the tensions this requirement sets up. I believe that the doctrine of internal relations can best be understood (indeed, can *only* be understood!) as a device to reconcile verbally these conflicting biases.

THE CONTINUITY/DISCRETENESS AXIS

This axis reflects divergent attitudes toward unity and plurality. The effects of these different preferences appear in every area of theoretical behavior—for instance, in theology, in ethics, and in metaphysics.

Thus, to cite a theological instance, what I call a strong discreteness-bias is operative in C. S. Lewis's criticism of William Blake:

Blake wrote the Marriage of Heaven and Hell. If I have written of their Divorce, this is . . . because . . . the attempt to make that marriage is perennial. The attempt is based on the belief that reality never presents us with an absolutely unavoidable "either-or"; that, granted skill and patience and (above all) time enough some way of embracing both alternatives can always be found; that mere development or

adjustment or refinement will somehow turn evil into good without
our being called on for a final and total rejection of anything we
should like to retain. This belief I take to be a disastrous error.
                              [C. S. Lewis, *The Great Divorce*, 1946, v.]

An exactly opposite, continuity-bias appears in F. H. Bradley's
attempt to show that, so far from being presented with "an absolutely unavoidable 'either-or,' " good and evil are incomplete in
themselves and necessarily combine in the Absolute:

> Goodness, since it must needs pursue the perfect, is in its essence self-
> discrepant, and in the end is unreal. It is an appearance one-sided and
> relative, and not an ultimate reality.
>   [F. H. Bradley, *Appearance and Reality*, 1902, p. 422.]

And the same, he argues, is true of evil. Ends that "we rightly
condemn as Evil . . . must be included" in the Absolute. In it,
every evil act "which is followed in opposition to the good, will
unite with, and will conduce to, the ultimate goal." Hence "the
opposition" between good and evil "in the end is unreal."

It is important to see that Bradley and Lewis come to diametri-
cally opposite conclusions about the relation between good and
evil not because they are looking at different sets of facts, but
because they occupy different positions along this Continui-
ty/Discreteness Axis. They are looking at the same set of facts—
human deeds and our appraisals of them; they interpret these facts
differently because one's preference disposes him to emphasize
continuities, "inclusiveness," and "identity in the end," while the
other's preference disposes him to emphasize discontinuities,
radical alternatives, and sharp "divorces."

One or two more examples of the effect of this axis may be
given: in metaphysics, contrast Spinoza and Leibnitz, for instance;
or Plotinus and Aristotle. In political theory, contrast Locke with
Burke. In theology, again, contrast Augustine and Aquinas. Pan-
theism is an obvious expression of a bias toward continuity and
unity; Christian thinkers who experience this preference often
have a difficult time combining it with the theological requirement for a transcendent God, and various verbal devices are introduced to effect a reconciliation. Once again I conceive of a wide
variety of possible bias positions between the one extreme of a
monism that "devours" all plurality and the other extreme of a

diversity in which (in Hume's words) everything is "loose and separate" from everything else and (in Bishop Butler's) "everything is what it is, and not another thing."

The Inner/Outer Axis

This involves another, and quite different, pair of contrasting value-attitudes. Here the contrast is between those who are satisfied with a relatively external relation to the objects of their experience and those who are satisfied only if they can, as it were, get inside them, i.e., who want to experience them as they experience themselves.

Carlyle's *Essay on Biography* contains a striking expression of the latter bias. The desire of the reader of biography, he says, is to know our fellow creature; to see into him, understand his goings forth, decipher the whole heart of his mystery; nay, not only to see into him, but also to see out of him, to view the world altogether as he views it, so that we can theoretically construe him, and could almost practically personate him.

Another example of the same inner-bias is Faust's demand:

> Dass ich erkenne, was die Welt
> Im Innersten zusammenhält,
> Schau alle Wirkenskraft und Samen,
> Und tu nicht mehr in Worten kramen.

[That I may know what holds the world together at its innermost point —see all creative energies and seeds and rummage around no more in words.   —Faust: *Nacht*, 11. 382–5]

On the other hand, we may take Goethe's Wagner to represent the antithetical, outer, bias. Speaking of the life of research and scholarship, he says with evident satisfaction:

> Ach! wenn mann so in sein Museum gebannt ist,
> Und sieht die Welt kaum einen Feiertag,
> Kaum durch ein Fernglas, nur von weiten ...

[Ah! When one is banished into his study and sees the world—hardly on a holiday—scarcely through a telescope—only from afar ...
                                                        —Faust: *Nacht*, 11. 530–2]

The same image occurs in *Women in Love*, where Ursula

(whose inner bias Lawrence himself obviously shared) refers scornfully to her sister: "Isn't it queer that she always likes little things? . . . She likes to look through the wrong end of the opera glass and see the world that way."

Another example of the influence of this axis is reflected in differences in styles of acting. In *To See the Dream* Jessamyn West has described her experiences in Hollywood as she supervised the filming of her novel, *The Friendly Persuasion*. Since the characters in the novel were all Quakers and since none of the actors knew anything about the sect, Miss West took each of the two leading actors to a meeting of the Society of Friends:

> I was interested in the difference between Dorothy McGuire and Gary Cooper in their approach to Quaker meeting. Cooper, when he went, became (as far as I could see) a Quaker. He didn't look about at all, but centered down into the silence. Dorothy, after her visit, spoke to me of the various attitudes and responses of the Quakers as she had observed them at the meeting and of those she intended to use in her portrayal of Eliza in the meeting scene. I was surprised at this use of the meeting and Dorothy was surprised at my surprise.
> "What else," she asked, "should I have done? I went to see the various ways in which those people worshipped and to choose for Eliza whatever seemed the most effective way."

It is interesting to note that Miss West herself shares Gary Cooper's inner-bias. But she is not so very far out toward the inner pole of this axis; her position is sufficiently mid-range for her to see both sides of the case. She comments:

> Pragmatically, [McGuire's] way may turn out to be better than Cooper's. But I understand Cooper's way better. I must become the character I write about, not put a set of observations on paper. However, there is no necessity for using either method exclusively.
> [*To See the Dream*, pp. 262–3.]

Or, to turn to some philosophical examples of differences along this Inner/Outer Axis, contrast Bergson, who believes that intuition penetrates to the inner core of nature and there experiences it as an *élan vital,* with Descartes, for whom intuition (the same term, but what a difference in meaning!) is a kind of searchlight illumining objects clearly and distinctly, but from without. Descartes is content to look at objects from a distance, like Goethe's Wagner and Lawrence's Ursula. His belief that animals are mere machines is suggestive in this respect.

The whole substantival way of thought, i.e., the disposition to take "substance" as a prime metaphysical category, is sustained by a preference for the outer view, for a substance, so far as it is defined as having independent existence, can hardly be got *inside* of. In this connection it is worthy of note, perhaps, that Hegel had an inner-bias—at least this is the inference I draw from his conception of the Absolute as taking up and including the finite thinker, who, in this way, somehow gets inside of the object of his experience. Thus Hegel and Bergson, who are poles apart on the Order/Disorder Axis, tend toward the same end of the Inner/Outer Axis.

One final observation in connection with this axis: Dewey's criticism of the traditional empiricism and the traditional rationalism as "spectator" theories of knowledge amounts to saying (rightly, I believe) that both rationalism and empiricism reflect an outer-bias.

The Sharp Focus/Soft-Focus Axis

Examples of this axis in the field of painting will immediately spring to mind: consider the differences between the ways in which Van Eyck and Holbein and Dürer see objects—each a clear and distinctly outlined image, regardless of its depth in the picture space, and with no "atmospheric" effects but exposed to view in even, steady light—with the ways in which the French Impressionists and Turner and Rembrandt see objects, with surfaces fuzzy in an intense glare of sunshine or else looming out of deep shadows.

But equally typical expressions of this axis occur in the handling of philosophical concepts. Descartes' insistence on the criteria of clarity and distinctness is an example of sharp-focus bias. Hume's reference of ideas back to impressions, which are supposedly distinguished by their vividness and clarity, is another example. Here again, incidentally, we see how different epistemological theories can be marked by the same bias: in Descartes we have a sharp-focus rationalist; in Hume, a sharp-focus empiricist.

Among contemporary philosphers Bertrand Russell has a sharp-

Sharp Focus

Hans Holbein

George Gisse, Merchant of the Steelyard, London

Soft Focus

Paul Cézanne

Victor Chocquet in an Armchair

focus preference. This shows up in many ways, for instance in what he says about his early dissatisfaction with Hegelianism:

If you watch a bus approaching you during a bad London fog, you see first a vague blur of extra darkness, and you only gradually become aware of it as a vehicle with parts and passengers. According to Hegel, your first view as a vague blur is more correct than your later impression, which is inspired by the misleading impulses of the analytic intellect. This point of view was temperamentally unpleasing to me.... I prefer sharp outlines and definite separations.
[Bertrand Russell, *Portraits from Memory*, 1958, p. 38.]

The point, of course, is not whether this is a "correct" description of Hegelianism, but that a dislike for fuzziness and for soft edges lies at the bottom of Russell's rejection of Hegel. It will be seen, incidentally, that discontinuity-bias is also at work here, in Russell's expressed preference for "definite separations" as well as for "sharp outlines."

On the other hand, Whitehead had a soft-focus preference. This is to be seen in an observation which, according to Russell, Whitehead once made to him:

You think the world is what it looks like in fine weather at noonday; I think it is what it seems like in the early morning when one first wakes from sleep.

[Russell, p. 39.]

A soft-focus bias far stronger than Whitehead's appears in a philosophical preference for what may be called "thresholds"—in the penumbra that encircles some (or, it may be claimed, all) experience. Thus Newman bases his proof, both of the existence of an external world and of God, on such threshold experiences:

... that there are things existing external to ourselves, this I do consider a first principle, and one of universal reception. It is founded on an instinct; I do call it, because the brute creation possesses it. This instinct is directed towards individual phenomena, one by one.... As then we have our initial knowledge of the universe through sense, so do we in the first instance begin to learn about its Lord and God from conscience; and, as from particular acts of that instinct, which makes experiences, mere images (as they ultimately are) upon the retina, the means of our perceiving something real beyond them, we go on to draw the general conclusion that there is a vast external world, so from the recurring instances in which conscience acts, forcing upon us importunately the mandate of a Superior, we have fresh and fresh evidence of the existence of a Sovereign Ruler....

[*A Grammar of Assent.*]

The whole argument rests on an appeal to a fugitive kind of experience ("mandate of a Superior") which a sharp-focus thinker would either disallow (on the grounds that he was unable to observe it) or declare to be too fuzzy to serve as a basis for inference, or trace back to other (*e.g.,* psychopathological) causes.

Many contemporary thinkers also show a soft-focus preference. Niebuhr, for instance, writes, "Mystery does not annul meaning but enriches it." [*Faith and History*, 1949, p. 103.] Philip Wheelwright declares that "Man lives always on the verge, always on the borderline of a something more," and he finds three types of thresholds—of time, of the world, and of the unseen. [*The Burning Fountain*, 1954, pp. 8–16.] W. T. Stace, discussing the experience of the "ineffable," insists that it is not limited to special people called "mystics": it is "not like . . . the taste of an onion to one who has never tasted it." Rather, its "source" is "the universal religious consciousness of mankind." If many people believe they do not experience it, this is because they do not attend to it, or because they refuse to accept anything as evidence that they cannot conceptualize. The ineffable " is such that it is in itself incapable of being conceptualized. . . . The nature of God is such that it cannot be enmeshed in concepts at all. If it is true that ordinary men do not have the mystic experience—and I think that in any absolute sense this is not true, but that all men have it in some degree—it is not this lack of experience which makes it incomprehensible to us. The fault [lies rather with our] discursive, discriminating, conceptual intellect. . . . [*Time and Eternity*, 1952, pp. 36, 45, 39.]

I do not mean, of course, to suggest that all these thinkers use threshold experience in exactly the same way, nor do I pass any judgment here on the cognitive value of the phenomenon. I merely call attention to the way in which differences in bias cause some thinkers to attribute major significance to aspects of experience that have no interest at all for other thinkers.

Soft-focus interest in thresholds is naturally not confined to philosophical theory. Wherever a present experience is felt to be saturated with more meaning that is immediately present, we have an expression of this bias. It may be, for instance, that the past is evoked in the present:

> There is a charm in footing slow across the silent plain,
> Where patriot battle has been fought, where glory had the gain;
> There is a pleasure in the heath where Druids old have been,
> Where mantles grey have rustled by and swept the nettles green.
> [John Keats, "Lines written in the Highlands after a visit to Burns's Country"]

A writer with a sharp-focus bias would have seen and enjoyed the plain and the heath, not the patriot battle or the Druids old. When Wordsworth wrote

> A primrose by a river's brim
> A yellow primrose was to him,
> And it was nothing more,
>
> [*Peter Bell*, I, 249–51.]

he was describing a man with sharp-focus bias—and expressing a characteristically soft-focus dislike of it.

The whole central core of the *Recherche du Temps Perdu* is of course threshold experience, to which Proust assigns the utmost importance as being revelatory of the inner meaning of both life and art. Take, as a single example, what he says about book collecting. Note that when we hold a book in our hands, we do not merely think about some earlier owner or some earlier experience of our own. "Association of ideas" of this kind is much more external and extrinsic than the experience Proust prizes. For him, the past is really "interwoven" with the present.

> ... if I had been tempted to be a book collector, as the Prince de Guermantes was, I would have been one of a very peculiar sort, seeking that beauty which is independent of the 'value' of a book, properly speaking, and which it possesses for booklovers because of their knowing the libraries it has passed through, or that it was given to this or that famous man by this or that sovereign on the occasion of some special event, and through their having followed it from sale to sale throughout its career; this historic beauty of a book, so to speak, would not be lost for me. But I would gladly extract from it the history of my own life.... I would seek for the novels old-fashioned bindings of the time when I read my first novels, in those days when my father used so often to say to me, "Stand up straight." ...
> The sight of the cover of a book one has previously read retains,

woven into the letters of its title, the moonbeams of a far-off summer
night. . . .   [trans. Moncrieff, ii, 1006–8]

It will be seen that the penumbra meanings of which those with
soft-focus bias are conscious may be either additional sense-experi-
ences, as with Proust; or they may be transcendental, adumbra-
tions of immortality, as with some of the philosophers we have
cited. In these differences we have an example of the interaction of
this axis with varying positions on still another axis, the This-
World/Other-World Axis, which we must now examine.

THE THIS-WORLD/OTHER-WORLD AXIS

The other-world bias can take many forms. In its simplest version it is no more than a discontent with the here-and-now, a
preference for the far away and strange, which beckon just because
they are far away and strange. When this bias is felt more intensely,
it may be proper to describe it as a form of escapism. There may
then be either a flight through time or a flight through space, and
the former may involve either an "antiquarian" escape into a past
very different from the present (*e.g.*, the Pre-Raphaelites, Gothic
revival) or a "futuristic" escape, a projection into a happier future:
the modern science-fiction story is, I suspect, a version of this latter
bias, but so also is, say, Shelley's dream of a new and better day
emerging for mankind.

Spatial escape may involve actual removal of oneself from the
here-and-now (*e.g.*, Gauguin); or there may be only an imaginative
removal. In general, this version of the other-world bias prizes
imagination and dreams—either day- or night-dreams—precisely
because they take us out of the here-and-now. And characteristically, such dream experiences are held to be more veridical than fully
conscious perception:

> . . . Sleep hath its own world,
> And a wide realm of wild reality,
> And dreams in their development have breath,
> And tears, and tortures, and the touch of joy . . .
> They do divide our being; they become
> A portion of ourselves as of our time . . .
> . . . What are they?

Creations of the mind?—The mind can make
Substance, and people planets of its own
With beings brighter than have been, and give
A breath to forms which can outlive all flesh.

[Byron, "The Dream"]

The other-world bias is not, of course, limited to a projection to other heres-and-nows; it may, more radically, reject the whole natural world in favor of some non-natural, or supernatural, realm. In this form, the other-world bias often combines with the static bias, and we have, accordingly, the perennial attraction of the Platonic realm of forms, conceived as more real and more valuable than the flux of spatiotemporal "shadows."

On the other hand, the other-world bias may combine with the dynamic bias; when it does, what is affirmed is a transcendent reality of movement or energy—for instance Schopenhauer's blind, struggling Will. *How* transcendent this reality, whether dynamic or static, is conceived to be, depends in part on the individual's position on the Continuity/Discreteness Axis. In general, a bias toward discreteness permits a sharp distinction to be drawn between this-world and the other-world—there will be a tendency toward some form of dualism. But a bias toward continuity requires the thinker to close the gap in one way or another; accordingly, changes will be rung on the relations between "appearance" and "reality." Since many thinkers seem to combine a fairly strong continuity bias with a fairly strong other-world bias, there is a good deal of tension on this point in western philosophy, and many different verbal constructions have been introduced to enable the thinkers in question to satisfy both biases at once. Hegel's use of the term "aufgehoben" seems to be a case in point. This play on words satisfies other-world bias by suggesting a "cancelling out," and "annulment"; it satisfies continuity-bias by suggesting "suspension" and "absorption."

It will be seen, further, that the This World/Other World Axis is closely related to the epistemological distinction between rationalism and empiricism, but they are not identical. The empiricist almost certainly has a strong this-world bias; the rationalist need not, but is likely to, have an other-world bias, since the epistemological demands that rationalism makes are hard to satisfy in this world. But certainly, it must not be supposed that all other-world-ers are rationalists; it is easy to think of philosophers who combine a strong other-world bias with biases toward dynamism, continuity and disorder (Plotinus, for instance).

In a word, positions on the This World/Other World Axis assume a great variety of forms. The most we can say generally is (a) the this-world bias is likely to show up as a hard-headed, "real-istic" (those with the opposite bias would probably characterize it as "cynical") attitude toward the facts: Machiavelli, in political philosophy, and Hobbes in metaphysics are examples. When Hobbes writes that "the subject of Philosophy is body" and that body is that "which, having no dependence upon our thought, is co-extended with some part of space," he is expressing a strong this-world bias.

On the other hand, (b) an other-world bias is likely to lead to an "idealistic" attitude (which those with the opposite bias will de-scribe as "impractical" and "utopian.") Other-worlders will insist that the material world, so far from (as with Hobbes) exhausting reality, is either unreal or at least incomplete and incomprehensi-ble. Thus Reinhold Niebuhr: "The Christian doctrine of creation *ex nihilo* calls attention to the fact that the temporal process is not self-explanatory." [*Faith and History*, p. 48.] Between these two positions, which represent biases fairly far out on the opposite ends of this axis, we may put a position like Kant's. His assertion that things-in-themselves exist but that they are unknowable represents a typical middle-of-the-axis bias, a compromise formula that tries to "do justice" to both extremes.

THE SPONTANEITY/PROCESS AXIS

This is the final pair of contrasting values that we will intro-duce. On the one hand there are those who insist on an element of freedom, of chance, or of accident in nature; on the other hand there are those who insist on the orderliness and the lawfulness of things. The most obvious example, perhaps, of a strong spontanei-ty-bias appears in the doctrine of the free human will; but this bias also turns up in all the various versions of "emergent" and "crea-tive" evolution, and need not involve claims of specifically human freedom. Nor need spontaneity be interpreted in any moral sense;

it may appear merely as an emphasis on there being an unpredictable element in human affairs. Thus H. A. L. Fisher formulated what he held to be the "one safe rule for the historian: that he should recognize in the development of human destinies the play of the contingent and the unforeseen." [*A History of Europe*, 1935, I, vii.] Philosophers of history, on the other hand, tend to have a fairly strong process-bias: whether they conceive the order as organic, mechanical, linear, or cyclical, they all play down contingency and spontaneity. As an example, consider the following:

> There is an immutable law—that each human society and all individuals participating in it strive to increase and perfect production. . . .

And

> In history, it is not important who implements a process, it is only important that the process be implemented. . . . The revolution created forces, leaders, organizations, and ideas which were necessary to it.
> [M. Djilas, *The New Class,* 1957, pp. 11, 41.]

It is interesting, as an example of the depth of such preferences in the personality structure, that this "process" aspect of Marxism has survived Djilas's illusionment with, and rejection of, most of the detailed economic and social theories of Marxism.

In political philosophy and, more generally, in basic attitudes toward politics, this axis clearly emerges. Riesman's "inside dopesters," and even more his "new-style indifferents," are likely to have a process-bias—to believe that the course of political events is too large, too massive, for the individual's efforts to have an effect. His "moralizers-in-power," on the other hand, have what I have called a spontaneity-bias; they believe that it *is* possible to change the course of politics.

Since this exposition of our seven biases has been complicated, I will repeat them in summary form. I have defined an axis of bias as a range of possible attitudes toward a pair of contrasting values. The seven dimensions proposed are:

(1) *The Order/Disorder Axis,* which consists in the range of attitudes lying between a strong preference for fluidity, muddle, and chaos and a strong preference for system, clarity, and conceptual analysis.

(2) *The Static/Dynamic Axis* in which, at one pole, there is a

preference for the changeless and eternal, and at the other pole, a preference for movement and for explanation in genetic terms.

(3) *The Continuity/Discreteness Axis,* which consists in the range of attitudes between a preference for wholeness and a preference for diversity.

(4) *The Inner/Outer Axis,* which consists in the range of attitudes between a demand to get inside the objects of one's experience and a tendency to be satisfied with an external view of them.

(5) *The Sharp-Focus/Soft-Focus Axis* in which the contrast is between a preference for clear and distinct experiences and a preference for threshold experiences.

(6) *The This-World/Other-World Axis,* in which a readiness to believe that the spatiotemporal world is self-explanatory is contrasted with a refusal to believe it is self-explanatory, and a contentment with the here-and-now is opposed to a preference for the other-in-time and the other-in-place.

(7) *The Spontaneity/Process Axis* in which, at one extreme, there is a strong preference for chance and novelty and, at the other extreme, an equally strong disposition to believe in the "lawfulness" of events.

QUESTIONS FOR STUDY

1. Define *temperamental bias, axis, overt, symbolism, construction, indeterminism, pejorative, dichotomy, genetic, cognitive, discreteness, monism, pluralism, archetypes, penumbra, fugitive, ineffable, discursive, veridical, epistemological, contingent.*
2. Define the contrasted terms *order* and *disorder.*
3. The quotations from Proust and James illustrate a preference for disorder. Give as specific an illustration of a preference for order.
4. The writer contrasts the static and dynamic axis largely in abstract, theoretical terms. Supply concrete illustrations.
5. Which sentence summarizes the writer's contrast of continuity and discreteness?
6. How does the reaction of the actors at a meeting of the Society of Friends illustrate the difference between inner and outer axes?
7. In response to experience, which actor parallels the characteristic

responses of empiricist and rationalist in John Dewey's interpretation of the terms?

8. What tie exists between sharp and soft focus and judgments or evaluations of ideas?

9. Why are the epistemological demands made by rationalism hard to satisfy in this world?

10. How does William James's contrast of the tough- and tender-minded parallel the contrast in the this-world and the other-world axis? In *Pragmatism* (1907), pages 11-12, James contrasted the rationalistic, intellectualistic, idealistic, monistic, and dogmatical emphases of "the tender-minded" with the empiricist, sensationalistic, materialistic, pluralistic, and sceptical emphases of "the tough-minded."

11. List synonyms for both *process* and *spontaneity*.

12. What method of development dominates the essay as a whole? What other methods appear frequently in the divisions?

CIVILIZATION AND THE SENSE OF QUALITY

Herbert Read

> *It is art that makes life, makes interest, makes importance, for our consideration and application of these things, and I know of no substitute whatever for the force and beauty of its process.*
>
> Henry James, *Letters*, II, 508

Art, as I have so often insisted . . . is one of those vague spheres of human activity which escape any very precise definition. Criticism is merely an approximation towards that unattainable end, an endless multiplication of distinctions. One such distinction more firmly established than most is that between *art* and *entertainment*. An entertainment is something which distracts us or diverts us from the routine of daily life. It makes us for the time being forget our care and worries; it interrupts our conscious thoughts and habits, rests our nerves and minds, though it may incidentally exhaust our bodies. Art, on the other hand, though it may divert us from the normal routine of our existence, causes us in some way or other to become conscious of that existence. Matthew Arnold defined poetry as the criticism of life—with a saving clause, if I remember rightly, about 'high seriousness.' I do not like the phrase, for its suggests that art is some kind of intellectual activity. Art is rather an expression of our deepest instincts and emotions; it is a serious activity whose end is not so much to divert as to vitalize. I avoid words like 'improve' and 'uplift' because they only apply to a special kind of art. Art is not necessarily a moral activity, and its tonic effect is made through the senses. Nevertheless, even in its purest, or most abstract—in Oscar Wilde's sense, its most *useless* forms: in one of Shakespeare's songs, or a minuet by Mozart, or a drawing by Boucher—even then art is radically different from amusement. It does not leave us without affecting us, and affecting us, according to some scale of value, for the better.

This virtue in art is shown by its survival value. Historically speaking, we cannot distinguish a civilization except by its art. At any rate, the more a civilization is subjected to the test of time, the more it is reduced to its works of art. The rest rots away. Even the remote periods of pre-history become vivid for a moment in some cave-drawing or fragment of carved bone. Historical civilization begins with the epic poems Gilgamesh, or the Bible, or Homer. Shards of pottery, painted or incised, are more eloquent than the names of emperors or fields of battle. Cities and fertile lands disappear, but buried in their ruins, in tombs and sanctuaries, we find a vase, a jewel, a few coins, made by the artists of those days, which speak to us in clear language and tell us of the status and character of that lost civilization. They tell us not merely that such and such a people worshipped the sun, or that they fought in chariots, or believed in the resurrection of the dead. These are incidental items of knowledge which we might possibly derive from some other source. But works of art speak more directly to us: for by their form and style they give us a measure of the refinement of a civilization. The aesthetic sense—the faculty by which we appreciate works of art—has its vagaries; at one moment we execrate, say, Gothic architecture, and a century later it is exalted above all other styles. But there is an ideal aesthetic scale of values, just as there is an ideal scale of moral values; and by the measure of this scale all civilizations are given their due rank.

The survival value of art may be readily admitted, but what, the cynic might ask, is the value of survival? What does it matter, what did it matter to the caveman of the Stone Age, or the sculptors of Assyria, or the potters of China, that some remote civilization would disinter their works and judge them good?

Here we face a problem which is fundamental to our faith in the future. It is a fundamental question that divides mankind into those who believe all human activity to be vain, leading to no realizable improvement in this world; and those who believe that man has acquired, however slowly and however tentatively, the instruments of self-improvement, and moves towards a more enjoyable life.

There is a phrase, the perfectibility of man (probably first used by Godwin or his disciple Shelley) which has been the object of much ridicule on the part of those who despair of mankind, and find perfectibility only in divine or unattainable realms of being. It is, obviously, an incautious phrase; a state of perfectibility would be a state of immobility, of final attainment; and it is difficult to conceive of life as thus stabilized. But the phrase does not represent the true doctrine of progress, which is not so much a doctrine as a *myth*. One can take a long view or a short view of the future of mankind. On a short view we can only be practical and realistic: if man improves, it is at a rate to which we cannot accommodate our immediate politics. A precise set of dogmas is probably as much as one generation can cope with. But a belief in progress belongs to a long view of mankind's future: it is a mythical conception quite parallel to the mythical conceptions of religion. It merely substitutes, for a supernatural Kingdom of Heaven to be attained in another world, a Golden Age to be attained in this world. And as a myth it is as good as any other myth; I would claim that it is much more sensible because it is much more human. The dogma of original sin, which is offered as an alternative, would be insupportable did it not have, as a corollary, the promise of salvation through divine intervention; and one may suggest without cynicism that in this case the wish is father to the thought. The myth of progress, on the other hand, has no illegitimate offspring. It is born as a wish, or as a will, and there is no attempt to disguise its innocent and hopeful nature.

The spirit of disillusionment which prevails in our war-ridden world is probably a reaction to the evolutionary optimism of the nineteenth century. Let us freely admit that much that goes by the name of liberalism is to be identified with that same spirit of optimism. But I think by now we have learned to distinguish between the freedom to do as we like and the duty to create a free world. Is see no reason at all why the right to create an artificial scarcity of goods, or the right to exploit native labour in the colonies, should be even remotely associated with the concept of liberty. Liberty and freedom, these values we are now defending, have no economic purpose: they are spiritual values, and as such depend on the fine perceptions of those who guard them. Just as the dogmas of religion depend for their interpretation on fallible human agents, so the ideals of liberty are subject to the same chance. You cannot put on one side certain ideals of life, of conduct, of social order, and say that these represent a divine dispensation to which all men must submit; and on the other side place all other ideals and condemn them as human. The choice is between the interpretation of dogma, supernatural or divine in origin, and the interpretation of the natural phenomena of life—between faith and reason. In either case the interpreting agent is a human being, and the fallibility inherent in our humanity extends to every range of thought and feeling.

We may therefore reaffirm a rational faith in human progress. But let us be very clear that we do not confuse spiritual with material progress; let us recognize the uncertainty of our aims and the feebleness of our agents; let us proceed with humility and measure. But let us at the same time declare, that throughout all the chances of history, in the face of defeat and despair, in spite of long epochs of darkness and retrogression, man has established faculties that enable him to distinguish between immediate satisfactions and absolute values. He has established a moral sense to guide him in his dealings with his fellow-men and an aesthetic sense to enable him to modify the life of reason; and though the life of reason is still subject to all manner of raids and rebuffs, it exists as a practical ideal, extending to wider and wider circles of humanity, and promising an earthly paradise never to be attained only because each stage toward its realization creates a superior level.

I have just defined the asethetic sense as the faculty that enables man to modify the quality of his environment. Quality is, of course, the essential word in this definition. There are other faculties, faculties which might be described as technical or practical, that enable man to modify the *quantity* of his environment: to produce more corn, to utilize more power, to conserve more energy. But these faculties, though they play an important part in the growth of civilization, are not our present concern. I freely admit that in some cases it is difficult to disentangle the two elements: the aesthetic appeal of the Gothic cathedral, for example, depends very directly on the solution of technical problems in building; more obviously, the quality of music has, within certain limits, been governed by the technical perfection of the instruments available.

If we make this distinction between art and the instruments of art, then I think we are bound to admit that whatever progress in art is discernible within historical times is due to an improvement in its instruments rather than to any change in the instinct that operates them. The difference between a bushman's engraving of an antelope and the drawing of a similar animal by Pisanello is fully explained by the difference between a sharpened flint working on the surface of a rock and a silver-point pencil working on parchment. The civilizations behind these two manifestations of the aesthetic sense bear no comparison; but the aesthetic sense is the same. Similarly, who would be bold enough to say that the poetry of Tennyson, or even of Shakespeare, showed any qualitative advance on the poetry of Homer? Whatever art we examine, we are driven to this conclusion: that the underlying faculty or impulse is relatively constant; that the variations are due to the accidents of time and circumstance which release this impulse or faculty. The faculty with which we are endowed must be educated, encouraged, provided with suitable instruments and a rewarding material. Art does not, like technical skill, arise from the necessities of a situation: it is not an invention. Alas, it is perfectly possible for the whole process of civilization to carry on without art. 'To carry on'—the phrase has a provisional ring; and from a wider point of view it is equally certain that a civilization without art will perish—perish materially and fade from the memory of mankind.

Art is grace, art is form, art is—among all possible manners of doing or making a thing—the most memorable. That particular manner of doing or making a thing is memorable because it stimulates our senses, because it brings human inventions within measurable distance of organic growth, because for a moment the will of man seems to be identified with the universal forces of life.

Art redeems our actions from monotony and our minds from boredom. We have to make things and to do things in order to live, but the routine of this endless repetition of menial tasks would dull the senses and deaden the mind unless there was the possibility of doing things and making things with a progressive sense of quality. That sense of quality is the aesthetic sense, and in the end the aesthetic sense is the vital sense, the sense without which we die.

QUESTIONS FOR STUDY

1. Define *civilization, vagaries, execrate, myth, cynicism, disillusionment, liberty, aesthetic.*
2. Why does the word *art* escape very precise definition? What definition is given here?
3. Contrast art and entertainment.
4. Why is art of first importance in any civilization?
5. The value one assigns art may be colored by what contrasted views of the meaning and value of life?
6. What illustrations of myth does the writer include?
7. Contrast the doctrines of progress and of original sin.
8. What choice may man make in the realm of speculative thought?
9. What, to Read, is human progress? What are its components?
10. What may cause "progress in art"?
11. What is variable and what constant in art?
12. In the last paragraph, what meaning does the writer give the word *quality?*
13. Outline the essay.
14. Write a paragraph on your understanding and appreciation of a specific work of art.

THE LAST THREE CENTURIES

Carl Becker

[From lectures delivered at Leland Stanford University in April, 1935.]

Surveying the activities of men during the last three hundred years of the Time-Scale [in this essay, 506,000 years: from Java man to A.D. 1935] we can see that this extension of the realm of matter-of-fact to include the intangible forces that are in and behind appearance is the chief contribution of the Europeans to the expansion of human power and intelligence. It is an extension of the common man's matter-of-fact apprehension, but it is a generalized and abstract extension, not well understood by common men, that can be effected only by exceptional individuals. We see them emerging, these exceptional individuals, a new class of learned men, differentiated from the official priests and scribes: humanists and historians—the mechanics of the intellectual realm, erudite accumulators of matter-of-fact knowledge of man's activities in a time sequence; natural philosophers—verifying and tabulating the observed recurrences in the behavior of material things; mathematicians, the high priests of the new science—rediscovering Archimedes' secret, noting with increasing refinement the relation between the behavior of material things and their unsubstantial idea forms. We note that these exceptional individuals "do not reply to their predecessors, they bid them goodby." They do not ask what is officially said to be true, or what tradition holds it reasonable to suppose must be so: observing what does in fact occur, what has in fact happened, they announce what as a matter of fact is true of this particular thing, of that particular event. We can see, what they could not, that they are dispensing with the assistance of the gods in the effort to find out for themselves what man has in fact done (History), how things do in fact behave (Science).

We see them emerging, these exceptional individuals: Copernicus and Kepler and Galileo, conveniently assuming that the earth and planets move around the sun, and thereby finding the calculations of their observed behavior much simplified. The assumption appears to "cover the facts" and is therefore taken for true: it need not declare the glory of God, since it lightens the burden of mathematicians. In this casual way the earth is displaced from the center of creation and takes its place as a minor planet, while man sees his stature diminish as the comprehended universe is infinitely expanded. The immense spaces affright him momentarily, but he reflects that "thought makes the dignity of man," and is not long disheartened by his apparent insignificance since he has himself discovered it: is encouraged rather, as he discovers that the universe of infinite spaces, insensitive to his fate though it may be, is amenable to his control. For there is Galileo, discovering the law of nature—measuring the accelerating velocity of falling bodies; and Newton, with the aid of the differential calculus, measuring the force of gravitation that holds the universe together. It is not the concept of natural law that they discover, but the law itself. The concept is old in tradition—is in Aristotle and the Stoics, the Jurisconsults and the Christian philosophers, who infer from the rational nature of God that Nature is not recalcitrant to Right Reason. But Galileo and Newton do not infer that Nature is lawful because God is rational; having transposed the verbal concept of natural law into mathematical formulae, they infer from the measured mechanical behavior of Nature that God is an engineer—the Great Contriver or Prime Mover, who has so constructed the universe of immense spaces that it may be mastered by the hand as well as contemplated by the spirit of man. In the law of falling bodies, Archimedes, if he were with us, would at once recognize the fulcrum for moving the world which he sought in vain.

While natural philosophers are disclosing an ordered and predictable outer world that is amenable to man's control, humanists and historians are disclosing a world of human activities that is ever changing, yet not necessarily for the worse. There are the humanists (from Petrarch to Erasmus and Montaigne) piously recovering and critically examining lost or forgotten works of ancient writers; and the historians (from Guicciardini to Montesquieu and Gibbon) filling in and making vivid the half-empty Time-Passed with a matter-of-fact story of man's activities from remote beginnings. In the light of recorded history, the revealed story of man's life and destiny fades away into the realm of myth, and the initial ideal state of man is transferred from the Garden of Eden to the Golden Age of Greek and Roman civilization. Dazzled by this brilliance, men for a moment distrust their own abilities and are afflicted with nostalgic regret for the vanished grandeur of the ancients. Yet only for a moment. The Dark or Middle Age intervening between them and the Romans is after all no more than a temporary decline and fall into barbarism and superstition, from which they see themselves rapidly emerging by virtue of having recovered all that the ancients knew. It occurs to them then that they themselves, the "moderns," are the true ancients, since they are the latest in the succession of generations, while the ancients whom they revere are the young, those who lived in the youth of the world. Surely the late-comers, having appropriated the knowledge and profited by the errors of past generations, should be able to surpass their predecessors; and, having surpassed them, transmit to future generations the accumulated experience which will enable their descendants to surpass the generations of men now living. They can therefore face the future with renewed confidence, revering their ancestors less as they think better of themselves and expect more of posterity.

Thus there emerges, within the European climate of opinion, and as a rationalization of the practical interests of a burgher society, the idea of human Progress. During five hundred years the adventurous Europeans have gradually pushed back the obscuring walls of the spatial and temporal universe until, by an imaginative flight from the here and now, man can see himself functioning within an ordered and predictable outer world that may be controlled, and within a developing social world that changes for the better with the increase and refinement of knowledge. Within this expanded Time and Space frame of reference, man and Nature appear once more in harmonious relation, since Nature is designed according to unvarying laws that reveal its meaning, and man is endowed with an intelligence capable of discovering that meaning for himself. There is then no need for a special revelation, since God has spoken to men through the articulated mechanism of Nature. We hear the pregnant question: "Is it natural, is it reasonable that God should go in search of Moses in order to speak to Jean Jacques Rousseau!" Man has only to read the open Book of Nature to learn the meaning of existence and to adjust his way of life to cosmic intention. The long-treasured vision of a Golden Age, once identified with the creation of the world by capricious, inscrutable gods, and then transferred to the beatific life after death in the Heavenly City, is at last identified with the progressive amelioration of man's earthly state by the application of his intelligence to the mastery of the outer world of things and to the conscious and rational direction of social activities.

In following the slowly accelerating expansion of human power and intelligence along a Time-Scale of 506,000 years, we thus arrive at the point where progress and the idea of progress are conjoined. We feel that the event should prove to be a notable one, and we are curious to see what will come of it. But time is running short, a scant three hundred years remaining on our Time-Scale; and we may think it unlikely that anything new and strange can occur in that brief moment of human history. Nevertheless, we need not despair of man's capacity to upset our expectations. Of all the inventions yet made by the ingenious Europeans, the doctrine of progress is the most effective, the most revolutionary and dislocating, since it transforms a Deo-Centric into a Homo-Centric universe, and thereby makes man the measure of all things. By liberating the mind from fear of the gods and the restraints of tradition, it invites men to pursue without inhibitions the call of their desires; while by locating perfection in the future and identifying it with the successive achievements of mankind, it makes a virtue of novelty and disposes men to welcome change as in itself a sufficient validation of their activities. If then the idea of progress emerges from progress itself, progress is in turn reinforced by the idea of progress that is in men's minds. Which is cause, which effect, we need not inquire: we note merely that during the brief three hundred years remaining on our Time-Scale there occurs an unanticipated and quite unprecedented expansion of human power and intelligence, a quite unprecedented acceleration of man's capacity to control the outer world of things and to modify his traditional ideas and social habits.

The beginning of this brief but momentous three hundred years we will place at the moment when Newton is formulating the universal law of gravitation, which is the moment when Newcomen is trying to devise a workable steam engine, the moment also when the idea of progress is disclosing to men the hope of a resplendent future. We note that, in the century following, men become increasingly conscious of living in an age of Enlightenment, of Clarification: common sense reason, and matter-of-fact knowledge, washed clear of enthusiasm and illusion, are exposing old errors and superstitions, justifying the ways of Nature to men's desires, disclosing the capacity of the natural man for moral and social perfection. Never did the universe appear less mysterious or more easily manageable; never did man appear more simple, more pliable to the persuasive influence of rational instruction. The answers to all of man's unanswered questions, the solution of all of his unsolved enigmas appear to be at hand: he has but to adjust himself to the laws of Nature and of Nature's God, which are also the laws of his own being. We hear Condorcet announcing the fact, "The perfectibility of man is really infinite." It is in this optimistic age of common sense that we see men becoming conscious revolutionists, with systematic deliberation turning their minds to the discovery of Nature's secret laws and to the regeneration of social institutions.

Observing the course of this revolutionary attack, we note that the optimism of those who rely upon unvarying natural law to give them control over the outer world of things is justified beyond all expectation, An ever increasing number of exceptional individuals, inspired by the success and guided by the method of Galileo and Newton, devote themselves with impersonal curiosity to the exploration of the physical world, and thereby rapidly create the systematic and co-ordinated body of matter-of-fact knowledge that takes the name of natural science. The expansive force of steam, long known, is made available by the laws of mechanics, and new sources of power (electricity and radiation) are discovered, reduced to measured control, and applied to practical use. The discovery of new sources of power calls for the invention of new implements of precision for measuring and exerting the power available; while the multiplication of machines, machine tools, and appliances that serve the practical activities reinforces the systematic pursuit of scientific knowledge by enlisting the interest and support of the dominant burgher class. Thus science serves industry, industry endows science, and both the pursuit of knowledge and of profits calls for an ever increasing class of engineers, technicians, statisticians, and mechanics whose minds are disciplined to the matter-of-fact apprehension and stored with the matter-of-fact knowledge of things that alone make the new power available.

Under the impact of this deliberate and concerted attack upon the secrets of Nature, the slow-paced routine of man's activities is accelerated and loses its familiar pattern. The new power discovered by scientists and mediated by engineers is applied to all the diverse activities of men, but its most notable manifestations are in the realm of the mechanic and industrial arts. Within this realm the function of the new power is to accelerate the movement of men and things and thereby increase work done in relation to the time and the man-power required to do it. Speed and power become the symbols, quantity and precision the measure of achievement: speed and power in the mass-production of things desired, in the mass-movement of men and things from place to place; precision in the intermeshing relation of men and things in a pattern that becomes ever more extended and intricate as technical improvements overcome inertia and diminish the obstacles of time and space. Observing this process, we note an unprecedented acceleration in man's capacity to create material wealth; we note also that as instruments of power and precision multiply and are improved, the man-power required to create wealth declines. Men are themselves aware of these significant facts, and they look forward to the moment when, with slight effort on their part, instruments of power and precision will supply all that is needed: the moment when common men, hitherto condemned to live by un-remitting labor, will have leisure for the pursuit of immaterial values, and can live—as in the mythical reign of King Chronos men lived—like the gods, free from toil and grief.

Nevertheless, from generation to generation the happy moment recedes, and the hopes of men are disappointed. The reason for this will perhaps appear if we contrast the revolution in scientific knowledge with the social revolution that runs parallel to it. To the philosophers of the century of Enlightenment the regeneration of society seems no different in character, and even less difficult to effect, than the exploitation of Nature's secrets: no different in character, since common-sense reason will disclose, in men as in things, the unvarying laws of Nature which God has imprinted on men and things alike; even less difficult to effect, since men, unlike things, will consciously cooperate in the adjustment of their social activities to these unvarying laws. "The constitution," we hear them announcing, "is already made since its eternal principles are engraved on the hearts of all men." This optimistic view is not justified in the events. It turns out that men are less tolerant of projects interesting to social reformers than things are of theories interesting to natural scientists. Unlike things, men are not indifferent to experiments made upon them, while those who carry through social revolutions do so, not with an impersonal matter-of-fact apprehension, but with an apprehension attentive to their own advantage. The social revolution is not carried through by philosophers standing apart from the men who are to be regenerat-ed, but by the men themselves; and so it happens that the eternal laws of Nature, which philosophers think God has engraved on the hearts of all men, are hardly distinguishable from the ideas im-printed upon the minds of the dominant social class.

We note then that the dominant social class, the bourgeoisie, finding its expanding activities hampered by the arbitrary power of kings and the privileges of nobles and priests, identify the eter-nal law of Nature with the freedom of the individual from royal and corporate and class restraints. Philosophers tell them that when everyone is free all will be equal, when all are equal everyone will have enough, when everyone has enough no one will be unreasonable or inhumane. During a hundred years the social revolution follows this path, inspired by this hope. Kings are deposed in favor of representatives chosen by the people; the individual is emancipated from the class status, relatively stable, that from time immemorial defined his rights, prescribed his occupation, and bound him to long-established habits and ideas. Nevertheless, a society of equal, and equally rational and humane individuals does not emerge. Within an industrial society of uprooted and freely competing individuals, in which wealth replaces birth and occupation as the measure of power and prestige, there emerge certain individuals, favored above others by intelligence and opportunity, who acquire control of the new implements of power, appropriate the surplus wealth created by them, and purchase the services of the many in a labor market where the demand for man-power declines as the efficiency of machine-power increases. Thus the new power discovered by scientists and mediated by engineers is placed at the disposal of the few, and employed by them in a competitive struggle to maintain and extend their private advantage.

As the social revolution discloses this harsh fact, philosophers cease to predict the infinite perfectibility of man, but still declare that the unvarying law of Nature sanctions individual freedom in the economic realm, since the private profit of the few is obviously a public benefit. This view serves for a time—so long as the many are not too distressed, so long as the brilliant success of scientific knowledge applied to the production of wealth obscures the ominous fact that its proper distribution is left to chance, to the uncertain operation of individual self-interest. Yet from decade to decade the public benefit of this discordant system becomes less apparent as the ruthless competition for private profit leads to disastrous class conflict within, and to still more disastrous war between the nations: so little apparent that philosophers, unable any longer to distinguish right and force, identify the law of Nature with the unconscious will of man, and progress with an unremitting struggle for existence and survival. We thus note that during a hundred years the expansion of human intelligence and power discloses a

significant contrast: while man's effort to control the forces of
Nature is accompanied by increasing success and mounting optimism, his efforts to regenerate society lead only to confusion and
despair.

This significant contrast is reflected in the activities of men as we
observe them at the very end of our Time-Scale. We see no lack of
fertile farms, of elaborate and fully equipped factories, no lack of
engineers and technicians and mechanics to operate the factories
and cultivate the farms, no lack of inventors with new devices for
making machine-power more automatic and man-power less necessary. Yet we note that the factories are running intermittently or
not at all, that the farms are cultivated only in part. It is not that
all have enough; for we see millions of men and women, lacking
the necessities of life, standing before the machines, competent and
eager to operate them; and yet, like the machines themselves,
standing idle and unsupplied. We see this, and something more:
while millions of men stand idle before idle machines, other men
in obedience to governmental decree, refrain from planting wheat
and plow growing cotton under ground. A survey of human history will often enough disclose millions of men starving in time of
famine: what we see now is something unprecedented—millions of
men destitute in the midst of potential abundance. For there are
the necessary instruments of precision, there are the engineers and
technicians and mechanics with the necessary power and knowledge conjoined, ready and eager to supply men with all that they
need, with much that they desire besides; yet there they stand,
waiting as it were, while the people engage in furious class struggle
and governments prepare for war and revolution.

> Blight—not on the grain!
> Drouth—not in the springs!
> Rot—not from the rain!
>
> What shadow hidden or
> Unseen hand in our midst
> Ceaselessly touches our faces?
>   [ARCHIBALD MACLEISH, *Panic,* 1935, p. 8]

There is clearly some failure in co-ordinating the expanding
activities of men, some radical discord between man's capacity to

control the forces of Nature and his capacity to subdue his social
relations to rational direction.

QUESTIONS FOR STUDY

1. Give the etymological meanings of each of the following pairs of
   words: *erudite* and *rudiment; stature* and *station; recalcitrant* and
   caulk; rational and *ration; capricious* and *taxicab; corporate* and
   corpulent.
2. What kinds of work, according to Becker, does the new class of
   learned men do?
3. How do they differ from traditionalists?
4. What illustrations of the work of the new class does Becker include
   to develop his point?
5. What illustrations of the work of humanists and historians?
6. What idea about the nature of history itself emerges from their
   inquiries and views?
7. Where and how does the writer define that idea?
8. What is Becker's evaluation of that idea and his reason for that
   evaluation?
9. Need man see his stature diminish as the comprehended universe
   is infinitely expanded? Give reasons for your answer.
10. The shift in orientation during the last three centuries has re-
    sulted in new attitudes and ways of life which contrast sharply
    with tradition. List, specifically, such opposites.
11. When, in Becker's interpretation, did the modern age begin?
12. What views characterized the earlier Enlightenment?
13. What, in this interpretation, are the symbols and the measures of
    achievement of the new power of technology? What have been the
    consequences of the new goals of power?
14. What has been the impact of the revolution in scientific knowledge
    on social institutions?
15. How does changing nature differ from changing institutions?
16. Across the recent centuries of change, what different meanings
    have proponents given the terms *the law of nature* and *progress?*
17. What evidence today, if any, may be cited to modify the statement
    made by Becker in 1935 that although man is increasingly success-
    ful in controlling nature, "efforts to regenerate society lead only to
    confusion and despair"?

18. What is Becker's analysis of attitudes toward solutions of economic problems in the production and distribution of commodities?
19. This essay is organized around two of man's hopes: to master the outer world of things, of nature; and to direct social activities rationally. In the full perspective of history, what other hopes and purposes appear?
20. This essay begins with the promise of man's controlling nature and society. On what relevant conclusion does it end?

THE CRITICISM OF DEMOCRACY

Leslie Lipson

THE NEGATIVE SUMMING-UP

There are three principal objections to the democratic form of government: that it invites the tyranny of the majority, that it constitutes the enthronement of ignorance, that it puts up a false front behind which an oligarchy really rules. Let us consider these points in turn.

The force of the first criticism depends, in the main, on what meaning one attaches to "tyranny." In this context, I take it to imply a ruthless treatment of a smaller number by a larger who deny them what they consider their rights. The essence of tyranny is the notion of unjust domination. It is an act of power, judged to be wrongfully exercised. Can this happen under a democracy, and does it? I think the possibility, and, sometimes, the actuality, has to be conceded. Every type of government requires the consolidation and use of power, which on occasion will be abused. Since democracies ordinarily entrust power to the majority, the chance that it may be used tyrannically cannot be denied, ignored, or explained away. The danger is built-in with the system. It is an element of risk which accompanies the advantages; and, when a majority becomes oppressive, it can admittedly be cruel.

Are there safeguards against this happening? Yes, there are some kinds of defense. But we would be deluding ourselves if we pretended that they are foolproof. One protection is to build the machinery of state in so complicated a manner that minorities find numerous ways of resisting. But this, when overdone, leads to the opposite evil—that no decisions can be taken, that government is powerless, and that the majority is forever thwarted. The better safeguard is that which relies, not on institutions working at cross purposes, but on the interplay of political forces opposing one another within a context of freedom. I am thinking especially of the party system, the existence of an organized and legitimate opposition, and open channels of opinion through which injustice, if it exists, can be exposed for what it is. In a democracy which remains alert, and which contains enough of the sort of people who respond to stirrings of conscience, such political conditions, while they may not prevent all abuses by a majority behaving tyrannically, may serve to mitigate the effects and evoke a counter action. This may sound like a statement of faith. But it is a reasoned faith, since the oppressive majority has in fact been known to encounter courageous opposition.

The second objection, that democracy places the ignorant in power, is a variant of the first. It is founded on an elitist conception of human nature and the government appropriate thereto. If you argue that ruling is an art which calls for knowledge and specialized skills, you may conclude that few are competent and qualified to govern wisely. On the same reasoning, the mass of men are considered too stupid and too ill-informed to reach the right decisions. Hence, when the untutored majority is supreme, knowledge is subordinate to ignorance. In this argument one must distinguish the assertions which are valid from the inferences which are not. It is true that good government requires a great store of technical information, together with accumulated experience. Those who possess such knowledge are experts, and they are few. But it is no less true that such expertise, while it provides the intelligent basis for policy, does not necessarily indicate what the policies should be. All kinds of factors—ethical, social, and political—may be relevant to the ultimate choice. On that plane, the expert is no different from any other citizen. A professional in his specialty, he is an amateur elsewhere.

Nor can it be demonstrated from history—which, after all, is the only reliable teacher—that the alternative political systems, which consciously enshrined the domination of the supposedly superior few, have been notably wiser and have committed fewer mistakes. One can readily think of tenacious oligarchies in the past, such as the senatorial families of the Roman Republic or the Venetian commercial plutocracy, which brought power and prosperity to the state they governed and within it preserved their own privileges. But one could equally compile a long catalogue of their errors and misdeeds. In modern times, the Nazi self-styled supermen despised the ordinary run of mankind and thought to enslave the world by determination and brute force. But mistake upon mistake brought them to the day of reckoning. Similarly, the Communist parties, whose dogma persuades them that everything can be calculated and planned by a disciplined few, have as many failures on their record as successes. How else does one explain their recurrent shifts in policy? Organizing the relation of knowledge to governmental power is a very tricky affair for which no guaranteed formula will ever be found. Democracy, to be sure, has its full quota of stupidities, but not more so than in other systems; and it is certainly exempt from the bloodier excesses of treachery and cruelty.

The third of the objections rests on quite a different premise. It cuts away the ground from under the democrat's philosophy by asserting that he is the victim of an illusion and that his creed is a sham. Popular sovereignty, on this view, is a fairy tale; the common man, a dupe or a fool. The people never rules in fact—even the majority does not govern—because in simple truth it cannot. Whatever the theory may be, all government is oligarchical in character. Realistically seen, ruling is a function performed by a few. Only they can wield the power. Democracy should drop its pretensions and abandon the disguise.

This criticism, like the others, has been with us for a long time, or at least for two centuries. Rousseau mentions in the *Social Contract* that it is contrary to nature that many should govern and only a few be governed. Late in the nineteenth century when the electorate was still expanding and parties were multiplying, writers like Mosca, Ostrogorski, and Michels pointed out that the institutions which serve a democracy were not exempt from the tendencies to oligarchy in big organizations. In recent decades, a school of behaviorists and quantifiers has been busy detecting elites and mapping the social landscape with pyramids of power. The equation of politics with *Who Gets What, When, and How* supplies the proof that the few get the most by skill and guile.

Where does this leave democracy? Are we foredoomed to futility by living in a dream and posing an unattainable ideal? Again let us seek to separate authentic fact from unwarranted inference. No one can deny what any statistical computation will show, that wealth, social status, and influence are unequally distributed in every society and that a small percentage of persons on the distribution curve enjoys a disproportionate share. Nor can we refute the evident truth that our increasingly complex society is managed by ever larger organizations whose structure becomes both hierarchical and bureaucratic. But let us not forget the insight in Acton's comment that modern democracy was derived neither from the medieval state nor from the medieval church, but from the conflict between the two. The exigencies of competition even between organizations which are controlled from the top contributes to the goals of democracy. For the atmosphere of publicity which surrounds their operations, and the criticisms which they must expect from rivals, compel the heads of those organizations ultimately to be answerable, not merely to their own members, but to the community at large.

When there is an alternative to which people may have recourse, an organization cannot, in monopoly fashion, bend them to its will. Instead, it must bid for their support. This holds true whether the institution in question is a church, a corporation, a trade union, or a political party. However, since the state bears the responsibility over all of promoting the public interest, the crucial competition is that which occurs within the political order. Hence, as I emphasized earlier, the indispensable political requirement for a democracy is always to have at least two major parties between which the voters can periodically choose. Nor can the discipline within these parties ever be made so tight that splits and revolts are impossible. Nor is the people a crowd of mere spectators who applaud or jeer the contesting teams, but otherwise are passive and take no part in the proceedings. Their function is more like that of a jury which hears the evidence as it is marshalled by professionals and then on election day delivers its verdict.

THE POSITIVE EVALUATION

Finally, there are the arguments in favor of democracy. Three will suffice, because these are the points which really matter. The democratic form of government has a claim on our allegiance for the reasons that it enhanced human dignity, it supplies a continuing civic education, and thereby in the broadest sense it helps humanity in becoming more civilized.

Respect for the dignity of its citizens is the cornerstone of democratic government. A democracy insists that the state and its personnel exist to serve the public. To enforce that principle, machinery is provided for changing the institutions and the officials. The whole body of the people discharges at stated periods the supreme responsibility of choosing the men and women who will direct the government and of approving the general policy they will pursue. Under this system, all have some share in the common enterprise. Therefore, everybody counts for something.

That is a statement of the ideal. It expresses the intent of the democratic man, the goal he sets before himself, the standard by which he judges his government and is prepared to be judged. Hence, it is true of actual democracies only to the extent that they are true to their own principles. Actual democracies vary in their degrees of approximation to what they aspire or profess to be. But this commitment to ideals serves as a regulator of practice. Certain things are done or avoided in a democracy because the democratic values demand or deny them. At rock bottom, all of this depends on the manner in which the citizens assert themselves. They can be pushed around or hoodwinked only if they allow themselves to be so treated. The processes and institutions of democracy afford to every man and woman more scope for participation and influence than any other system. How they use their opportunity depends on the character of the people. Their dignity is what they make of it.

Because they do count for something and are expected to participate, the people of a democratic community enjoy the benefit of a continuing civic education. Public affairs are constantly engaging their attention. They are consulted and canvassed, polled and propagandized, because they have votes which they will one day cast. The debate over issues of common concern goes on without respite, and those who read and listen, learn. They also learn by doing. The work of the myriad associations which citizens form among themselves helps to knit the community and to train its members in the exercise of responsibility. The political system which places a premium on the voluntary activity of its members grows stronger as their experience augments their education. It is in this sense that Pericles was correct in stressing the educative value of the democratic process.

For this reason also, although the people will err periodically, and will sometimes be the victims of deception, the system includes the means of discovering the errors, unmasking the frauds, and exposing the charlatans. Lincoln expressed this vividly in his remark that you can fool some of the people all of the time and all of the people some of the time, but not all of the people all of the time. It is this certainty which saves democracy from the worst effects of its own misjudgment or misplaced trust. With freedom will come mistakes, but our education, individual and civic, consists in learning not to repeat them and in striving to improve on past performance.

Therein, finally, lies democracy's greatest contribution to humanity. Open inquiry, criticism, and searching are stimuli to achievement and appraisal. By the laws of its being, democracy is dedicated to a concern for the general welfare. The rhythm of parties alternating in office encourages each to vie with others and promotes, along with exposure of faults, a constructive balance between experience and experiment. The ideals of democracy are dynamic because their contents admit of progressive redefinition. Hence, as a community advances, not only in knowledge and techniques but also in the level of its ethical aspirations, the politics of the democratic state enables its government by positive measures to translate the increment into policy and program. This is what I have meant throughout this book by calling my subject *The Democratic Civilization*. The state which responds to the citizens' awareness of their needs will help them to raise the standard of the good life, as their education equips them to envision it, and because its powers are derived from all, its civilizing benefits are distributed among all.

Democracy, its critics reiterate, is not a government by the best and wisest. But of all forms of government known and tried, democracy is the wisest and the best.

QUESTIONS FOR STUDY

1. Outline the essay. What are the main divisions? The subordinate points under each division?
2. Define *oligarchy, elitist, quantifiers, increment, exigency.*
3. What are the democratic safeguards against a tyranny of the majority?
4. Does the popular phrase "majority rule, minority rights," cover the case adequately?
5. What illustrations support the point that a supposedly superior few may be wiser than the many?
6. In spite of "its full quota of stupidities," what has been a significant difference between democracy and other systems of government?
7. What checks against oligarchy exist?
8. How does democracy enhance the dignity of the individual beyond allowing him to take part in the frequent elections of officials?
9. How does democracy augment civic education?
10. What characteristics of a civilized society are implied in the paragraph beginning "Therein, finally . . ."?
11. What methods of amplifying ideas does the writer use most frequently?

Part II

On Developing Ideas

CHAPTER 1

Ideas: Sentences and Paragraphs

Man is a reed, the weakest in nature, but he is a
thinking reed.   —Pascal, *Thoughts*, 1670

Noon, boat, footprint, and *sand* are names for a time of day and objects. We may identify each object by its name, separately, to give it alone a name. Under appropriate circumstances, however, we may combine objects, by their names, with other objects to convey larger areas of our awareness. As we perceive objects, we may relate them, one to another, and unite them: "As I was going toward my boat at noon, I saw footprints in the sand." No one need ever be tongue-tied. If he looks, the visible world is before him and he may report what he sees in language. What he sees outwardly may move him inwardly:

It happened one day, about noon, going towards my boat, I was exceedingly surprised with the print of a man's naked foot on the shore, which was very plain to be seen in the sand. I stood like one thunderstruck, or as if I had seen an apparition.
                              —Daniel Defoe, *Robinson Crusoe,* 1719

He may not only recall and report his experiences, outwardly and inwardly. He may judge them:

To the University of Oxford I acknowledge no obligation, and she will as cheerfully renounce me for a son, as I am willing to disclaim her for a mother. I spent fourteen months at Magdalen College; they proved the most unprofitable of my whole life.
                              —Edward Gibbon, *Autobiography,* 1796

From the past he may isolate historical or biographical facts:

In the village of Domremy, near Vaucouleurs, on the borders of Lorraine, there lived a country girl of twenty-seven years of age, called Joan d'Arc, who was a servant in a small inn.
                    —DAVID HUME, *History of England*, 1754–62

John Wilmot, afterwards Earl of Rochester, the son of Henry, Earl of Rochester, better known by the title of Lord Wilmot, so often mentioned in Clarendon's *History*, was born April 10, 1647, at Ditchley, in Oxfordshire.
    —SAMUEL JOHNSON, "Life of Rochester," *Lives of the Poets*, 1781–83

And by language he may direct future actions as well:

The Fifty-third and the Tenth Divisions will establish battle headquarters at or near Jalud and Selfit respectively tomorrow afternoon at five o'clock.

He may make known his sense of himself in his relationships with others:

The notice which you have been pleased to take of my labours, had it been early, had been kind; but it has been delayed till I am indifferent, and cannot enjoy it; till I am solitary, and cannot impart it; till I am known, and do not want it.
                    —SAMUEL JOHNSON, letter to Chesterfield, 1790

Or he may express the pathos in the lives of all men:

Man that is born of a woman hath but a short time to live, and is full of misery. He cometh up, and is cut down, like a flower; he fleeth as it were a shadow, and never continueth in one stay. In the midst of life we are in death.
                    —*The Book of Common Prayer*, 1549–1662

Facts and events, the perception of objects, and the awareness of emotional responses are all conveyed by linking together in grammatical units words which designate separable but related aspects of them. The substance of experience, however, is not limited to facts, events, perceptions, and emotions. Being a thinking reed, man abstracts qualities from his experiences, reflects on their nature, relates them to other qualities.

CONCEPTS

In his awareness of existence, man's ideas and concepts may be as dominant as his percepts. He can neither see nor feel diversion as he could a tennis ball, and yet he knows the meaning of the word which denotes a generalized sense of play, *diversion*. Science is not a Bunsen burner with tapering flame, and yet millions work in the name of science. *Virtue, skepticism, philosophy, people, business, motive, education, suggestibility, belief, knowledge, literature, value, life, nature, style, language, democracy,* and *opinion*—all, as words, denote concepts.

Thinking is inquiring into the nature of, comparing, and relating concepts, one with another, and concepts with percepts. A word designates an object, an idea, a concept; a sentence, a relationship or relationships between them; a paragraph, an expansion or development of that relationship by a fuller exploration of its many aspects. The phrase *the United States,* designating a government and not a geographical area, names a concept; so does the word *democracy.* The two may be brought together in one sentence: "The United States is a democracy." Why? Because *democracy,* in *intension,* is interpreted as meaning the existence of multiple parties and representational government and the United States, as a political unit, has multiple parties and representational government. In his thinking one relates concepts by discovering the points they have in common and the ways in which they are unlike, their likenesses and their differences.

The sentence in which a writer or speaker expresses that relationship is a proposal that the relationship exists. Unlike poetic utterance, it invites the reader to test it in his own thinking. It does not state a fact—"I see footprints in the sand"; "John Wilmot was born April 10, 1647"; nor does it report an emotion—"I am solitary, and cannot impart it," "he fleeth as it were a shadow." Its meaning it offers for consideration, acceptance, or adoption. It is a proposition, a conclusion, a judgment. The sentence "Pennsylvania is a part of the United States" states a fact in its geographical, political, and other senses. In contrast, the sentence "The United States is a democracy" states a conclusion, a judgment, reached, if understood, by reflective thought. Its meaning is neither intuitive nor emotional, but logical. That is because it centers in the implications of and the inferences to be drawn from an awareness of the qualities or the concepts it joins.

COMBINING CONCEPTS

Contrast the two following statements:

1

Yes, sir, we were married just fifty years ago the seventeenth day of last December and my daughter and son-in-law was over from Trenton to help us celebrate the Golden Wedding. My son-in-law is John H. Kramer, the real estate man. He made $12,000 one year and is pretty well thought of around Trenton; a good, steady, hard worker. The Rotarians was after him a long time to join, but he kept telling them his home was his club. But Edie finally made him join. That's my daughter.

—RING LARDNER, "The Golden Honeymoon," 1926

2

To understand that we have souls is to feel our separation from things visible, our independence of them, our distinct existence in ourselves, our individuality, our power of acting for ourselves this way or that way; our accountableness for what we do.

—JOHN HENRY NEWMAN, "The Immortality of the Soul," *Parochial Sermons*, 1834

The first passage achieves its purpose quite well, but that purpose is not to record reflective thought. It is to give the flow of an old man's remarks, remarks unsystematic, uncontrolled, and uncritical. There is no centralizing subject. There is only a flow of free association from the Golden Wedding, the identity of the son-in-law, his salary, his characteristics, his hesitancy to join a club, to the name of the daughter. The second passage, however, illustrates an ordered sequence of concepts: systematic, controlled, and critical. It selects and relates concepts to a centralizing subject: evidences of the existence of the soul. One's accountability for his actions, his power of self-determination, and his individuality are interpreted to affirm the existence of the soul.

A sentence which conveys a thought may name only two concepts: "The United States is a democracy." Or it may include several, as the sentence quoted from Newman does (although they are reducible to two: evidence and soul). A sentence may present such a compression of meaning that will, upon close analysis, reveal many proposals. One, however, should be dominant and the others subordinated to it.

Analyze the assumptions or conclusions in this sentence:

Unless an opinion is freely discussed, the grounds for holding it are likely to be forgotten; so that even if the opinion is true, it is likely to give way before the slightest semblance of argument.

A few of the implicit conclusions in this passage will illustrate the degree of compression in thought that it presents. The separate ideas conjoined in the underlying assumptions are given in parentheses after each restated assumption.

1. An opinion may be discussed. (Opinion and discussion)
2. The discussion of an opinion may be unrestricted. (Discussion of an opinion and freedom from restriction)
3. An opinion may be forgotten. (Opinion and forgetfulness)
4. Useful opinions should be remembered. (Useful opinions and remembering)
5. The worth of an opinion is determined by the grounds for holding it. (Worth of an opinion and grounds for holding an opinion)
6. An opinion may be true. (Opinion and truth)
7. An opinion may be false. (Opinion and lack of truth)

The assumptions may be further isolated. These, however, are enough to illustrate the complexity of the meaning of a sentence. What concepts control the entire statement? Freedom of discussion and truthful opinions. What relationship is conceived here as bringing the two together? The effect of the former on the latter, a tendency to preserve. Hence, the central major conclusions is *Freedom of discussion helps to preserve truthful opinions.* All minor concepts, such as grounds for belief, forgetfulness, remembering, truth, and lack of truth, are subsumed.

This sentence is deliberately taken out of context, separated from other sentences around it. For that reason, one cannot be certain of the purpose it furthers in a paragraph made of many such sentences. From it alone, therefore, one may extract other central major conclusions which provide different emphases.

THE NATURE OF PROPOSITIONS

Thus, *A knowledge of the grounds for holding a truthful opinion helps to preserve it in an argument.*

Contrast the meanings of the following statements:

> All men create their own world.
> No man is created by his environment.
> Some men create their own world.
> Some men are not created by their environment.

The implications of these statements, the inferences that may be drawn from them are varied. If you hear or read the third, "Some men create their own world," you will report it incorrectly if you give it as the first, "All men create their own world." For the third separates men into two groups: those men who do create their own world and those who do not. The first statement considers all men as a unit and the second concept, that of creating a world, is there said to be applicable to all without exception. The first is *universal;* the third, *particular.* The second is *universal* also, but *negative.* The fourth, *particular,* but *negative.* Whether the proposal implicit in any sentence may be rightly interpreted as *universal affirmative* or *negative, particular affirmative* or *negative* conditions the meaning it conveys.

To overlook a condition which qualifies a statement and still consider its meaning as conclusive is to distort it. Similarly, in attempting to understand or to report what one has said, to exclude one of the two alternatives and consider the other alone is to misunderstand it or to report it incorrectly. Only those statements which are made unconditionally and conclusively can be so considered or reported. Only they are *categorical.* The statement "Of all modern and ancient poets, Shakespeare had the largest and most comprehensive soul" is a categorical one. The statement "There can be no enlargement of mind unless there be a comparison of ideas one with another as they come before the mind and a systematization of them" cannot rightly be interpreted to mean "There can be no enlargement of mind." It gives the indispensable *condition* of enlargement. The statement "You have made a monstrous charge against me: direct, distinct, public. You are bound to prove it directly, distinctly, publicly, or to own that you cannot" cannot correctly be said to mean "You cannot prove the monstrous charge." The statement names alternatives: "You must prove the charge you have made or you must admit that you cannot."

THE TESTING OF PROPOSITIONS

To understand that propositions, proposals, or conclusions are stated as being true of all groups or of particular groups, or that they are *categorical, conditional,* or *disjunctive* (that is, *either-or*), is not to conclude that they are therefore true—that they represent the actual condition of the subject they present. To test the truth of any proposition, you may ask these questions:

1. May the proposition be understood? May it be related to known concepts and observations?
2. May it be verified? Does it report existing and known conditions?
3. Is it useful? Does it contribute to man's comprehension of the world and the circumstances of his life?

Ask these three questions of each of the following statements. Under such questioning, what is each statement worth?

a. Only those with physical defects or perverse subjective leanings attempt intellectual pursuits.
b. Men create their environment and are not created by it.
c. If the human race is to survive as "human," knowledge, reason, and sympathy must triumph over ignorance, impulse, and hatred.
d. Economic institutions alone determine the quality of men's ideas.

THE DEVELOPMENT OF IDEAS IN PARAGRAPHS

A paragraph of several sentences, no less than a single sentence, may express a definite relationship between two major concepts. More subordinate aspects of each may be included, to be sure, but the meaning of the entire paragraph may be summarized in one sentence, which states the central point of the entire unit. This *topic* or summarizing sentence may be implied or it may be expressed directly at any point in the paragraph. The rest of the sentences in the paragraph, if they are relevant, represent the development of one or another of the aspects of its controlling meaning.

Consider this paragraph:

[1] In this age of ours, when the form of government has become the

most momentous of the issues that divide men and nations, we have peculiar need for clear thinking about democracy. [2] If we defend it we should do so without misunderstanding what it is; if we attack it we should know what we attack. [3] To question and to seek the truth is still our democratic privilege. [4] In defending democracy one need not and should not be blind to its limitations and to its defects. [5] Public opinion is no wiser, no better than the people who hold it. [6] The people are easily led by demagogues. [7] They are beset by prejudices, moved by slogans, deceived by specious sentiments. [8] They are often inert and often confused. [9] They are often roused by things that matter little and often unresponsive to things that matter much. [10] Let us freely admit all this, but let us equally admit the fact that we do not get away from the prejudices and the confusions of the people by resorting to dictatorship. [11] In the modern world every system of government must rest on the general consent of the mass of the people. [12] On this score everything that is said in the indictment of democracy applies with yet greater force against dictatorship, since the latter must use every technique to prevent the people, on whose mass emotions it depends, from becoming more enlightened.
—R. M. MacIver, *Leviathan and the People*, 1939

After you have read the paragraph, you may recall many propositions or conclusions. Some representative ones are:

a.   The most momentous of the issues that divide men and nations has become the form of government.
b.   Public opinion is no wiser than the people who hold it.
c.   People are easily led by demagogues.
d.   In the modern world every government must rest on the general consent of the mass of the people.

These ideas, to be sure, may be debated and tested. They are part of a rhetorical and not a poetic discourse.

Upon further analysis, you will observe the inclusion of many concepts in the paragraph. A condensed list of some of them as they occur includes:

the form of government
issues that divide men
need for clear thinking
democracy
defending or attacking
   democracy
understanding or misunder-

admitting limitations and
   defects of democracy
public opinion
creators of public opinion
public opinion under a
   dictatorship
government

standing democracy	general consent of the people
seeking the truth	suppression of enlightened
democratic privilege	public opinion

Some of these concepts, obviously, are more recurrent and dominant in the paragraph than others. Which are they? Attacking democracy? The public's inertia? Issues that divide men? Clear thinking? Or others? The dominant ones should appear in the summarizing sentence. All the others are details which help make them clear. What, essentially, does the paragraph say? How may it be summarized?

The context of the paragraphs which make up the essay from which this paragraph is isolated may become a factor in giving a final answer to the last question. Here, however, consider this paragraph as an isolated one. The progression of ideas in it may then be represented in these summarizing sentences:

Since the form of government is the most momentous issue today, clear thinking about democracy is needed. In admitting the limitations of people in a democracy, one must still admit that dictatorship offers no remedy for such limitations. A dictatorship is to be indicated more than a democracy, for it uses many techniques to prevent its people from thinking clearly.

To what conclusion in the entire paragraph does this point? To the statement "We have peculiar need for clear thinking about democracy." But why do we have that need? Because the form of government (the most momentous issue today) rests on the general consent of the people. That government which rests on the enlightened opinion and consent of the people has fewer limitations than that which rests on unenlightened opinion; hence, we have peculiar need for clear thinking. This paragraph, then, develops various aspects of the proposition *Today we have peculiar need for clear thinking about democracy.*

The topic may be stated differently. If it is reduced to its simplest form, however, it will contain two major ideas, *our peculiar need today* and *clear thinking about democracy* and an expressed relationship between them. And if it is the true topic of the paragraph, either expressed within the paragraph, as it is here, or implied, all the sentences will have direct bearing on it, will develop some aspect of it.

WAYS OF DEVELOPING IDEAS IN PARAGRAPHS

A writer may use various means of developing a single proposition or topic into a full paragraph. Using the statement "We have
peculiar need today for clear thinking about democracy" as the
central meaning which links together all the details of the quoted
paragraph, we may ask how each sentence is related to it. The first
part of the first sentence offers *proof* of the existence of the need:
the form of government is the most momentous issue that divides
men and nations today. The second and third sentences emphasize
clear thinking, understanding, and misunderstanding, in the
choice, attack or defense, forced on us by the issue. They offer
further proof of the conclusion, the topic of the paragraph. The
limitations and the defects of a democracy which the writer brings
forward in the fourth sentence also prove the need. The next five
sentences, the fifth through the ninth, are an *analysis* of the characteristic shortcomings of the people. The tenth sentence contains a
comparison, in one respect, of a democracy and a dictatorship,
which is completed in the twelfth. The eleventh is further proof of
the need for clear thinking about democracy. The writer, therefore, has developed the governing idea of his paragraph by using
several means: proof, analysis, and comparison. Proof, however, is
the dominant means; comparison and descriptive analyses are used
to expand particular aspects of the problem which prove the basic
proposition. The paragraph is developed largely by what is offered
as proof.

The foregoing analysis is of a paragraph which is abstract in
substance. It includes no concrete details, no figurative language,
no specific, readily perceivable instances. The following paragraph
centers around an abstract idea, as does the foregoing paragraph;
but the writer develops it by listing specific *illustrative* cases.

It is always very difficult to decide whether it was the artist who
created the national atmosphere or whether the national atmosphere
had actually made the artist. Our most typical negro songs were written
by a white man, Stephen Foster. What we call typical Hawaiian music
was really written by a Prussian band master. Most people associate
Carmen and the Bolero with everything typically Spanish, but Bizet
and Ravel were Frenchmen. The best tangos have been written not by
Argentines but by Germans, and Dvorak, a Czech, wrote the best
known of all purely American symphonies.

—HENDRIK VAN LOON, *The Arts,* 1937

The topic sentence of the paragraph is the first. The other sentences give cases in point. The paragraph is developed by *illustration*. No final decision, no proof, is offered; difficulty of decision concerning the relationship between an artist and national atmosphere is stressed by the writer's including numerous examples.

In addition to proof, analysis, comparison and contrast, and illustration, there are other ways of developing a subject: cause, definition, classification, and analogy. Although the amplification of any governing idea may—indeed, usually does—require two or more of the methods, each of the following paragraphs is confined to just one.

THE TOPIC SENTENCE

The topic or summarizing sentence of a paragraph may be implied or it may be expressed directly at any point in the paragraph.

1

The topic, Many tonal perceptions are fusions, is developed by *illustration:*

Many tonal perceptions are fusions. The processes constituting a chord melt into one another so completely that they tend to lose their own specific qualities in favor of the total character of the chord itself. The chord frequently appears as a simple or unanalyzable experience. Smell and taste qualities often fuse together. The perception of the taste of coffee, to take another illustration, is a fusion made up of a certain bitter-sweetness, a certain temperature quality, and perhaps several olfatory qualities. Many of the cutaneous perceptions are also fusions. Wetness, dryness, sharpness, bluntness, oiliness, roughness, and smoothness are cutaneous perceptions made up by the fusion of cutaneous qualities, or cutaneous and kinaesthetic qualities. Dizziness is another illustration for it is experienced as something qualitatively different from any of the processes we have described.
—COLEMAN R. GRIFFITH, *General Introduction to Psychology*, 1923, p. 21

2

The topic may be developed by *contrast:*

The classical Latin is pagan, quantitative, and unrimed; the mediaeval Latin is Christian, accentual, and rimed. And whereas classical Latin is national and local, singing the pride of Rome, mediaeval Latin is necessarily without national values, and hymns the pride of the universal Church.

—JOHN BERDAN, *Early Tudor Poetry*, 1931

3

The topic, the nature of the scientific method, is here developed by *analysis:*

Correct scientific method is made up, according to Galileo, of four parts: (1) observation brought to the highest possible development by the prolonged special training of the observer; (2) the isolation of phenomena in laboratories for the purpose of experimentation; (3) the use of steadily improved precision instruments such as scales, barometer, telescope, etc.; (4) the scientific hypothesis as an avenue for penetrating into the unknown but conscientiously treated as pure hypothesis until fully confirmed by the evidence.

—FERDINAND SCHEVILL, *A History of Europe*, 1951

4

The *classification* of types in a phylum follows:

Because of the kinship of the grasshopper and the crayfish, scientists have placed them in the same great group, or phylum. The phylum to which they belong is called Arthropoda, which is derived from the two Greek words: "arthron," a joint, and "pous," a foot. All of the animals which have jointed, or hinged, appendages are placed in this phylum. There are also other characteristics, as we have seen, which are common to all members of this group. The phylum includes such animals as the lobster, crab, prawn, barnacle, honeybee, centipede, and spider. These animals are built on the same general plan as the grasshopper and the crayfish. All animals which possess these general characteristics belong to the phylum Arthropoda.

—CHARLES JOHN PIEPER, WILBUR L. BEAUCHAMP, and ORLIN D. FRANK,
Everyday Problems in Biology, 1932

5

Definitions of *credit* are considered in this paragraph:

From the point of view of the buyer of goods or the borrower of funds, credit is purchasing power made available in the present in the consideration of a promise to repay its equivalent in the future. From the point of view of the seller of goods or the lender of funds, *credit* is the right to receive specified sums of money, or equivalent values, at specified future dates. Such rights are secured by guarantees which may be specific or implied. From the legal point of view, *credit is a contract*

—a promise to pay in return for value received, which constitutes a claim or lien upon the present or future resources of the debtor enforceable by due process of law. As an economic concept, *credit is a medium of exchange* and may be described as *a form of purchasing power which serves to supplement the supply of money.* It is based fundamentally upon values incorporated in actual or potential goods which are directly or indirectly pledged as security for the exchange value of the credit.

—RICHARD THEODORE ELY and RALPH H. HESS, *Outlines of Economics,* 1937

Is the topic stated or implied?

6

Causes of changes in the surfaces of the earth are the subject of this paragraph:

Since marine sedimentary rocks underlie large areas of the present continents, even in the highest mountains and plateaus, manifestly there are powerful forces within the Earth that cause widespread uplift and thus tend to offset the wearing away of the lands by destructive surface agents. These internal forces, whose origin and mode of operation are still in large part mysterious, elevate and depress large areas by gentle bending or *warping* of the crust, a process that has repeatedly caused emergence and submergence of large land masses in all the continents. The forces within the Earth also cause violent crumpling and breaking of the rocks in mountain zones, which rise as great welts above their surroundings. At the same time, localized heat causes the development of great bodies of melted rock, some of which break through to the Earth's surface, forming lava flows and other volcanic products. Heat from igneous reservoirs causes profound change or metamorphism of adjacent rocks in the crust; metamorphism results also from the Earth's great deforming pressure in the mountain zone.

—CHESTER RAY LONGWELL, ADOLPH KNOPF, and RICHARD F. FLINT, *Textbook of Geology,* 1939

Is the topic stated or implied?

7

Three phenomena offer *proof* that the earth and not the sun moves in an orbit:

That, relative to landmarks among the stars, it is the earth and not the sun that moves in a great orbit is shown by three different phenomena, the discovery of which required exact measurements with instruments that were not available until long after the time of Copernicus. These are the aberration of light, discovered by the English astronomer Bradley in 1727; the annual parallactic displacement of the nearer stars, first detected by Bessel in Germany in 1837; and the annually periodic variation in the radial velocity of stars, which has been observed since the first work of Sir William Huggins on stellar spectra in 1864.   —JOHN CHARLES DUNCAN, *Astronomy*, 1935

Which sentence states the topic?

EXERCISE I

Which of the following statements convey verifiable facts? Events? Personal preferences or emotional responses? Ideas?

1. Colleges should bring students face to face with the decisions made by their elders in order that they may meet the questions of human existence and find their answers for them.

2. According to Manlius, in *Locorum communium collectanea* (1562), Faustus was born at Knittlingen in Württemberg; the popular legend says Rohda in Saxony.

3. When I look upon the tombs of the great, every emotion of envy dies within me; when I read the epitaphs of the beautiful, every inordinate desire goes out; when I meet with the grief of parents upon a tombstone, my heart melts with compassion; when I see the tombs of the parents themselves, I consider the vanity of grieving for those whom we must quickly follow; when I see kings lying by those who deposed them, when I consider rival wits placed side by side, or the holy men that divided the world with their contests and disputes, I reflect with sorrow and astonishment on the little competitions, factions, and debates of mankind.
   —JOSEPH ADDISON, "The Tombs in Westminster Abbey"

4. In August, 1519, five ships and two hundred and eighty men started with Magellan; in July, 1522, the *Vittoria,* with a remnant of thirty-one men aboard, returned up the Atlantic to her anchorage near the Mole of Seville, in the river Guadalquivir.

5. Parallel quarto and folio texts exist for fourteen of Shakespeare's plays.

6. To transfuse emotion—not to transmit thought but to set up in the reader's sense a vibration corresponding to what was felt by the writer—is the peculiar function of poetry.
   —A. E. HOUSMAN, *The Name and Nature of Poetry,* 1933

7. As Alice said these words her foot slipped, and in another moment, splash! she was up to her chin in salt water. She soon made out that she was in the pool of tears which she had wept when she was nine feet high.

— LEWIS CARROLL, *Alice in Wonderland*, 1865

8. Talk is one of the few unspecialized talents still left in a mechanical world.

— RANDOLPH BOURNE, *The History of a Literary Radical*, 1920

9. I cannot see the wit of walking and talking at the same time. When I am in the country I wish to vegetate like the country. I am not for criticizing hedgerows and black cattle. I go out of town in order to forget the town and all that is in it.

— WILLIAM HAZLITT, "On Going a Journey," *Table Talk*, 1821

10. In March, 1845, Thoreau borrowed Alcott's axe, cut down some tall, arrowy pines for timbers, studs, and rafters, bought a shanty for boards, built a hut at Walden.

EXERCISE II

A. Each of the following sentences expresses a relationship between the concepts named by it. Thus, between the two concepts *succeeding generations* and *bubbles* the relationship may be thought of as expressed in "One generation blows bubbles, and the next breaks them." That sentence conveys its meaning figuratively. Translated into its literal meaning, it might read: "Every generation devises explanations, theories, or customs which, to the next generation, prove to be incorrect, inadequate, or worthless." But what quality links the theories of one generation and bubbles? Both the theories or customs and the bubbles are too fragile to hold together. The link between the concepts of bubbles and theories then is fragility. The link between generations and bubbles is a succession of constructing and destroying.

In each of the following sentences name the quality which brings the two concepts together.

1. Human life is an isthmus.
2. Man's nature runs either to herbs or weeds.
3. Their friendship was for summer weather only.
4. His threats are a wooden gun.
5. Time is a pretty toy.

B. By considering the meaning, both in extension (denotation) and in intension (connotation), of each of the words in the pairs of words given below, try to establish some one quality that the paired words have in common. Then express in a single sentence of your own invention that relationship. Make the relation as direct as possible; avoid the fanciful. For example, *words* and *clothes* can remind you that both go out of style. Thus, "Words, like clothes, become old-fashioned." Consider a second case: two notions, first that of reaching correct decisions in a world of uncertainties, and second, that of a cat, are joined in this statement: "Reaching correct decisions in a world' of uncertainties is being able to see in the dark, like a cat."

1. affected speech, a load of bandboxes
2. clouds, procession
3. rain, fury
4. night, cave
5. man, mushroom
6. life, bubble
7. an excited person, a leaf
8. a stupid excuse, a broken clock
9. language, algebra
10. corporation, conscience

EXERCISE III

Four conditions of meaning are named in the following key sentences:

a. The meaning expressed by the predicate applies to all of the things named by the subject.

b. The meaning expressed by the predicate applies to none of the things named by the subject.

c. The meaning of the predicate is applicable to some, not all, of the things named by the subject.

d. The meaning of the predicate is not applicable to some of the things named by the subject.

Indicate which of the four conditions listed above—a, b, c, or d,—applies to each of the sentences:

1. Men are thrown into groups by their different inferences from the same experiences.
2. The power of watchwords consists in the clusters of suggestions which have been fastened upon them.
3. The aim of all institutions in the modern state is to please the average man.
4. Education which produces faith in life comes through personal influence and example, not from books.
5. Outwitting an enemy by any means possible is praiseworthy.
6. Men are scoffers.
7. Newspaper commentators who live in and write from Europe hold distorted views of the United States.
8. True citizens do not respond to flowery speeches and fantastic promises.
9. Might has made all the right which ever has existed or now exists.

10. Whales are not pachyderms.
11. No wise man ever wished to be younger.
12. Some men, under the notion of weeding out prejudices, eradicate virtue, honesty, and religion.
13. Some people take more care to hide their wisdom than their folly.
  —11, 12, and 13: JONATHAN SWIFT, *Thoughts on Various Subjects Moral and Diverting,* 1711
14. Men were not intended to work with the accuracy of tools, to be precise and perfect in all their actions.
  —JOHN RUSKIN, *The Stones of Venice,* 1851–53

EXERCISE IV

Which of the key sentences given below—a, b, or c,—correctly describes each of the following sentences:
  a. The sentence involves a supposition, a condition, or an assumption.
  b. The sentence names alternatives.
  c. The sentence contains an unconditional assertion.
 1. Democracy rests upon the equality of men.
 2. If one is sensitive and not callous, he finds immortality in the vividness of life.
 3. Ritual is the perfect form of drill.
 4. Man must choose either a policy of virtue or a policy of success.
 5. If the newspapers of America fall very far short of keeping all channels of information clear, the fault lies largely with the reader.
 6. The announcement meant that the two factions had quit the fight, that one had given in, or that both had made compromises.
 7. If the writers not only did the dialogue but also worked out the sequences, they should be credited with the most perfect screenplay of the year.
 8. The success of any undertaking alone determines whether it is good or bad.
 9. A patriot is either a real defender of his country's freedom or a factious disturber of the government.
10. Realism shows the meanness of greatness, the other side of virtue, the weakness of heroes.
11. The task of an author is either to teach what is not known or to recommend known truths by his manner of adorning them; either to let new light in upon the mind, and open new scenes to the prospect, or to vary the dress and situation of common objects, so as to give them fresh grace and more powerful attractions, to

spread such flowers over the regions through which the intellect has already made its progress, as may tempt it to return, and take a second view of things hastily passed over, or negligently regarded.

—SAMUEL JOHNSON, *The Rambler,* 1750–52

12. I have just left the observatory of one of the most learned astronomers in the world, who have spent forty years in unwearied attention to the motions and appearances of the celestial bodies, and has drawn out his soul in endless calculations. . . . His comprehension is vast, his memory capacious and retentive, his discourse is methodical, and his expression clean.

—SAMUEL JOHNSON, *The Rambler,* 1750–52

EXERCISE V

Of the group of things named by the subject of each of the following sentences, the meaning expressed by the predicate applies to

a—all, without question
b—all, probably
c—none
d—some, at least
e—some, but not all
f—some, and possibly all
g—the percentage actually named

1. Men attain success by deceit.
2. There are no universal and absolute facts; knowledge is subject to unlimited verification and revision.
3. Some sports are really dangerous.
4. During the last few years, magazines designed for masses of readers have undergone many changes.
5. The minds of men dwell more on misfortune than on prosperity.
6. Too few of the minority who use the public libraries know what they read.
7. Men want only a fair chance.
8. Current problems are not always economic.
9. Only artists know fully the vividness of life.
10. Forty per cent of the counties in the United States, containing 17,-000,000 persons, do not have a registered general hospital.

EXERCISE VI

Ask these three questions of each of the following sentences: Can it be understood? Can it be verified? Is it useful?

1. Errors, as well as facts, perpetuate themselves by their usefulness.
2. Freedom, justice, truth, right, and reason are but the weirdest and most ineffectual voodoo incantations unless they are operative and observable in the actions of men.
3. Thinking is interfused with emotion; the rational with the irrational. Understanding a thought or an idea requires a knowledge not only of its substance (its expressed subject) but also of its emotional coloring (the habits of mind and the desires of the author which it reflects).
4. Action based on faith in impulse or in self-appointed authority is superior to action based on reason and a full knowledge of the causes and the consequences of one's actions.
5. To enslave an individual is to make him bear another's burden; to coddle him is to bear his burden for him; to liberate him is to protect his right to bear his own. The last is the desire of a free people.
6. The promise of any group to aid and defend the whole people must be tested by the acts of that group; even at the outset, action alone can give value to statements of creeds and programs.
7. The political freedom of a people rests basically in their right and in their ability to choose or to reject their political leaders.

EXERCISE VII

For each of the following paragraphs, point out the topic sentence, or if it is implied, write one. By what means is each paragraph developed?

1

Death meets us everywhere, and is procured by every instrument and in all chances, and enters in at many doors by violence and secret influence, by the aspects of a star and the stink of a mist, by the emissions of a cloud and the meeting of a vapour, by the fall of a chariot and the stumbling of a stone, by a full meal and an empty stomach, by watching at the wine or by watching at prayers, by the sun or the moon, by a heat or a cold, by sleepless nights or sleeping days, by water frozen into the hardness and sharpness of a dagger or water thawed into the floods of a river, by a hair or a raisin, by violent motion or sitting still, by severity or dissolution, by God's mercy or God's anger, by everything in providence and everything in manners, by everything in nature and everything in chance.

—JEREMY TAYLOR, *The Rule and Exercises of Holy Dying,* 1651

2

If we compare the grasshopper with the crayfish, we find several

likenesses. In each animal the body is segmented and divided into three regions. The appendages are jointed. The nervous system consists of a chain of ganglia resting on the ventral surface. The heart is located on the dorsal surface. The digestive tract extends from the anterior end to the posterior end, and is nearly a straight tube. The body is covered with a hard exo-skeleton which must be shed at frequent intervals. It is thus evident that the two animals are built upon the same plan. Because of this similarity of structure, scientists believe that at some time in the remote past the crayfish and the grasshopper had a common ancestor; that is, they are descended from the same stock.
—CHARLES JOHN PIEPER, WILBUR L. BEAUCHAMP, and ORLIN D. FRANK,
Everyday Problems in Biology, 1932

3

We should think a carpenter very foolish who cut all his lumber with a jackknife because he thought it too much trouble to learn to use a saw. Students in their school life are workmen, and their most important tools are *words.* Each subject taken up, like different kinds of carpenter work, requires the use of a certain number of new tools (words). These must be learned before the student can do his work efficiently.
—TRUMAN JESSE MOON and PAUL BLAKESLEE MANN,
Biology for Beginners, 1921

4

The Peace of Westphalia is, from the variety of matter which it treated, one of the most important documents of modern times. First, it determined with what territorial concessions in Germany, France and Sweden were to be persuaded to retire from the war; second, it laid a new basis for the peace between Protestants and Catholics, and third, it authorized important political and territorial readjustments within Germany.
—FERDINAND SCHEVILL, *A History of Europe,* 1938

5

Chlorine, bromine, iodine, and fluorine exhibit such close resemblances as elements and in their compounds that they are grouped as a family of "halogens." Of all the elements they are the least like the metals. The name "halogen" means "salt-former," given because they all react with metals to form salts, such as sodium chloride.
—HARRY N. HOLMES, *Introductory College Chemistry,* 1939

6

The word *planet* is derived from a Greek word meaning wanderer. The word as now applied means an opaque body that shines by reflected sunlight and that moves around the sun in a nearly circular orbit.

—JOHN CHARLES DUNCAN, *Astronomy*, 1935

7

It is a commonplace of history that war between Charles V and Francis I was inevitable, and certainly there were enough causes for friction to make peace between them impossible in that age when the personal or family interests of rulers were considered sufficient reason for war. In the first place, France was surrounded by the Hapsburg territory, and its king felt it necessary to break the Hapsburg power in self-defense. Then, too, Charles and Francis had conflicting dynastic claims to territory in half a dozen places. . . . And as if these various grounds for conflict were not enough, the two young rulers had been rival candidates in the imperial election, which created a strong personal animosity between them.

—WALLACE K. FERGUSON and GEOFFREY BRUUN,
A Survey of European Civilization, 1947

8

The rotation of the earth is demonstrated by simple experiments. If a body is dropped from a high tower, it does not fall to a point immediately beneath that from which it fell. Instead, it always falls a little to the east of the point from which it started. This is explained as follows: If the earth rotates, any point must move faster than any other point which is nearer its center, for the same reason that a point on the rim of a wheel moves faster than a point between the rim and the hub. If the earth is rotating, the top of the tower must be moving forward faster than the bottom. In this case, the falling body, starting from the top of the tower, has a forward velocity greater than that possessed by the base of the tower. Under these circumstances, the falling body must gain on the base of the tower in the direction of rotation; that is, if the earth rotates to the east, the falling body will be farther to the east, relative to the base of the tower when it reaches the ground than when it started; it seems to fall away from the tower to the east. Since such a body always falls to the east, and since nothing but the rotation of the earth to the east seems to explain this fact, it is taken as proof that the earth rotates in that direction.

—ROLLIN D. SALISBURY, *Physiography*, 1907; 1931

EXERCISE VIII

After you have read each of the following statements, first, indicate whether it is open to objection by using the tests given in Exercise VI of this chapter. Second, suggest a method or methods which would best develop its meaning. The methods to be named here are illustration, analogy, comparison or contrast, analysis, classification, definition, causal analysis, and proof.

1. Most sorts of diversion in men, children, and animals are an imitation of fighting.
2. Science has to do with things, literature with thoughts; science is universal, literature is personal; science uses words merely as symbols, but literature uses language in its full compass.
3. True virtue lies between opposite vices.
4. Man is easily governed.
5. Skepticism has entered too deeply into our souls ever to be replaced by faith, and we can never forget the things which the new barbarians will never need to know.
6. There is a world of difference between industry conceived as a social process and trade conceived as a private end.
7. The service of philosophy, of speculative culture, towards the human spirit is to rouse, to startle it to a life of constant and eager observation.
8. People are willing to help the man who can't help himself, but as soon as a man is able to help himself, they make his life as uncomfortable as possible.
9. Hunger, vanity, love, and fear are the great motives of human action.
10. Popular education is a system of selecting outstanding men.
11. What hurts business hurts the public.
12. Suggestibility is the natural faculty of the brain to admit any ideas whatsoever, without motive, to assimilate them, and eventually to transform them rapidly into movements, sensations, and inhibitions.
13. Men justify their beliefs intuitively, not rationally.
14. Knowledge which brings applause is acquired before knowledge which conduces to personal well-being.
15. One studying a work of literature must discover four of its elements.
16. Critics of the skyscraper hold divergent views of its value.
17. The many activities in the life of man fall into five groups.
18. The larger natures among men are distinguished by the great breadth of their power of laughter.
19. From 1820 to 1860 the Greek style in architecture appeared in America.
20. As a discipline, the study of science is superior to the study of language.

CHAPTER 2

Illustration

It is a figure called Illustration, by the whiche the forme of things is so set foorth in words, that it seemeth rather to be seene with the eies, then heard with the eares.

—JOHN MARBECK, *A Book of Notes and Commonplaces,* 1581

THE NATURE OF ILLUSTRATION

In Shakespeare's play *Timon of Athens,* after all Timon's friends have deserted him and he has gone to the woods, bandits come seeking gold. He then says to them:

I'll example you with thievery:
The sun's a thief, and with his great attraction
Robs the vast sea; the moon's an arrant thief,
And her pale fire she snatches from the sun:
The sea's a thief, whose liquid surge resolves
The moon into salt tears: the earth's a thief,
That feeds and breeds by a composture sto'n
From general excrement: each thing's a thief . . .

Timon's examples of thievery and thieves are not the ones men commonly associate with the words. More immediately recognizable are the blackmailer, the burglar, the embezzler, the shoplifter, the land pirate, the cattle thief, the hijacker, the strong-arm man. And not the sun, the moon, the sea, and the earth itself. We cannot say, however, that the latter examples are too fanciful and far-fetched. They develop Timon's purpose. He is thinking of thievery in no ordinary sense. He is reflecting on the nature of the world, and the presence of thieves gives him an occasion to express his bitter and cynical views: "All that you meet are thieves." Thus, thievery extends in his mind from the common bandits before him to the entire world. By citing sun, moon, sea, and earth, he gives appropriate expression, figuratively and poetically, to his conviction.

In contrast, observe the purpose and the illustrations in this passage:

Over immense departments of our thought we are still, all of us, in a savage state. Similarity operates in us, but abstraction has not taken place. We know what the present case is like, we know what it reminds us of, we have an intuition of the right course to take, if it be a practical matter. But analytic thought has made no tracks, and we cannot justify ourselves to others. In ethical, psychological, and aesthetic matters, to give a clear reason for one's judgment is universally recognized as a mark of rare genius. The helplessness of uneducated people to account for their likes and dislikes is often ludicrous. Ask the first Irish girl why she likes this country better or worse than her home, and see how much she can tell you. But if you ask your most educated friend why he prefers Titian to Paul Veronese, you will hardly get more of a reply; and you will probably get absolutely none if you inquire why Beethoven reminds him of Michael Angelo, or how it comes that a bare figure with unduly flexed joints, by the latter, can so suggest the moral tragedy of life. His thought obeys a *nexus,* but cannot name it. And so it is with all those judgments of *experts,* which even though unmotivated are so valuable. Saturated with experience of a particular class of materials, an expert intuitively feels whether a newly-reported fact is probable or not, whether a proposed hypothesis is worthless or the reverse. He instinctively knows that, in a novel case, this and not that will be the promising course of action. The well-known story of the old judge advising the new one never to give reasons for his decisions, "the decisions will probably be right, the reasons will surely be wrong," illustrates this. The doctor will feel that the patient is doomed, the dentist will have a premonition that the tooth will break, though neither can articulate a reason for his foreboding. The reason lies embedded, but not yet laid bare, in all the countless previous cases dimly suggested by the actual one, all calling upon the same conclusion, which the adept thus finds himself swept on to, he knows not how or why.

—WILLIAM JAMES, *The Principles of Psychology,* 1890

James's purpose is here to make clear and concrete his observation that men can seldom give real reasons for their preferences or

ILLUSTRATION   217

actions. Thus stated, that observation (only implied in the paragraph) is general and abstract. To make it known, James begins with abstractions: immense departments of our thought. These he narrows somewhat in the phrase "ethical, psychological, and aesthetic matters." But these are subjects; what people are unable to think analytically? The uneducated in mere matters of likes and dislikes. Then a specific instance: the Irish girl's choice of country. But, you may say, the uneducated are not supposed to be able to think analytically, rationally. The educated make no better showing, as another specific instance indicates: your most educated friend who prefers Titian to Veronese. Not the educated alone, but even the expert, as in the old judge's advice to a new one or in the doctor with a sense of doom and the dentist with a premonition of a broken tooth.

All these illustrations or cases give the reader a precise, concrete sense of the meaning James wished to convey.

Illustration is here used to include both *instances* and *examples*. Instances never refer to objects, but illustrate facts or events; they point out cases. Those cases are less representative than examples, which are usually interpreted as typical of the principles or class of objects they illustrate, and which are samples belonging to a larger group. In the preceding chapter, the topic sentence, "Many tonal perceptions are fusions," was illustrated by examples: in general, perceptions of sound, smell, taste, and touch, but, specifically, the sound of chords, the smell and taste of coffee, and the sense of wetness, dryness, oiliness. In paragraph 1 on page 211, the topic sentence, "Death meets us everywhere," was illustrated by instances: by the sun or the moon, by sleepless nights or sleeping days, by water frozen or by water thawed, by a hair or a raisin.

THE CRITICISM OF ILLUSTRATIONS

Contrast these two paragraphs:

1

Most sorts of diversion for men and children are an imitation of fighting. The competitive spirit is one of the most predominant of man's instincts. From checkers to football or from bridge to boxing, the main objective is the pitting of minds or muscles against one another. Both basketball and chess are based on the competitive spirit to fight and to win. Even the plays and motion pictures of to-day entertain us, to a great extent, through the presentation of opposing forces in the narrative.

2

But the interesting pessimistic and critical note in our current litera-ture is by no means confined to representations of country life and the small town. Take Mrs. Wharton's pictures of metropolitan society, from *The House of Mirth* to *The Age of Innocence,* remembering only that Mrs. Wharton cannot be classed as a Jacksonian; then consider the dreary wide wilderness of Mr. Dreiser's picture of big business; Ben Hecht's story of a city-editor in *Erik Dorn;* Mr. Cabell's *Cream of the Jest;* Mr. Norris's broad picture of the California scene in *Brass;* Mr. Fitzgerald's account of the younger generation in *The Beautiful and Damned;* Mr. Hergesheimer's admirable new novel, *Cytherea,* and, finally, Mr. Lewis's *Babbit.*
                —STUART P. SHERMAN, *The Genius of America,* 1923

As illustrations of its topic, "The pessimistic and critical note in current literature is not limited to representations of country life and the small town," the second paragraph contains not only titles of novels but also an indication of their content. In contrast, the illustrations in the first paragraph—checkers, football, bridge, boxing, basketball, chess, plays, and motion pictures—do not give the reader a sense of particular cases or of characteristics which illustrate the topic. The writer should have given more specific details of the sports mentioned or of motion pictures. The illustra-tions given in the development of a topic should not be so gener-alized as to be vague and abstract. They should be specific and concrete. Stuart Sherman names novels which contain pessimistic or critical views.

If you are explaining a color sensation in psychology, you will give as illustrations red, green, blue, or yellow. You will not be likely to refer to heliotrope, mauve, dubonnet, magenta, or char-treuse. If you are illustrating the combining power of oxygen, you will probably mention copper, iron, mercury, sulphur, or carbon, and not selenium or tellurium. The illustrations should not be exceptional but typical. They should be familiar and immediately recognizable. The cases here are well chosen for the purpose:

In winter the noble inhabitants of the castle enjoyed a variety of indoor games, most of which have a strangely familiar modern sound.

ILLUSTRATION   219

Chess was very popular, as also checkers, backgammon, various dice games, and the simple round games now relegated to the nursery.
—WALLACE K. FERGUSON and GEOFFREY BRUUN,
A Survey of European Civilization, 1947

Examine the range of illustrations in the following paragraph:

Most sorts of diversion for men and children are an imitation of fighting. The most popular games of true fighting are settlers and Indians, cops and robbers, forts and armies, snowball fights, and slapping, tussling, and kicking.

All the illustrations given are restricted to games in which children are physically active; none is a case of diversion for men, such as fencing, boxing, and wrestling:

To illustrate the topic "The test of truth lies in its ability to withstand ridicule" with two cases, Judaism and Mormonism, is to restrict the principle to religious beliefs. Examples of the principle operative in other fields would make its general applicability more evident. To give as examples of the topic "Many men have tried to conquer the world" only Alexander, Genghis Khan, Tamerlane is to limit the time needlessly. Notice the spread of cases in this paragraph:

Devastating diseases almost invariably come in the troughs of wars, famines, political and economic collapses, and other violent upheavals in society. Historians have pointed to the correlation between the outbreak of the plague in Justinian's time and the fall of the Roman Empire. Similarly it has been suggested that the plague which over-swept Europe in the fourteenth century marked the breakup of medievalism and harrowed the ground for modern civilization. There were destructive epidemics in the early nineteenth century, following the Napoleonic wars. In the 1830's, great waves of influenza troubled Europe and America. Other influenza epidemics followed in 1847 and 1889, and then after three decades of quiescence came the vast outburst of 1918 which showed what influenza can do on a truly global scale, with not merely a continent but the whole planet the stage of its action. In the present state of international and economic affairs one cannot but wonder what pestilence we may get from another world war —or as the aftermath of a prolonged period of mass anxiety.
—GEORGE W. GRAY, "The Problem of Influenza," *Harper's Magazine,*
CLXXX (1940), 166

From the foregoing cases the four principles which control the choice of illustrations become apparent:

1. The illustrations must be relevant.
2. They must be, not generalized, but as specific and as concrete as possible.
3. They must present typical and not exceptional cases.
4. They must give the range of cases required by the topic.

ILLUSTRATION AND PROOF

The development of a paragraph by illustration and by proof must be distinguished. One type of proof, as will be shown, rests on the accumulation of a number of cases. In such instances, other principles than those given above apply. Here, the illustration or the specific case is considered as a means of making the meaning of the topic sentence immediately evident. The difference in the use of illustration as a means of *clarifying* a point and as a means of *proving* it may be observed in these two passages:

1

By a use of modern methods and equipment adapted to natural conditions, large-scale farming, under efficient management, may be profitable. The apple orchards of several hundred acres in the Shenandoah Valley are cases in point, as are the 25,000-acre rice farms in Louisiana.

2

Apple orchards of several hundred acres in the Shenandoah Valley; large citrus orchards in Florida and in California; a 25,000-acre rice farm in Louisiana; a half-million acre hay and cattle ranch in Montana; large mechanized cotton farms in Texas and Oklahoma and in certain areas in the Old South have conclusively proved the profitableness of large-scale farming under efficient management, by the use of modern methods and equipment adapted to natural conditions.

—WILLIAM G. ROYLANCE, "How Big Should the Farm Be?," *The New Republic,* CI (1939), 138

EXERCISES

Which of the following paragraphs are developed by illustration and which are not? In the light of the principles given in this chapter, evaluate those which are.

1

Men seek diversion in recreation and entertainment. Some of the most popular of these entertainments are football, with two teams

ILLUSTRATION   221

matched against each other—their aim the other's goal; and boxing, with one man trying to knock out the other. Even though there is no contact of bodies in baseball, in racing, and in card games, the aim always is to beat the other fellow. As soon as children are old enough they learn the games of cops and robbers and cowboys and indians, both imitations of fighting. Dogs run, tussle, and roll each other over and over, snapping and growling in play.

2

What hurts business hurts the public. During depressions business is compelled to cut down on labor, to restrict production, to pare expenses wherever possible. This makes necessary an increase in price level. Such an increase immediately reduces the buying power of the public, and thus creates stagnancy. Therefore, any influence or situation, such as excessive taxes, bottlenecks in production, or decrease in demand for goods, exerts a direct influence upon the public by raising price levels in order to meet production costs. Conversely, it is true that prosperity increases the buying power of the public and stimulates business.

3

Men justify their beliefs intuitively, not rationally. Principles and prejudices are often confused, and when men insist that they think, they merely feel, and the strengths of their feelings are the more powerful as they are the more irrational. Prejudices lose their strength in the processes of rational thinking; therefore, in order that their beliefs may be justified, men dispense with reasoning and become subservient to their feelings. Thus, dictators gather disciples.

4

Latin and Greek have greatly influenced the English language. By a study of an English dictionary, one will discover that over half the words are derived from one of those languages. Most of the words added to the language from time to time have come from one of them. This is especially true of the names of new inventions. Such words as *submarine, automobile, telephone, tractor, motor, turbine* are of this class. Further, the special terms used in law, medicine, chemistry, botany, physics, and other scientific studies are of Latin or Greek origin.

5

Greek words have been early adopted into the popular vocabulary, and have undergone the strange transformations that popular words undergo. Learned names for diseases and flowers are peculiarly liable to be affected by this process; thus *dropsy* stands for the Greek *hydropsis, palsy* for *paralysis, emerald* for the Greek *smaragdos; athanasia* has become *tansy,* and *karuophyllon, gillyflower* in English. This process still goes on whenever a Greek word comes into common and popular use; *pediment* is believed to be a workingman's corruption, through *perimint*, of *pyramid; banjo* has come to us through the pronunciation of negro slaves from the Spanish *bandurria*, which is ultimately derived from the Greek *pandoura;* and we are now witnessing the struggle of the Genius of the Language with the popular but somewhat indigestible word *cinematograph.*

—LOGAN PEARSALL SMITH, *The English Language,* 1912

TOPIC SENTENCES TO BE DEVELOPED BY ILLUSTRATION

1. Fire is one of the natural phenomena most beneficial to man.
2. Many diversions of men and children are imitations of fighting.
3. Latin and Greek words have greatly enriched the English language.
4. Men justify their beliefs intuitively, not rationally.
5. What hurts business hurts the public.
6. The test of truth lies in its ability to withstand ridicule.
7. Man's accomplishments are fragile and insignificant when confronted by forces of nature.

CHAPTER 3

Analogy

> Analogy . . . is a good servant, but a bad master;
> for, when master, it does more to blind than it may
> previously have done to illumine. Most of us . . .
> have chanced to observe a bee buzzing up and down
> within the four sides of a window-pane vainly en-
> deavouring to escape by the only obvious way—the
> way most light comes; whereas by merely traversing
> the dark border of the window frame it might at
> once reach the open casement.
> —JAMES WARD, *Naturalism and Agnosticism*, 1899

THE NATURE OF ANALOGY

A paragraph begins with the general observation "The blackness
of night may become strikingly evident." It then continues: "Once
when there were only clouds, no stars and no moon, the lights on
our automobile went out and we had to walk in the dark to a
farmhouse to telephone." That sentence is an illustration of the
observation expressed in the topic sentence, an instance. The
blackness of night, however, the writer may make known, with
differing purposes, in other ways. He may use a simple comparison:
"Tonight is blacker than any other I've seen." Or he may use a
figure of speech: "The night is like pitch," a simile, or "Night is an
endless cavern," a metaphor. The phrase "pitch-black night" adds
to the first two concepts—night and cavern, night and pitch—a
third, black, a characteristic of both.

Still more intricate is this statement:

223

Hope, like the gleaming taper's light,
Adorns and cheers our way;
And still, as darker grows the night,
Emits a brighter ray.
—OLIVER GOLDSMITH, *The Captivity: An Oratorio,* 1820

Four basic concepts are implicit in these lines: the strength of hope, the uncertainty of the future, the growing darkness of night, the gleaming taper. But what relationship ties them together? The meaning of the passage may be expressed thus: "Hope is to the uncertain prospects of the future which engenders it as a gleaming taper is to the darkening night." Or: "The greater the darkness, the brighter the taper; the more uncertain the future, the stronger the hope." The two pairs of concepts—darkness and taper, hope and future—are joined on the basis of one similarity: the increase of the power of the taper and of hope in the presence respectively of darkness and concern with the future. Goldsmith might have said, "Our hopes increase with our uncertainties." That abstract statement lacks the vividness of imagery which the resemblance or *analogy* supplies.

An *analogy* does not, as does an illustration, give a particular case or instance of a general group or of a principle named by the topic sentence. It expresses relationships between separate objects not commonly thought of together. It does not identify them, as does a metaphor, but suggests or states likenesses in the relationship existing between four paired concepts. A simile expresses a likeness between two dissimilar objects; an analogy expresses a likeness in a relationship operative in two distinct instances. Upon analysis, the analogy may be read, as illustrated in the preceding paragraph: the first concept is to the second as the third to the fourth.

The contention that since children ought not to rebel against parents, colonies ought not to rebel against the mother country, schematized becomes: "Colonies are to the mother country as children to parents." That is, both pairs of concepts imply obedience and are thus related, one to the other. Here the analogy is given the force of proof. Its most useful function, however, is, as is that of illustration, to clarify meaning, to make vivid the abstract. Observe that function in this case:

History is like a tree, with roots of past and myriad branches of present and more growth or decay to come, flowers and fruit and tree-diseases—no flowers, perhaps, or flowers without fruit. No, not one tree but many, one overhanging the other, an awful thicket of them rooted in rotted centuries, a muddled jungle in which at times not one of us likes to move alone, a sacred wood where, even before entering, the best of us mystically or superstitiously bows down.
                    —GLENWAY WESCOTT, *Fear and Trembling,* 1932

That is, "History is to the reader as a thicket in a muddled jungle or a sacred wood is to the traveler. Both are bewildering tangles of the fruitful and the fruitless, of growth and of decay."

The following statement, however, is a comparison, not an analogy: "As Henry II is remembered for the growth of the common law, so his descendant Edward I is remembered for the growth of Parliament." The paired persons and concepts are closely related, but the first does not illumine the second.

THE CRITICISM OF ANALOGIES

To clarify and illumine the proposition it develops, an analogy must bring together two distinct pairs of concepts which are observed to have at least one point in common. What pairs and what common point appear in this paragraph?

A man with a definite goal in mind finds himself tied as if by bonds to the work he has attempted. To become proficient, he must undergo strenuous labor that he may either like or dislike. The thing that prods him on is the desire for perfection; often he feels he might break under the strain. Such a man is not truly freer than the slave who, in order to live, must labor under the insistent drive of an overseer.

The two pairs here—ambitious man, definite goal, slave, overseer—and the common point—the restraining power the goal and the overseer have over both the ambitious man and the slave—are not sufficiently distinct for the second to lend concreteness and clarity to the first. The statement is a comparison of two members of the same class of beings, man.

Notice, in contrast, that in the previous paragraph by Glenway Wescott, history does not belong to the same class as tree and that, as in the initial quotation in this chapter, the bee buzzing on the window pane does not belong to the same class as man blinded and mastered by analogy. As in these two cases, distinctly different sets of concepts are necessary for an analogy.

Observe how the second pair in this analogy brings sharply into focus the vague enormousness of the first:

The earth is entirely surrounded by a layer of nitrogen and oxygen which we call the atmosphere or the "air." This layer is supposed to be about three hundred miles thick and it turns around together with the earth just as the skin of an orange turns around with the inside of the orange which it protects.

                          —HENDRICK VAN LOON, *Geography,* 1932

The point the two pairs of the analogy have in common must be clear, familiar, and relevant. In which of these three passages is it?

1

The modern automobile is like a cocker spaniel whose legs force it to scamper and scurry, but an airplane is like a great Dane, a picture of liquid motion skimming over the earth.

    automobile: airplane : : cocker spaniel: great Dane?

2

Most of us regard apple pie as an enjoyable dish. The piece of cheese eaten with it, however, makes it a most satisfying dessert. Likewise, life may be a happy experience if one is able to receive a college education. With the training received in college, one may enjoy life more fully because of his understanding and appreciation of art and literature.

    cheese: apple pie : : college education: life?

    cheese: apple pie : : art and literature: college education?

3

The public is easily convinced by propagandistic schemes that the opinions and beliefs of others are true. Its mind is willing to receive ideas already formulated rather than to examine them. Most families purchase their clothing already made as one of the necessities of living. It is a time-saver and is less expensive to buy than to weave and make the clothes. Opinions are to the public as clothing is to the family.

The analogy, by its concreteness and vividness and by its revelation of a relationship not commonly observed, should throw light on the subject it develops.

Contrast the clarity of the relationships pointed out in the three passages that follow:

1

If a hen sets on her eggs, she will have a perfect hatch. If everyone were to consider this simple occurrence, many dispositions would take a turn for the better. Nothing is more harmful for a cheerful disposition than a constant meditation about one's misfortunes. Such meditation will result in much more unhappiness than one wanted. The hen thus teaches a lesson: if you brood over your troubles, you'll have a perfect hatch.

2

Many were the wit-combats betwixt him [Shakespeare] and Ben Jonson; which two I behold like a Spanish great galleon and an English man-of-war; master Jonson (like the former) was built far higher in learning; solid, but slow in his performances. Shakespeare, with the English man-of-war, lesser in bulk, but lighter in sailing, could turn with all tides, tack about, and take advantage of all winds, by the wuickness of his wit and invention.

—THOMAS FULLER, *Worthies of England,* 1662

3

A man who is learning French, or chess-playing or engineering has his hands full with his particular occupation. He would be confused and hampered by constant inquiry into its effect upon character. He would resemble the centipede who by trying to think of the movement of each leg in relation to all the others was rendered unable to travel.

—JOHN DEWEY, *Human Nature and Conduct,* 1928

The effectiveness of an analogy is heightened by its freshness and originality. Triteness, consequently, should be avoided. Here is an analogy which has lost its value from overuse:

The nature of the environment during childhood determines the character of the adult. As the twig is bent, so is the tree inclined.

To clarify the significance of the subject, then, an analogy should meet these requirements:

1. Its two pairs of concepts must be distinct, must belong to a different genus or class of things, and must have at least one point in common.
2. The common characteristic must be clear, familiar, and relevant.
3. The analogy should throw light on the subject.
4. It should not be trite.

ANALOGY AND PROOF

To infer that since the groups in an analogy have one characteristic in common, they therefore have others is to misuse the analogy. By force of analogy, children learning the language may say *gooder* and *badder* rather than *better* and *worse,* just as they rightly say *higher* and *lower.* An analogy is not a proof. Things alike in one respect are not necessarily alike in any other. The value of analogy derives from its power to suggest and clarify, not to prove.

EXERCISE I

State the four basic concepts in each of the following analogies and the point which joins each group. Then evaluate the analogy.

1

The constitution is to the country as a rulebook is to a football game. Without the rulebook a football game would become a hopeless jumble of confusion and disagreement as would the country without its constitution.

2

A carburetor is to an automobile motor as a chain is to a bicycle. The carburetor is one of the most essential parts of an engine. Without it, there would be no way to mix the air and gasoline before sending it into the cylinders. Thus without a mixture, the spark would not explode the gasoline. It would be impossible to operate a bicycle without the gears. The essential in the gearing of the bicycle is the chain, which connects the pedal sprocket with the rear wheel sprocket, thereby completing the gearing system. Without the chain there would be no gears.

3

Modern education puts students through school in the same manner as mass production builds automobiles on an assembly line. In modern education, knowledge is pursued by a large group; this group cannot be held back by slowness. Mass production works in the same manner; it cannot be held up by slowness anywhere along its production line.

Both, due to their efficiency and the amount of work they handle at one time, make it possible to render their services at a low cost per item.

4

A student confronted with a difficult trigonometric proof is like a sailor caught in a storm. At first the sailor flounders a bit, but then, using the skill afforded by past experience, he takes stock of the situation and starts slowly tacking forward in the direction his intuition tells him is toward home. His course may be slightly wrong and take him out of the way, but the general direction is correct. Finally, seeing a familiar landmark, he comes about and sails into the harbor to drop anchor. Likewise, the student, not positive he is right, but with a hunch as to the correct procedure, uses his knowledge of the laws of sines and cosines until suddenly he finds an equation that looks familiar, and with ease puts down the rest of the figures until, with a victorious smile, he writes Q.E.D.

5

The mind is a lamp which, when filled with the oil of knowledge and lit with labor's flame, burns and sheds forth its light upon the dark corners and gloomy recesses in the room of thought. When the fuel becomes exhausted, the lamp flickers and goes out, leaving the room blanketed in the thick darkness of ignorance. Even when the smoke outlet is closed, the lamp chimney clouds up, dimming the rays of light. The wick will, in time, cease to burn, although there is an abundance of fuel. Thus it is that the mind grows stagnant and useless if its knowledge can be put to no good use. In the minds of the great thinkers there is a constant fuel supply to a neatly trimmed wick which burns with a low, steady flame in a clean, polished chimney.

6

When you come to a good book, you must ask yourself, "Am I inclined to work as an Australian miner would? Are my pickaxes and shovels in good order, and am I in good trim myself, by sleeves well up to the elbow, and my breath good, and my temper?" And, keeping the figure a little longer, even at cost of tiresomeness, for it is a thoroughly useful one, the metal you are in search of being the author's mind or meaning, his words are as the rock which you have to crush and smelt in order to get at it. And your pickaxes are your own care, wit, and learning; your smelting furnace is your own thoughtful soul. Do not hope to get at any good author's meaning without those tools and that fire; often you will need sharpest, finest chiselling, and patientiest fusing, before you can gather one grain of metal.

—JOHN RUSKIN, *Sesame and Lilies,* 1865

EXERCISE II

Reduce to its simplest form and judge the validity of the following analogy:

In order of time, decoration precedes dress. Among people who submit to great physical suffering that they may have themselves handsomely tattooed, extremes of temperature are borne with but little attempt at mitigation. An Orinoco Indian, quite regardless of bodily comfort, will yet labor for a fortnight to buy pigment to make himself admired. An Orinoco woman who would not hesitate to leave her hut without clothing would not dare to commit such a breach of decorum as to go unpainted. Wild tribes, voyagers uniformly find, prize colored beads and trinkets much more than calicoes and broadcloths. When they are given shirts and coats, they turn them to some ludicrous display. With them, the idea of ornament predominates over that of use. A traveller tells of having seen in Africa natives who strutted about in their goat-skin mantles when the weather was fine, but when it was wet, took them off, folded them up, and went about naked, shivering in the rain! Indeed, the facts of aboriginal life seem to indicate that dress is developed out of decorations. And when we remember that even among ourselves many think more about the fineness of the fabric than its warmth, and more about the cut than the convenience—when we see that the function is still in great measure subordinated to the appearance—we have further reason for inferring such an origin.

It is not a little curious that the like relations hold with the mind. Among mental as among bodily acquisitions, the ornamental comes before the useful. Not only in times past, but almost as much in our own era, that knowledge which conduces to personal well-being has been postponed to that which brings applause. In Greek schools, music, poetry, and rhetoric, which had but little bearing upon action, were the dominant subjects; knowledge aiding the arts of life had a subordinate place. In our own universities and schools at the present moment the like antithesis holds. We are guilty of something like a platitude when we say that throughout his life a boy, in nine cases out of ten, applies Latin and Greek to no practical purposes. The remark is trite that in his shop, or his office, in managing his estate or his family, he is very little aided by the knowledge he took so many years to acquire. If he occasionally quotes Latin or alludes to some Greek myth, it is less to throw light on the topic in hand than for the sake of effect. If we inquire what is the real motive for giving boys a classical education, we find it to be simply conformity to public opinion. Men dress their children's minds as they do their bodies, in the prevailing fashion. As the Orinoco Indian puts on his paint before leaving his hut, not with a view to any direct benefit, but because he would be ashamed to be seen without it; so, a boy's drilling Latin and Greek is insisted on, not because of their intrinsic value, but that he may not be disgraced by being found ignorant of them—that he may have the education of a gentleman, the badge marking a certain social position, and bringing a consequent respect.

—HERBERT SPENCER, *Education*, 1861

TOPIC SENTENCES TO BE DEVELOPED BY ANALOGY

1. The public adapts opinions as it buys clothing.
2. Emotion rather than reason often determines men's actions.
3. A constant reader is like a bee.
4. Impulses in human beings are like rivers.

CHAPTER 4

Analysis

> Analysis of a thing means separate attention to each
> of its parts.
> —William James *The Principles of Psychology,* 1890

THE MEANING OF ANALYSIS

John Ruskin represented reading as a metallurgical process, a digging and reducing of ores, but William Ellery Channing here affirms it to be more:

Truly good books are more than mines to those who can understand them. They are breathings of the great souls of past times. Genius is not embalmed in them, as is sometimes said, but lives in them perpetually.

What characteristics of books justify the belief that they contain the "breathings," the stimulating opinions and ideas, of the past? What benefits may readers derive from books? To answer that question, Channing then directs his reader's attention to distinct uses of books; he *analyzes* the values of reading. He continues:

The great use of books is to rouse us to thought; to turn us to questions which great men have been working on for ages; to furnish us with materials for the exercise of judgment, imagination, and moral feeling; to breathe into us a moral life from higher spirits than our own; and this benefit of books may be enjoyed by those who have not much time for retired study.
—WILLIAM ELLERY CHANNING, "On the Elevation of the Laboring Classes," 1840

Briefly stated, his analysis reveals three values of books: first, they

233

make men think about first and last questions; second, they supply materials for the exercise of men's capacities; and, third, they awaken within men a sense of purpose in living.

There is no illustration here of the subject, the value of books; and a dissimilarity to mining together with a similarity to breathing which might have been stated analogously are both expressed metaphorically. The subject is expanded by dividing it into some of its parts.

That division, however, does not exhaust the possibilities of analysis. Consider these divisions of the same subject, the value of books: first, the rarity of a book on a significant subject may make it a collector's item; second, the paper, the type used in printing it, and the binding may increase its value; and third, so may the date on which it was printed.

An analysis, it becomes evident, is a division of a unit of meaning into its parts on the basis of a controlling purpose. What factors make books valuable? That question cannot be answered until a definite purpose gives meaning to both *books* and *value*. *Books* as objects, printed and bound, or books as the recorded ideas of their writers? *Value* in terms of money or in terms of the effects on readers?

A chemist may say, "This gunpowder contains 75 per cent potassium nitrate, 14 per cent carbon, and 11 per cent sulphur"; but a manufacturer of explosives, with a different interest and purpose, may say, "This powder contains enough nitrogen and carbon dioxide to drive a shell through a wall." No matter whether object, event, or thought be analyzed or divided into its component parts, the purpose of the person making the analysis governs it. It determines both the range of the details included and the principle linking the divisions. In his analysis of gunpowder, the chemist includes all constituents because his purpose is to enumerate the nature and the proportions of the ingredients. The manufacturer, however, is thinking more directly of the driving power of the explosion and hence limits his analysis to the gases which will, when liberated, supply it.

THE CRITICISM OF ANALYSES

The problem of analyzing the types of human beings is too general to be undertaken without qualifications. One person may say, "There are two types of men: those who always tell the truth and those who tell lies." Another may say, "There are five types of men: brown, white, black, yellow, and red." These divisions are based on distinctly different *principles,* the first, honesty, the second, color. Analysis of the types of men as "Caucasian, doctors, children, Mongolian, and Ethiopian" is obviously inconsistent in that it shifts from one principle to another: from physical traits, to profession, to age, and back to physical traits. The purpose of the analysis will suggest the principle which will link the divisions together. Ethnologists have found the form of the hair, the color of the skin, and the shape of the skull to be useful and significant principles in dividing men into racial groups. For other purposes, they could be divided on such bases as professions (doctors, lawyers, merchants, thieves); ages (consult tables of payments for life insurance policies); interests (those who do and do not play golf, bridge, and tennis, as the hostess who plans a house party will know); or rank (captain, lieutenant, or private; freshman or sophomore). No matter the purpose, the analysis must be centered in a single principle of division.

Sports might be divided into those played on land or in water, indoors or outdoors, by children or by adults, in winter or summer; thus, place, age, and season might be principles of division. In this paragraph, it is none of these:

The first of two types of competitive sports consists of those in which actual physical contact is predominant. Representative of this group are football, soccer, lacrosse, boxing, wrestling, and fencing. In the second, contact of bodies is infrequent, if present at all. Representative of it are track, swimming, tennis, and golf.

What principles are the basis of the division in the following paragraph?

Astonomers speak of four principal types of stars. The first group is composed of white or bluish-white suns, like Sirius, Vega, and Rigel, which have surface temperatures ranging from 20,000 to 30,000 degrees Fahrenheit and radiate light from hydrogen and helium. To the second group belong about half the stars, including our sun; they are yellow. The two remaining groups contain stars, among them Betelgeuse, of increasing redness and coldness.

If one principle is not followed consistently through the analysis, the divisions will overlap and become meaningless. Thus, if one says, by employing the principles of race and profession, that there are two types of men: Caucasians and doctors, it is obvious that some Caucasians are doctors and that some doctors are Caucasians, and that, the divisions, consequently, overlap and are false.

Examine this paragraph:

Wind instruments consist of two groups. The first includes the oboe, the bassoon, the English horn, and the saxophone. They are all made of wood and their tones are produced by a reed. The second group is composed of instruments made of brass. Their tones are produced by the vibration of the player's lips against a mouthpiece. To this group belong trumpets, cornets, tubas, French horns, and trombones.

In this paragraph, no overlapping of divisions occurs.

If a writer proposes to analyze mankind on the basis of physical traits, he must consider and find a place for all groups of men. His analysis will not be complete if he names only Caucasian and Mongolian. When added together the divisions must make up the entire unit named by the subject. Consider this paragraph:

In this age of flying, as people see thousands of airplanes shuttling across the sky, few realize how many types of aircraft exist. Basically, there are two. The first group, gliders, employs the lifting power of wings to keep them afloat. The second, planes with engines, combines the power of wings with that of the propeller. This group is far more common than the first.

Here the purpose is to analyze the existing types of aircraft, but that purpose is not achieved, for gliders and airplanes do not exhaust the types. The divisions added together do not equal the unit named in the topic sentence.

Contrast this paragraph:

In this age of flying, as people see thousands of airplanes shuttling across the sky, few realize that basically only two types of aircraft exist. The first group is made of craft lighter than air and employs the lifting power of gas to overcome the force of gravity. The most common of this group are free and captive balloons and dirigibles. The second type, heavier than air, employs the lifting power of wings alone or combined with that of the propeller or jet propulsion.

The analysis must be as exhaustive as the topic sentence indicates. If it clearly shows that the purpose of the writer is there to consider only *some* divisions, the analysis may be restricted to *some*. If not, *all* parts must appear.

Asked to analyze the columns of political comment which appear in newspapers today in order to reveal their substance, one could not use to advantage the family names of the writers as a principle of division. To say that there are three groups of columns —first, those written by all writers from Aaron through Folkner; second, Fulton through Opdyke; third, Padget through Walton— is merely to draw up an alphabetical list which might be useful in a directory, but which does not reveal the nature of the contents of the columns. To say, however, that there are three types of columns, those which reflect conservative, liberal, and radical views, is to be more informative. The principle of division, and hence, the divisions themselves, must throw light on the nature of the subject.

Contrast these two analyses:

1

Matter may be divided into two groups: materials strongly resistant to pressure and materials not resistant. Stones, metals, woods, and ice are examples of the first; water, air, cloth, and vapor illustrate the second.

2

At standard conditions of temperature and pressure, all matter may be placed under three main headings, according to the motion of the molecules: gases, liquids, and solids. The molecules of solids, such as iron, zinc, and sulphur, maintain their mean positions with respect to one another. Those of liquids, such as mercury and bromine, have free movement among themselves. The atoms of gases, however, tend to scatter and their bulk to expand, as in oxygen, hydrogen, and chlorine.

The four standards by which one may judge an analysis are these:

1. The analysis must be based on a single principle.

2. The divisions must not overlap.
3. Considered together, the divisions must correspond to the unit named in the topic sentence.
4. The divisions must throw light on the nature of the subject.

EXERCISES

In the light of the four criteria, or standards of judgment, just named, evaluate each of the following analyses.

1

The chief things that Justinian seems to have aimed to bring about were as follows: (1) to make the power of the emperor absolute; (2) to end the schism with the papacy; (3) to reconquer the lost possessions of the Empire in the West and restore the ancient Roman Empire "to the limits of the two oceans"; (4) to insure the existing Empire from attack by skillful diplomacy with the barbarians, by constructing and repairing numerous fortifications in the Balkan peninsula and throughout the East, and by avoiding war with Persia and the barbarians as far as possible; (5) to reform the imperial administration and secure good government; (6) to finish the work which Theodosius II had barely begun in his Code of 438, and to preserve the Roman law in a permanent and consistent form; (7) to be a great builder like the emperors of old.
—LYNN THORNDIKE, *The History of Medieval Europe,* 1917

2

A piece of music must pass through several important processes before the thought of the composer reaches our minds. In the first place he must develop and arrange his ideas, select the proper vehicle to display the tones which he has imagined, and record the result in musical notation. . . . The first stage it has undergone is composition. Inspiration, knowledge of musical form, instrumentation and notation have all contributed to the result. Now the music must be performed by someone with skill on the proper instrument and the ability to read musical notation. His performance must be accurate in execution of the notes and in interpretation of the spirit of the work. If it is not, we shall not be in entire communication with the thought of the composer.
—DOUGLAS MOORE, *Listening to Music,* 1932

3

The activities of the individual plant are two-fold: vegetative activities and reproductive activities. The vegetative activities are those which have to do with the growth and preservation of the individual. Important vegetative activities are the (1.) absorption of raw materials from soil and air, (2.) transfer of the raw materials in the plant, (3.) food manufacture, (4.) assimilation, (5.) respiration, and (6.) transpiration. Reproductive activities are those which have to do with the continuation of the species of plants to which the individual belongs. These actions include the production of many new individuals of the species which will survive the parent plants and thus tend not only to insure the survival of the species but also to increase its numbers and spread the species over wider areas of the earth's surfaces.
—RICHARD M. HOLMAN and WILFRED W. ROBBINS, *A Textbook of General Botany*, 1939

4

Of all the imaginative works of man, the most appealing, it seems to me, is great painting. Nothing in the other arts offers itself so directly to the mind, or opens up, in such small compass, so many avenues of interest. For painting reveals itself as a whole, not as a succession of parts; it stands before us in all its glory, apprehensible and undisguised, a complete statement of the infinite surmises and adventures of the human spirit. It weds the past to the present and conceives the future; it deals with experiences as old as time, and always, when it is living and useful, in the terms of some special civilization: always casting its materials in the predominant pattern of the period, but tracing into that pattern the individual variations of genius which make the behavior of the race endlessly dramatic and fascinating throughout the ages.
—THOMAS CRAVEN, *A Treasury of Art Masterpieces*, 1939

5

Each of four kinds of newspapers is printed for a distinct group of people. The journal which has the largest circulation usually serves the upper part of the middle class. It is alert and progressive. Its articles breathe political death to bosses and other offenders of the public. Its features are varied. The lowly question box may give all sorts information and its serialized stories may be worth reading. Its first page contains about one column of foreign and national news and seven of local.

The second group of newspapers is read mostly by the lower middle class. The outside pages are often green, yellow, pink, or orange. Many times they are printed in two colors. Pictures and accompanying articles about murders, divorces, accidents, and feminine beauty abound. No foreign news is printed. The paper is entirely local in interest.

The highest type of publication is for a small group of people who demand the truth about all interesting news, no matter its origin. Its editorial page is a balanced unit of opinion, thought, and suggestion. It contains no screaming headlines. All of its stories are well-written and accurate; none of them is sensational. It reflects a conscious effort to present a dignified, reliable record of events.

The tabloids are friends to morons. Everything about them bespeaks stunted mentality. Pictures explain what people will not read. And the pictures are about anything that the owners believe will make the paper sell.

TOPICS TO BE DEVELOPED BY ANALYSIS

1. Musicians, Athletes, or Teachers I Have Known
2. College Dining Halls
3. American Newspapers
4. Metals
5. Popular Music
6. Growth in the Animal Kingdom

CHAPTER 5

Comparison and Contrast

> Happiness . . . is a fancy—as big, as little, as you
> please; just a thing of contrasts and comparisons.
> —George du Maurier, *Peter Ibbetson*, 1891

THE NATURE OF COMPARISON AND CONTRAST

An analysis reveals the divisions of the subject, no matter whether it is object, event, or thought. It separates it into its parts and is concerned with it alone. A comparison or contrast, however, includes two objects, events, or thoughts which belong to the same class, not, as in the case of analogy, to distinctly different classes. A comparison makes known either similarities or both similarities and dissimilarities of the things compared; a contrast shows differences only. Either a comparison or a contrast may be helpful in clarifying for the reader the meaning of the writer.

How do young men and young women differ in their thinking? Differences in height and weight, in the clothes they wear, and the magazines they read are obvious. Less so their modes of thought. Here is a contrast:

A young woman of twenty reacts with intuitive promptitude and security in all the usual circumstances in which she may be placed. Her likes and dislikes are formed; her opinions, to a great extent, the same that they will be through life. Her character is, in fact, finished in its essentials. How inferior to her is a boy of twenty in all these respects! His character is still gelatinous, uncertain what shape to assume, 'trying it on' in every direction. Feeling his power, yet ignorant of the manner in which he shall express it, he is, when compared with his sister, a being of no definite contour. But this absence of prompt tendency in his brain to set into particular modes is the very condition which in-sures that it shall ultimately become so much more efficient than the woman's. The very lack of preappointed trains of thought is the ground on which general principles and heads of classification grow up; and the masculine brain deals with new and complex matter indi-rectly by means of these, in a manner which the feminine method of direct intuition, admirably and rapidly as it performs within its limits, can vainly hope to cope with.

    —WILLIAM JAMES, *The Principles of Psychology*, 1890

The woman's intuitive promptitude of reaction, her formed likes and dislikes, and her fixed opinions James here takes as evi-dences of her preappointed trains of thought. Because of them, her character has become well defined; that of the young man, howev-er, to James, is gelatinous. He lacks preappointed trains of thought. That lack, however, is here said to provide ground for the develop-ment of principles and classifications which enable him to cope with new and complex matter, matter with which the direct intui-tion of the young woman cannot cope.

This paragraph is not an analysis, for it does not divide the thought of either the young man or the young woman into its several aspects. It is not a comparison, for it shows no similarities in the way each reaches conclusions. Restricted to two basic differences—forming opinions and solving new problems—it is a contrast.

Some may say, "It is not true!" Whether it is or not can be shown only by observing the behavior of the subjects it character-izes, not in two cases, but in enough to merit such a generalization, enough to begin to consider proof. Although it does not prove a point, contrast or comparison, however, as a method of making one's ideas known, may be tested in more immediate ways.

THE CRITICISM OF COMPARISONS AND CONTRASTS

The subjects of both comparison and contrast must be not momentary insights, but likenesses and differences worthy of sustained consideration. The reader might find significant charac-teristics of both lighthouses and Dutch windmills in a comparison of the two, but not in a comparison of Dutch windmills and the theory of valence, or of electricity and a Boston terrier. Some illumination might result from such pairings in figures of speech, but a comparison is analytical and extensive, both in the number of cases it considers and in the range of its inquiry. It does not point out single likenesses intuitively. One may gain little clarification of the nature of a desk and that of a cat by comparing them; but one may disclose the natures of a cat and a dog by comparing or contrasting them.

A dog differs from a cat in having a looking-glass self. He is interested in what you are thinking of him, studies your eye, acts little plays for your approval. A cat cares for you only as a source of food, security and a place in the sun. Her high self-sufficiency is her charm. She is an egoist; the dog, sometimes, an egotist.
—CHARLES HORTON COOLEY, *Life and the Student,* 1927

Things are comparable when their likenesses and differences make them members of the same general group. They are obviously not comparable when their differences are so great as to make contrasts unrewarding. Twins upon comparison may be called identical in most respects; but upholstered chairs and telephone bells belong to distinctly different categories and are not contrasted.

Given two comparable objects, events, or thoughts, the writer must make evident the points on which they are compared. He can complete neither a comparison nor a contrast before he has analyzed each of the things compared. He must know the characteristics they have in common—in the case of young women and young men, the ability to respond mentally to experience—before he can point out similarities and dissimilarities. In the contrast of the cat and the dog the controlling principle is the relation of each to human beings. Other purposes might require that they be compared in weight, color, or usefulness. In any case, the point or the points on which they are compared must be clear.

In this paragraph, they are not:

As a discipline, the study of science is superior to the study of language. The problem of interpretation enters into the study of language whereas in science the procedure must be exact. A problem in language may be correctly solved in any of several ways, but in science there can be but one correct solution. Therefore, because of the greater leeway in language, science is superior as a disciplinary study.

Here the comparison is offered as proof, but no clear basis of comparison appears. Interpretation enters into the study of science; procedure in the study of language must be exact. The correctness of the solution of problems lacks clarity. It may be as applicable to one as to the other. Leeway in what respect? The precise points on which the study of language and of science are being compared are not evident.

Contrast this paragraph:

> In many respects respiration and burning are essentially alike. Glucose will burn freely if supplied with sufficient oxygen. The burning of glucose and its respiration in the cells of a living plant or animal have the following similarities: oxygen is necessary for both processes; the substances produced in the two processes are the same, carbon dioxide and water; and in both cases energy is liberated. Both in burning and in respiration the stored chemical energy of the glucose molecule is released. Respiration is clearly different from burning in that it does not take place outside of living protoplasts and goes on at temperatures much below that necessary for burning.
> —RICHARD M. HOLMAN and WILFRED W. ROBBINS, *A Texbook of General Botany,* 1928

The ways in which respiration and burning are essentially alike and the ways in which they clearly differ are immediately evident.

The objects, cases, or instances chosen for comparison must be typical of the group they represent. If they do not represent a fair sampling, the value of the comparison is highly questionable when its purpose is to reveal general and not exceptional likenesses and differences.

As a discipline the study of science is superior to the study of language. I remember a boy in preparatory school who never did well in English, Latin or French during his first two years. He hated to memorize vocabularies and verb forms; he could not interest himself in them. Then, in his third year, he studied physics and botany. He became greatly interested, and for the first time, really learned to study. That year he did well not only in physics and botany but also in French and English. The study of science, therefore, is superior as a discipline to the study of language.

This contrast of the two periods of the boy's work in preparatory school, granted that it is a complete and a truthful story of his case, does not justify the generalization stated at the outset and repeated in the last sentence. His case must at least be proved to be typical and not exceptional if it is to support contrast and judgment of two kinds of study.

Further, the basic point or points in the comparison or the contrast must actually be present in two or more of the things compared. The likenesses and differences must be observed, and not imagined. Consider this paragraph:

As a discipline the study of science is superior to the study of language. Science is restricted by inductive reasoning, going from particulars to generals, and involves a knowledge of definite facts and logical organization before research can produce a scientific law. The study of language involves emotions, feelings, and the imagination, and may easily include sophistry or irrational thought; it is like a chameleon that can change color to suit its environment and purpose.

Here is confusion. The restriction of logic to the study of science and of the irrational to the study of language is an imagined difference. The student of language has to guard against the irrational no less than the student of science. In fact, the serious study of language may become a science. A knowledge of linguistic processes and a knowledge of natural phenomena are both subject to logical principles.

Observe the care and the precision with which the contrast in this paragraph is made. The presence of the twinkle in stars and its absence in planets is not an infallible distinction between the two, and it is, accordingly, not represented as being such.

A planet may be distinguished from a star in three ways: First, the stars twinkle and the planets usually do not; this rule, however, is far from infallible. Second, when magnified by a telescope, the planets show disks of perceptible area, while the stars appear as glittering points. This distinction holds for all the principal planets, but fails for most of the many minor planets, or asteroids. Third, and most important, the stars maintain practically the same relative positions for years while a planet changes its position among them perceptibly from night to night or, seen in a telescope, in the course of a few hours or even minutes.

—JOHN CHARLES DUNCAN, *Astronomy*, 1935

Finally, the comparison or contrast must throw light on the nature of the subject. That it may do if the foregoing principles are followed, or it may not. For this criterion emphasizes the function of the comparison or contrast in terms of the writer's purpose. The likenesses and differences may be evident and unquestionable, and still, their precise relevance or value to the point the writer wants to make may be vague, as may the point itself. Comparison and contrast, properly used, should emphasize the writer's meaning: they are not advantageously used, when the hearer may rightly say, "I understand the likenesses and differences, but not what I am to conclude from them."

Observe the relation between the purpose and the comparative details in each of the following paragraphs:

.... In broadest outlines, however, such records as we have of the lives of Lincoln and Altgeld reveal much not only of common circumstance but of common experience. Each was born of humble parents and reared in country poverty; each bore a heavy yoke of hardship and deprivation in his youth; each was chiefly self-educated by grace of a passion for reading. Later, each had experience as a soldier and as a common laborer. Each turned to the study and practice of law, settled permanently in Illinois, went into politics, and eventually wrote his name high in the annals of his adopted state....

Now consider this comparison in its context:

"My early history," Abraham Lincoln once said, "is perfectly characterized by a single line of Gray's Elegy: 'The short and simple annals of the poor.'" John Peter Altgeld might have said the same thing with equal truth. Indeed, in his case the annals are even shorter and simpler than in Lincoln's. They are also much more obscure, despite the fact that Altgeld was born nearly forty years later and was the contemporary of many who are still living. In broadest outlines, however, such records as we have of the lives of Lincoln and Altgeld reveal much not only of common circumstance but also of common experience. Each was born of humble parents and reared in country poverty; each bore a heavy yoke of hardship and deprivation in his youth; each was chiefly self-educated by grace of a passion for reading. Later, each had experience as a soldier and as a common laborer. Each turned to the study and practice of law, settled permanently in Illinois, went into politics, and eventually wrote his name large in the annals of his adopted state. But certain inspiriting influences that shone from both within and without upon the young Lincoln never lightened Altgeld's early years. No innate harmony with environment, no confidence bred of high animal spirits and unusual physical strength, no previsions of a great destiny, no whole-hearted devotion of a noble mother or encouragement of a sympathetic father, no congenial comradeships, ever gladdened or fortified *his* youth. He was a stepchild of fortune, a lonely alien for more in spirit than by birth amid conditions that were not merely hard and unpropitious but for the most part aggressively hostile.

—WALDO R. BROWNE, *Altgeld of Illinois,* 1924

These then are the five criteria of comparison and contrast:

1. The subjects must be comparable; they must belong to the same general group of objects, events, or thoughts.
2. The point or points on which the things are being compared or contrasted must be made evident.
3. The objects, instances, or cases chosen for comparison must be typical of the group they represent.
4. The basic point or points in the comparison or contrast must be actually observed and not imagined.
5. The comparison or contrast must clarify and emphasize the writer's purpose and meaning.

THE ARRANGEMENT OF DETAILS IN COMPARISONS

The details in a comparison or contrast may be arranged in either of two ways. The writer may gather them around the points in which the things compared or contrasted are similar or dissimiliar. Thus, if one is contrasting modern and Victorian houses, he may divide his paper in this way:

The exterior design of the houses
  The walls, windows, and porches
    Of the Victorian house
    Of the modern house
  The roof
The interior design of the houses
  The handling of utilities: plumbing, heating, lighting
    Of the Victorian house
    Of the modern house
  The floor plan
    Of the Victorian house
    Of the modern house

Or, in a comparison, the writer may group their likenesses and their differences. Thus, in comparing the ordinary house of the 1880's and the 1940's, he may arrange the details in this way:

Similarities between the houses of the 1880's and the 1940's

The size of the lots on which they are built
The chief building materials (wood or brick)
The largely unchanged floor plans
Dissimilarities between the houses of the 1880's and the 1940's
Heating, plumbing, lighting

Exercise (Questions for study follow the article)

Two Decades of Depression (the 1930's and the 1870's)

1. In recent years [1930's] investors, speculators and economists have
    been busily engaged searching the records of the depression of 1921
    for a series of economic events which can be used for forecasting
    purposes. If they can find some common index which led in the
    decline and subsequent rise of the business cycle of 1921 and in the
    decline of 1929, they believe that they will be enabled to predict
    the future. Aside from the fact that such a correlation would be a
    mere coincidence of doubtful forecasting value, such attempts
    involve a serious error, for the two periods are not comparable.
    The depression following 1873, however, may legitimately be
    compared with the present one. [This article was first published in
    1931] The similarity of this post-Civil War period and its panic to
    the post-World War period and the panic of 1929 is indicated by
    the major events of the two periods.
    1. A major war. (1861–65: 1914–18)
    2. A trade depression resulting from the readjustment of industry
        to peacetime demands. (1866: 1921)
    3. A period of industrial boom characterized by expansion, inven-
        tions, optimism, speculation and talk of "new areas." (1867–73:
        1923–29)
    4. A stock-market crash believed in each period to be a technical
        reaction. (September, 1873: October, 1929)
    5. A long period of depression. (1873–77: 1929–?)
2. By tradition the Americans are a speculative people. Forced in
    their early environment to exploit a land of opportunity, they
    have come to be ever on the lookout for possibilities of accumulat-
    ing wealth quickly. Consequently their history is a chain of specu-
    lative endeavors. Hardly had the Atlantic coast been decently
    populated before the more venturesome began to speculate on the
    future of the frontier lands. As civilization moved westward,

the California gold rush, the development of the railroads, the rise of the petroleum industry, the organization of the trusts, the invention of the automobile, and in recent years the advent of the radio and the airplane—each in turn gave further vent to the national speculative mania. As each of these occupied the center of the stage, "new eras" arose to dwarf and eclipse by their newness all previous ones. It is almost impossible for a participant in our most recent boom to realize that there existed in American history other periods of productive advance comparable to the late one. Yet it is doubtful if the historian of the future will feel that the world of 1930 with its marvelous inventions is economically as far removed from that of 1920 as the nation of 1870 was from that of 1860.

3. At the beginning of the Civil War Americans used iron, had but 30,000 miles of railroads and valued their industrial equipment at a billion and a half. A decade later steel was rapidly replacing iron, railroad trackage had increased to 60,000 miles and the value of industrial equipment had doubled. Remarkable progress in the technique of production had been made all along the line. The invention of refrigeration, the settlement of the Western plains and the extension of railroad facilities made it possible for Armour and Morris to begin meat packing on a large scale. A similar shift from small to large-scale production was also taking place in the flour industry at Minneapolis. Meanwhile the petroleum wells of Pennsylvania, sunk to produce quack Indian medicines, were pumping to capacity to meet the new demands for lubrication and illumination. The old method of hauling the oil to market in wagons had been replaced by pipe lines and steel tank cars. Progress in the production of shoes was the most amazing. A single workman using the new machinery could turn out three hundred pairs of shoes in 1870 against six pairs in 1860, while an American factory could produce as many shoes as thirty thousand French shoemakers. The progress made in this decade probably surpasses that of any other.

4. The new industrial setup supplied the common people with better food, clothing and shelter at lower prices and was the basis of the orgy of spending and extravagance that followed. For the first time members of the lower classes found themselves able to indulge in some of the luxuries which previously had been reserved for the rich. Within a few years their homes were crammed full of marble-topped tables, Roger's groups, red-plush albums, whatnots, sea shells, bric-a-brac and other imitations of art and culture. Their leisure time was spent at the theatre, the race track or the professional ball games. Lawn tennis and croquet were popular fads. Now, for the first time, they found it possible to take vacations

once a year. Those who failed to consume the whole of their income invested the remainder on slender margins in Wall Street, where fabulous fortunes were being created overnight. Public participation in stock speculation was common. One of the popular periodicals operated a department for the accommodations of its subscribers, who were encouraged to exchange their government bonds for good railroad securities. There was present in this prosperity spree of 1868–73 every symptom of the "new era" fever. Old production records had been shattered, the standard of living had been raised to unprecedented levels and the public was duped into believing that poverty had been permanently replaced by ever increasing and never ending prosperity.

5. It was the custom at that time for Western banks to deposit excess reserves in New York, withdrawing them only in the autumn to finance the movement of crops. Whenever such withdrawals began, tight money conditions resulted temporarily. The stringency of money during the fall of 1872 had been more severe than usual, but it was believed that a solution for the trouble had been discovered and that the old malady would not show itself in 1873. However, when the movement of crops set in, bankers experienced trouble in liquidating their call loans. As a result, under August withdrawals, reserves melted from twelve million to less than a half million. The seriousness of the situation was not realized. The leading financial journal of the day pointed out that had the "withdrawal of deposits been for any other ground than a business revival, it might be regarded with apprehension," and Harper's Weekly wrote that "the Western wheat crop will be the largest every harvested . . . Thus far everything looks well and bright. Large crops and good trade mean general prosperity."

6. The first rumblings of the approaching storm were heard on Monday, September 8, 1873, when the New York Warehouse and Security Company closed its doors because of its inability to collect $1,-250,000 loaned at call to the M. K. and T. railroad. Even this disaster did not cause concern about the future. The Independent in commenting on the events of the week said:

Wall Street has gone through a series of excitements from causes which would have been quite sufficient to create a panic; but notwithstanding the excitement, there has been no panic for the reason that the business of the country is in so sound a condition that any ordinary commercial calamity cannot disastrously affect the general interests.

7. On September 18, the failure of Jay Cook and Company was announced and within a few hours came similar announcements from sixteen other firms. Stock quotations wilted, bank loans were called and call money soared to 1,100 percent. Friday brought runs on the New York banks and by Saturday the best stocks were

selling at half their former quotations, while many could not be sold at any price. Because of the demoralized state of affairs, the directors decided to close the stock exchange.

8. An appeal was made for government aid and President Grant met with a number of prominent bankers to discuss methods of reëstablishing order. It was decided that the government would purchase $13,500,000 worth of bonds from the banks, that the New York Clearing House would issue $10,000,000 in clearing-house certificates, that the savings banks would require thirty days' notice of withdrawals and that the stock exchange would remain closed for a time. Upon the opening of the exchange two weeks later, stock values continued to sink until late in November.

9. As soon as the excitement of the panic had subsided, discussion of the after effects began. A few newspapers suggested possibilities of a business depression, but the majority filled their columns with the usual soothing statements. "The stoppage of the mills is only a temporary disarrangement," writes one, "and as a whole the mercantile community is beyond a doubt in a better condition than for years." The panic, referred to as the "Wall Street flurry," was said to be a "mere accident." It was believed that a large amount of the money which had been diverted from mercantile borrowers to speculation would now be released to legitimate business. According to Harper's Weekly "our general commerce was never in a more prosperous condition," and four years before stock prices touched bottom The Commercial and Financial Chronicle felt that prices of good dividend-paying stocks were still too low, and it was to be doubted if the current prices would be seen again for years. In general it was believed that the situation presented no symptom of a particularly malignant character.

The present panic is near its limits. Everyone knows that the fluctuations in the stock market do not affect the commercial solid interests of the country. Prices may go up or down but the real wealth, the solid permanent productive power represented by such hundreds of millions of securities, remains pretty much the same. Since the close of the War there has never been a time when the mercantile community has been in a better condition than now. The outlook for the next season is more promising than for several years.

10. The reaction was expected to set in within a week. The prevailing idea was that when the bankers recovered, the demand for merchandise would gradually reassert itself. That the purchasing power of the unemployed might have any bearing on the recovery did not occur to them. By November they were certain they were near the outskirts of the storm, but six weeks later there was less confidence. "This panic is remarkable for the slowness of its recovery and for the languor which it has left behind it," writes one

journal. Expectations of the early revival of business returned with the new year, but three months the signs were less certain. It was now five months since the panic, yet no tendency toward improvement was discoverable. The return to normality was being delayed only because "the capitalists are timid and the people are economizing."

11. The coming of April found the "indisposition to engage in new negotiations" still present, and by May it was admitted that there was a depression. The prevailing philosophy was accordingly modified. It was now known that "brief periods of stagnation in trade, suspended industries and reduced prices have always followed upon great financial panics. They are the natural effects of the excess which precede and cause panics." In fact, "stagnation is really a natural and wholesome reaction from previous overexcitement." Being natural, there was nothing to be done about it, for "as the world grows older and wiser, men are getting to recognize more and more the marvelous wisdom of the great doctrines of the French economists *laissez-faire et laissez-passer*."

12. During the summer there were indications of a revival, but these too proved deceptive. In September The Commercial and Financial Chronicle hailed the beginning of the "real revival," and expressed surprise that shrewd business men had failed to recognize the fact that business had already turned the corner. This illustrated, so they thought, "the danger of having too much confidence in the prophets of evil."

13. A month later, however, it was admitted that this start, too, was a false one, and by November even the most optimistic of prophets had become uneasy about the future. It was hoped that the spring of 1875 would bring the return of prosperity. But such hopes, too, proved futile, for three years later crowds of workless and hungry men still tramped the streets and joined in the parades of protest. It was computed by Harper's Weekly that there were in 1877 some three millions of idle people in the country who would gladly work for fifty cents a day.

14. It is little wonder then that the discouraged laboring men seized the first opportunity for violence. The explosion came when the railroads announced a 10-percent cut in wages. Workmen at Baltimore struck, and when their places were eagerly taken by the unemployed, the strikers proceeded to stop all trains. Railroad employees at Martinsburg, West Virginia, also blockaded the system. The Governor appealed to the federal government for aid and, after considerable fighting, road service was reëstablished only to be interrupted at Newark and Columbus, Ohio. By this time Pennsylvania employees at Pittsburgh had struck. In an attempt to protect the railroad's property there, soldiers killed sixteen civilians. When the news spread through the city, twenty thousand

citizens assembled in the downtown section, five thousand of them armed. The federal soldiers took refuge in a roundhouse while the mob destroyed the depot, a hotel and a thousand tank cars, the damage amounting to well over seven million dollars.

15. Rioting then broke out all over the country: a train was burned at Baltimore; thirteen were shot at Reading; fifteen were killed at Chicago; and fighting took place at St. Louis and San Francisco. On July 24 and 25 not a train operated in the territory north of Virginia between the Mississippi River and the Atlantic Ocean. The attitude of the press toward the workers' troubles is exemplified in the following quotation:

Society does not owe any particular rate of wages to anybody. Common sense insists that if a man refusing to work for seventy-five cents a day refuses also to let others take his job, that he be refuted with gun, powder and ball.

16. In 1929 a generation of Americans celebrated the birth of another "new era." This time the radio, the talkie, the airplane, electric refrigeration, twenty-five million automobiles and over two million miles of good roads were numbered among the achievements. For a decade fads had swept the nation in fast succession, first mah jong, then crossword puzzles, flagpole sitting, miniature golf and backgammon. Homes had been luxuriously furnished with modern electrical devices and delapidated antique furniture. Speculation had been rampant. Millionaire, mechanic, banker and bookkeeper had eagerly scanned the latest editions of the newspapers to see how far their favorites had gone up. Day after day stocks had risen and more had been purchased because they rose, until three- and four-million share days came to be accepted as usual. Brokers' loans reached dizzy heights, yet the market climbed on. If activity slackened, it was stimulated to an accelerated pace by the statements of the "new era" economists that we could go on increasing productivity indefinitely "as long as the crash upon employment will have been passed during the next sixty days." But in April, when quarterly reports began to appear, the stock market slumped again and prospects for an early revival disappeared. Another start was made in the fall of 1930 and still another in the spring of 1931, but both these, like the others, proved false, so that the summer of 1931 finds mobs of discouraged men still tramping the streets in search of work. Thus far there has been no violence, but the depression may be yet young. How long it is to last no one knows. Economists and forecasters predict an early upturn but they have been prophesying this continuously for almost two years.

17. Sooner or later, however, economic conditions must improve and another industrial boom grow out of the present ruins. New inventions and new techniques will then raise the standard of living even higher than it was in 1929, and when this has come to pass,

economic prophets will arise to preach again eternal prosperity and the gospel of the "new era." Human beings do not learn from history.

—WILFORD J. EITEMAN, *The New Republic,* LXVII (1931), pp. 222–5

QUESTIONS FOR STUDY

1. Why are the periods of 1921 and 1929 not comparable?
2. Why are the depressions of 1873 and 1929 comparable?
3. List the similarities between the periods that are here named. Are any dissimilarities mentioned? Why?
4. Are the bases of the comparison implied or stated explicitly? Illustrate.
5. Cite evidences of the author's efforts to give a fair sampling of cases.
6. What reason do you have for believing that the likenesses here mentioned are not imaginary?
7. How are the details arranged: point by point; likenesses, then differences; or those of one period, then those of the other? Why? Give the main sub-divisions of each major division.
8. This article is a comparison. The author, however, uses other methods of developing the various aspects of the subject. Give illustrations of contrast, analysis, and illustration.
9. Account for the absence, comparatively, of personal opinions.
10. What conclusion does this comparison clarify and emphasize?
11. Would the author's statements about the depression of 1929 have been as clear and meaningful if he had omitted those about the depression of 1873? Why do his statements about 1929 follow those about 1873?
12. Does the author attempt to provide a series of observations which may be used for forecasting events? (See paragraphs 1 and 17.)

SUBJECTS TO BE COMPARED OR CONTRASTED

1. Two Department Stores
2. Gasoline and Diesel Engines
3. High School and College
4. The Study of Science and the Study of Language
5. Oratorio and Opera
6. Saturday and Sunday
7. The Average Man and the Genius
8. Two Decades: the 1930's and the 1960's

CHAPTER 6

Classification

> The object of all classification . . . is to bring to-gether those beings which most resemble each other and to separate those that differ.
> —William B. Carpenter, *Zoology*, 1847

The Nature of Classification

As impressions of them flow through one's consciousness, objects, persons, or ideas may have no perceptible order. They may be represented by a sequence such as this one:

alarm clock, snow, book, coat, genus *Paramecium,* lamp, camera, freedom, cloud, carpet, bracelet, bed, picture, truth, newspaper, purple, giraffe, bicycle, toothbrush, rain, dog, typewriter, compass, liberty, telephone, tie, green, desk, blanket, democracy

Such a sequence, without order or design, does not, however, represent a person's active, alert attention, which controls experience in a more systematic way. It associates and dissociates objects on the basis of resemblances and differences. It brings many objects together in groups. It may provide a sense of knowing what any one thing is merely by knowing to what class it belongs. "He is a doctor," one person says. "Oh, I see!" another replies.

Alarm clock and snow do not commonly belong to the same group, for they have no commonly recognized likenesses. Nor do book, coat, and genus *Paramecium.* An analysis of each of these things separately will disclose such marked differences in qualities or characteristics as to make a contrast unrewarding. However, if one wishes to know what varieties of details such as those in the preceding sequence may flow through man's consciousness during a few seconds, he may expediently group those which resemble one another in distinct classes. The thirty items may be classified in nine divisions:

Natural phenomena: snow, cloud, rain
Animal life: *Paramecia,* dog, giraffe
Clothing: coat, tie
Personal effects: bracelet, toothbrush
Colors: purple, green
Abstract concepts: freedom, truth, liberty, democracy
Printed matter: book, newspaper
Furnishings: lamp, carpet, picture, desk, bed, blanket
Mechanical contrivances: bicycle, alarm clock, camera, telephone, typewriter, compass

He may classify them in other ways as well: things outside the room: bicycle, rain; things inside the room: bracelet, alarm clock, bed; subjects of study: freedom, *Paramecia,* giraffe, colors. Or he may choose to divide them into abstract and concrete things.

Both the nature of an object and the reason for classifying it determine the basis of the classification. Thus, some might put the forms of animal life under three headings: the intelligent, the average, and the stupid. Upon occasion, such a classification might be of use. The zoologist, however, finds classifications, like vertebrates, arthropoda, and protozoa more suitable for his purpose.

A classification is a grouping together of objects, persons, events, or ideas on the basis of a common characteristic or of common characteristics. Those characteristics one may discover by analysis and comparison. Analyzed as separate objects, oak, pine, spruce, elm, hickory, and poplar are all found to be woody perennial plants with trunks, branches, and foliage, and they may be rightly grouped as trees. But one could make other classifications: trees, stunted or hearty; trees, living or dead. Here, obviously, the basis of the classification changes. It is no longer the meaning of tree in intension, the logical connotation of the word. It has become, respectively, the degree of firmness and strength, and the continuation or cessation of the processes of life.

Classifying the items of our experience is a convenient form of labeling them. It results from our analyzing and comparing them. The druggist generally keeps alarm clocks, cigars, cosmetics, magazines, and drugs in different sections of his store. College officials may group students on the basis of the number of years they have attended school, their grades, their sex, their major subjects, the dormitories in which they live, or the states from which they come. The purpose of the classification determines which basis is used.

Classifications make widely varied details manageable. The chemist can discuss oxides without naming each oxide; the physicist, gases or solids, without naming any or all of them. The classification focuses the attention on the distinctive characteristic or characteristics of the group in which each item is placed.

Here are names of some American painters of this century: Thomas Benton, Georgia O'Keeffe, Rockwell Kent, Glenn Coleman, George Bellows, Preston Dickinson, Edward Hopper, Niles Spencer, Charles Burchfield, Stefan Hirsch, Charles Sheeler, John Stewart Curry, John Sloan, Charles Demuth, Stuart Davis, and Peter Blume. Even though we may know some of their paintings, such a listing tells us nothing of the relationships between them, of the distinctive characteristics of the movement or movements they may represent. In contrast, how much does the following classification tell us about them?

There are two groups of painters whose inspiration is the American scene. One group is not concerned with realism as such, but with an interpretation of the American scene in highly personal idioms. These men range from the practitioners of a selective realism, amounting almost to a formal purism with some of them, to abstractionists and inventors. The pioneers of this group are Charles Sheeler and Charles Demuth. Sheeler's work is remarkably pure and selective, reducing realism to the sheer elements of design, with a spatial arrangement that is precise and harmonious. Demuth, whose best expression is in watercolor, has elegance of formal pattern, inventiveness, and a feeling for the human episode when he chooses to be concerned with it that makes his illustrations the very best things of their kind which America has produced. Georgia O'Keeffe, one of the striking personalities of American art, who simplifies forms and uses color in a very personal way and articulates the design of her pictures as clearly as the veins in a leaf, must be included with this group. So must the late Preston Dickinson, who used the pastel medium with power and virtuosity, and who had an almost Oriental sense of spatial arrangement and color relation. Others are: Niles Spencer, whose work is characterized by clarity of conception, sound execution, and relevance to the contemporary scene; Stefan Hirsch, a master of his craft, clear and precise, with a fine decorative sense and a feeling for formal harmony; Stuart Davis, a realist of the abstract who practices a very personal kind of legerdemain with rectangular contours and proportions; Peter Blume, a fine draughtsman with a feeling for contours and architectural contrasts and a telling pattern of light and dark; Henry Billings, who is close to Blume, but with more feeling for pigment; George Ault, who has a good eye for architectural arrangement and is directly related to the early American school; Elsie Driggs, Charles Goeller, Arnold Wiltz.

The other is a group of realists who preserve for us moments of our history. The leaders of this group are John Sloan, the ablest of our etchers, and Glenn O. Coleman. Their notations of contemporary life in paintings, etchings, and lithographs are among the fine contributions to American contemporary art. Related to them as men who draw inspiration directly from the American scene are Edward Hopper, a realist whose bare understatement always has a hint of satire, and Charles Burchfield, who is more avowedly satirical and literary. Burchfield has done his best work in watercolor. Others who may be classified with this group are the late George Bellows with his harsh and powerful transcripts from American life; Thomas Benton who has done pioneer work in mural painting; Guy Pene DuBois with his hardboiled simplifications of modern types; Reginald Marsh whose greatest promise seems to be in etching; Rockwell Kent, important as an illustrator; Boardman Robinson, Richard Lahey, Jerome Myers, William J. Glackens, Randall Davey, John Steuart Curry.

—HOLGER CAHILL, "American Art Today," *America as Americans See It*, 1932.

EXERCISE

Classify the following items into distinct groups. Explain the purpose and principle which controls each classification.

Apples, red, glycol, calculus, peaches, glycerine, white, beans, algebra, Keats, pears, orange, benzene, geometry, Shelley, corn, lemons, formaldehyde, trigonometry, Tennyson, oranges, blue, potatoes, dimethylamine, statistics, plums, Coleridge, carrots, purple, peas.

THE CRITICISM OF CLASSIFICATIONS

A college student may be a freshman, sophomore, junior, or senior; passing or failing; man or woman; a major in fine arts or in economics; from Virginia, New Hampshire, or Montana. All these groupings result from analyses based on different principles: year, grades, sex, major, or native state. Suppose a person classifying forty students on the basis of what they want most to do said,

"Sixteen want to play tennis; ten, to produce a play; eight, to do extra work in the laboratory; three, to read novels; and three are failing." The classification becomes immediately faulty because it does not maintain categories based on the same principle: what the student wants most to do. A new principle, academic standing, appears. Since classification rests on divisions or groups, a single principle must be followed. Any shift in principle results in a new classification, as is evident in the case of the three failing students.

Notice how accurately the author observes this requirement in the following paragraph:

> These six arts can be classified in several different ways with reference to their respective primary media. Music, the dance, and literature, for example, are "temporal" arts in the sense of unfolding themselves to the percipient in a determined temporal order and at a tempo more or less dictated by the composition itself; in them time plays a role which it does not play in architecture, sculpture, or painting. Again, music and literature are "auditory" arts, whereas the other major arts are "visual." This means that the latter are spatial in the sense of actually existing, in one way or another, in space.
> —THEODORE MEYER GREENE, *The Arts and the Art of Criticism*, 1940

If any aspect of the things being classified which the purpose makes significant is not included, the groupings are faulty; the parts do not equal the unit implicit in the subject. How complete is this classification?

The daily activities of the average college student may be arranged in two groups. In the interest of self-cultivation, he reads, writes, speaks (more or less formally), listens, thinks, memorizes, works problems—in general, he studies. Not to be forgotten, however, are the hours he spends every day keeping himself alive, healthy, and neat. He must brush his teeth, eat, bathe, sleep, comb his hair, and keep his clothes in order. Thus, he devotes his time to his body and his mind.

The fault in the following classification is immediately evident: chair, bed, stool, chest of drawers, ineptitude, and table. Ineptitude lacks the quality which joins the others in a group: furniture. In any classification, every item should possess the distinctive characteristic or characteristics of the group in which it is placed. All the items in the group, therefore, will have one or more qualities in common. Observe both the definiteness and the precaution with which such qualities are pointed out in this statement:

But what is a virus? Nobody knows. The term is difficult to define. We can say that most of the infectious diseases may be roughly classified under three headings according to the nature of the causal parasite: (1) the protozoal diseases, such as malaria and amoebic dysentery, which are caused by the invasion of microscopic animals; (2) the bacterial diseases, such as tuberculosis, meningitis, and the thousand and one infections which are spread by cocci, bacilli, spirilla, and other microscopic plants; and (3) the virus diseases, whose agent is neither like any of the little animals we know nor yet like any of the little plants, but appears to be of an entirely different order of organization. A few years ago the viruses were commonly known as the filter-passers, but this term ceased to be significant when it was found that certain bacteria could also pass through the fine pores of a porcelain filter and that some of these bacteria are as small as some of the viruses; i.e. the virus of smallpox.
—GEORGE W. GRAY, "The Problem of Influenza," *Harper's Magazine,*
CLXXX (1940), 172

Every item should be classifiable in only one division at the same degree of extension. If it is classifiable in two or more, the principle which controls the classification has been changed. Contrast these classifications: frogs, toads, salamanders, and whales; whales, cats, cows, dogs, and apes; whales, salamanders, ostriches, cats, dogs, lizards, lamprey-eels. If the first is intended to represent a class, amphibia, whale does not belong. It does not live on land and is not cold-blooded. All of the items in the second belong to the same class, mammalia. Amphibia and mammalia represent the same degree of extension; as classes, both stand between orders and subphyla. Whales cannot belong to each of them. The third classification represents the subphylum vertebrates; and whales may rightly belong to both it and the second.

Is it possible to reclassify the items in each of the three following groupings in either of the other two? Why?

On the basis of their purpose in writing, authors may be classified into three general groups. First, those who, desiring primarily to entertain the reader, produce works of fiction, drama, and poetry. The second group takes in those writers whose chief purpose is to inform the reader. In this group are the news reporters, some news commentators, authors of textbooks, biographers, and writers of encyclopedias and technical works. The third class is made up of those who want to control the opinions of the reader or to affect his course of action. Included here are the political propagandists and advertisers.

May the items in each of these three divisions be classified in either of the other two? Why? Suggest other bases for classifying these books.

The books on my shelf may be classified into three groups. The first, including *Moby-Dick, Ulysses, Think Fast, Mr. Moto,* and *Modern American Poetry,* I read on my own initiative. The second, *A Survey of European Civilization, Listening to Music, A Brief Course in Trigonometry, A Textbook of Zoology,* I read according to the assignments and the requirements of my instructors. The third group, my thesaurus, dictionaries, *World Almanac,* I use from time to time for reference.

Finally, the classifications should further the purpose controlling them. The reason beneath it should be readily evident. Any effort to issue license plates to owners on the basis of the color of their automobiles or to catalogue books on the basis of their colors or sizes would prove unrewarding. License fees are commonly determined by the horsepower of the automobile, which is linked with both its weight and its speed, and hence, presumably, its effect on the road. Librarians classify books by subjects, not color or size, because readers are more commonly interested in their subject matter than in their greenness or their smallness. To some, obviously, other classifications might be more useful: the binder may be concerned with color, the printer with sizes.

If analysis of an object discloses all its details, it will remain apart from all other objects, *sui generis.* Classifying it as belonging with other groups abstracts it from all its individuality and the circumstances of time and place in which it exists. In that way, classification may be said to check analysis and, for convenience, to group together things similar in readily apparent ways. Classification, therefore, is an artifice built on average and not exceptional cases. It is wrong to suppose that since a thing belongs to a class, it will invariably have all the markings or qualities commonly associated with that class. Not all swans are white.

As an ordered arrangement designed to bring large and divergent numbers of items into manageable form, a classification may be tested by the following principles:

1. The divisions or groups throughout the classification must conform to a single principle.
2. The groupings must include all aspects of the things being

classified which the purpose makes important and useful.
3. Every item should possess the distinctive characteristics of the group in which it is placed.
4. Every item should be classifiable in only one division at the same degree of extension.
5. The classification should further the purpose which controls it.

EXERCISES

On the basis of the standards of judgment of classifications given in this chapter, evaluate each of the following:

1

The instruments of the modern symphony orchestra are divided into four groups. The strings, which are the backbone of the orchestra, are composed of violins, violas, cellos, and basses. The woodwinds are flute, oboe, clarinet, and bassoon. The brasswinds are trumpet, French horn, trombone, and tuba. Finally, the percussion section, which has the greatest variety of instruments, contains the tympani, snare drums, glockenspiel, and many others.

2

Angles may be classified into three groups: right angles which contain ninety degrees, straight angles that contain 180 degrees, and oblique angles which are any angles other than a right or a straight angle. Oblique angles may be either acute, less than ninety degrees, or obtuse, an angle greater than a right angle and less than a straight angle.

3

In general, the talent of three types of composers is recognized today throughout most of the world. First, the work of the members of the "old school" has been tested by time and proved everlasting. To this class belong Bach, Beethoven, Chopin, Haydn, and Mozart. Then, the durability of the works of more modern writers is as yet uncertain. In this number are Shostakovitch, Sibelius, Rachmaninoff, Debussy, and Ravel. Finally, there are the composers of popular swing music, which appeals to the people more universally, but which has failed to stand the test of time. Here are included George Gershwin, Cole Porter, and Irving Berlin.

4

The show windows of a typical ten-cent store contain a miscellaneous collection of articles ranging all the way from chocolate drops to linoleum rugs. Part of the space is devoted to clothing, such as brightly colored socks, striped neckties, baby bonnets, and fifty-nine-cent sweaters. In another section of the window, various foods are displayed. Lollipops, peanuts, gumdrops, and popcorn are arranged in glass dishes beside artificial chocolate sodas. Still another section contains glasses of pencils, book satchels, notebooks, and other school supplies, beside shelves of toothpaste, soap, perfume, hairpins, and various additional toilet articles. Finally, one comes to a display of toys and household furnishings, which includes rubber balls, six-shooters, dolls, window curtains, floor lamps, bath towels, and a twenty-four-piece dinner set.

5

In the course of the revolutionary wars they [the German states] had been steadily reduced by a process of fusion till in 1815 there were only thirty-eight states left. They were divisible, on the score of size, into three groups: a group of two great powers, Austria and Prussia, a group of five middle-sized states, Bavaria, Württemberg, Baden, Saxony, and Hanover, and a final group of petty principalities, like Weimar and Hesse, together with the city-republics of Hamburg, Bremen, and Lubeck.

—FERDINAND SCHEVILL, *A History of Europe,* 1938

6

At the top of the series (vertebrates) are placed the Mammalia, usually known as *animals* or *beasts*. Among the representative mammals are man, the apes, monkeys, bats, moles, rats, mice, rabbits, dogs, cats, cows, sheep, horses, whales, sloths, opossums, and the peculiar duckbill and spiny ant-eater of Australia. They are vertebrates which possess hair, and, with a few exceptions, nourish their young with milk secreted by mammary glands. They breathe air by means of lungs, and are said to be warm-blooded, since their body temperature is nearly 100° F., regardless of the temperature of the surrounding medium.

—ROBERT W. HEGNER, *College Zoology,* 1931

7

Bark gives the names to shagbark hickory, striped maple, and naked wood. The color names white birch, black locust, blue beech. Wood names red oak, yellow-wood, and white-heart hickory. The texture names rock elm, punk oak, and soft pine. The uses name post oak, canoe birch, and lodge-pole pine. The tree habit is described by dwarf juniper, weeping willow, and weeping spruce. The habitat by swamp maple, desert willow, and seaside alder. The range by California white oak and Georgia pine. Sap is characterized in sugar maple, sweet gum, balsam fir, and sweet birch. Twigs are indicated in clammy locust, cotton gum, winged elm. Leaf linings are referred to in silver maple, white poplar, and white basswood. Color of foliage in grey pine, blue oak, and golden fir. Shape of leaves, in heart-leaved cucumber tree and ear-leaved umbrella. Resemblance of leaves to other species, in willow oak and parsley haw. The flowers of trees give names to tulip tree, silver-bell tree, and fringe tree. The fruit is described in big-cone pine, butternut, mossy-cup oak, and mock orange.

—Julia Ellen Rogers, *The Tree Book*, 1931

Subjects for Classification

1. Classify flowers (a) for a garden with flowers blossoming all summer and fall; (b) by colors.
2. Suppose you are the superintendent of a general hospital. Classify the patients there on any one day in at least four ways.
3. Classify the schools you might have attended.
4. Suppose that you, as an engineer, are assigned the problem of reducing noises in a city. Classify the types of noises.
5. Suppose that you are the manager of a factory which employs five hundred people. Classify them. Show the usefulness of both your purpose and the principle of division.
6. Classify crops for a year on the basis of (a) need for a particular type of soil; (b) the time the seed should be planted.
7. Classify motor vehicles and re-route them through the center of town in order to speed up traffic.
8. Every subject in a college catalogue includes many subdivisions. Thus, zoology includes anatomy, histology, embryology, ecology, and other subsciences. Group the details of the subject with which you are most familiar into subdivisions.
9. Compare the ways in which fire insurance agents and real estate agents classify houses.
10. Contrast the natural and the Linnaean classifications in botany or the classifications of man made respectively by Linnaeus and by Huxley.

CHAPTER 7

Definition

> A definition is the enclosing a wilderness of idea within a wall of words.
> —Samuel Butler, *Note Books*, 1912

What is a crystal? Contrast these three definitions:

1

A crystal is something that glitters in the sun.

2

9. *Chem.* and *Min.* A form in which the molecules of many single elements and their natural compounds regularly aggregate by the operation of molecular affinity: it has a definite internal structure, with the external form of a solid enclosed by a number of symmetrically arranged plane faces, and varying in simplicity from a cube to much more complex geometrical bodies.

> —*Oxford English Dictionary*

3

Crystal is a word with misleading implications, and I suppose I should devote some space to brushing these away. The really important feature of a crystal, which is the ordering of the atoms in it, is a thing which no man ever sees, not even with the most powerful microscopes; and the things which are seen are often unimportant and not even confined to true crystals. For instance, we often use the word to denote the piece of glass over the face of a watch. This is a most unlucky habit, for if there is any solid substance in the world in which the real distinction of a crystal is feeble or missing, glass is certainly it. The earliest meaning of the Greek word *crystallos* was apparently *ice,* and this is not so bad, for ice is crystalline, though nothing in its outward aspect suggests that. "Crystal clarity" and "crystal purity" are just nonsensical phrases to a physicist, who knows that many an admirable crystal is opaque. There is, however, one idea associated with the word, which verges upon the essential.

Even in popular speech, "crystal" is likely to suggest a piece of matter which is not only glassy and transparent, but shaped into a strange and lovely form; a cube or column or a minaret, a pyramid or a pinnacle, with lustrous surfaces of exquisite smoothness divided from each other by arêtes of knife-edge sharpness. A perfectly formed crystal looks more like a creation of intelligent design than anything else in inorganic Nature; one would almost think it expressly contrived as a pleasure for the eye. It is a pleasure for the mind as well, for its surfaces and angles declare the inner truth. Glassiness and transparency have nothing whatever to do with this—they are practically accidents; but the shape is a sign of that which is fundamental, the arrangement of the atoms. And yet, there may be a crystalline arrangement of the atoms, and no curiosity of outward form to suggest it. A perfectly rough and shapeless hunk of matter may be just as good a crystal as the loveliest diamond that ever was found. This I say to bring out the fact that, far from being infrequent, the crystalline state is almost universal among solids. Stones are mostly crystalline; a metal is a mass of tiny granular crystals, one or more of which may be increased to great size by techniques which are well known; sand is pulverized crystal, brick is a mass of clay crystals baked together, and even wool and hair and cotton are crystalline to some degree.

Now, to state the essential feature of a crystal: It is a piece of matter in which the atoms are disposed in a superbly regular array in a neat geometrical pattern. The atoms of a crystal stand in ranks and files like soldiers on parade, instead of being huddled together in a disorderly crowd or sprinkled at random in an open space. Only, the parade is in three dimensions instead of two, and this makes analogies difficult to find. Regular arrays—"lattices," they are called—in two dimensions are rather familiar to everyone. The classic illustration is wall-paper, in which a design is repeated over and over again, both up and down and sideways; this is still usual in English books, but the trend of the art of interior decoration has made it less useful in America. The squares of a chessboard form a lattice, very limited in extent; the intersections of the streets in most American cities form lattices, though seldom perfect ones; the windows on the face of a very large skyscraper often make a magnificent two-dimensional lattice of vast expanse. But for examples of three-dimensional lattices, I have been able to think only of the intersections of the girders of a steel-frame building, as one sees them when the masonry coating is not yet on; and a friend suggested the piles of cannon balls which are stacked up by ancient war memorials.

—KARL K. DARROW, *The Renaissance of Physics*, 1936

The first definition is not very helpful. A crystal may glitter in the sun; but so may a lake, and a lake is not made of crystals. The first is not a definition. It does not help us in establishing the identity of crystal.

The second tells us that it is, in a ninth sense, a technical word (*Chem.* and *Min.*) which designates a solid aggregate of molecules with definite internal structure and with the external form of a solid enclosed by a number of symmetrically arranged plane faces. This is a *logical definition*. It places the thing being defined, crystal, in the class to which it belongs, matter, and, further, tells how it differs from other members of that class, other forms of matter —that is, in its having symmetrically arranged plane faces.

The third contains a *logical definition*—a crystal is "a piece of matter in which the atoms are disposed in a superbly regular array in a neat geometrical pattern"—but it contains much more. It may be called an *extended definition;* for, in addition to the strictly logical definition, it makes known the meaning of crystal by giving the etymology of the word *crystal,* descriptive analyses of the thing crystal, contrasts, and illustrations. All these are fitting and proper in a definition.

VERBAL AND REAL DEFINITIONS

To state the meaning one may assign to a *word* is to give, rightly or wrongly, a *verbal definition:* "A traitor is any man who changes his political party for any reason whatsoever." Giving the nature of a *thing* represented by a word is called a *real definition:* "A traitor violates his allegiance to his country and betrays it." This distinction indicates the power men have to use words to stand for meanings convenient to them but not necessarily to anyone else and not to which all may agree. That power may and often does block genuine communication. Beyond revealing individualized meanings, however, the distinction also shows that the only link between a thing and the word used to designate it is the historical association between the two. Pronouncing the word *rain* will not bring rain, the thing. At times, the association between a thing and the word used to name it may become so strained and so burdened with a variety of meanings that the word no longer represents anything precise and definite. The author who uses it, therefore, has at the outset to give it a *verbal definition* to make his discourse intelligible. What does *free enterprise* mean?

In the third definition of crystal, Darrow, you will observe in the first paragraph, gives both verbal and real definitions. What specific "misleading implications" make these two types of definitions necessary?

THE LOGICAL DEFINITION

Since things possess common characteristics, they may be associated together in groups. All plane figures with four sides and four angles are quadrilaterals. All four-sided figures with opposite sides equal and the same distance apart at all points are parallelograms. If the angles of such figures are all right angles, the figures are rectangles. From such likenesses and differences arise groupings, which the logical definition employs. It tells what a thing is by placing it in the group to which it belongs and then showing how it differs from other members of the group. The thing being defined is a member, a *species,* of a larger group, the next in extension, the *genus.* The difference between the thing being defined and the other species is the *differentia.* Thus, a logical definition may be schematized in this way:

The	SPECIES	is the	GENUS	plus the	DIFFERENTIA.
A	parallelogram	is a	quadrilateral	with	opposite sides equal.
A	rectangle	is a	parallelogram	with	four right angles.

THE CRITICISM OF LOGICAL DEFINITIONS

1. The genus must be neither too large nor too small.
   A crystal is *something* with plane faces.
   A crystal is a *formation of quartz* geometrically patterned.
2. The species being defined must be differentiated from other members of genus.
   A crystal is a form of matter. Of amorphous matter?
   A garage is a building. A house or a store?
3. The term being defined or a derivative of it must not be repeated in the definition.
   A crystal is a form of crystalline matter.
   A parallelogram is a quadrilateral with parallel sides.

4. A descriptive comment must not be substituted for genus and differentia.

EXERCISE I

In each of the following definitions, indicate whether (a) the genus is too large; (b) the genus is too small; (c) the term is not adequately differentiated from other members of the genus; (d) the term itself or a derivative of it is used in the definition (e) the object is commented on and not defined logically; (f) the definition is logical.
1. A degree Fahrenheit is 1/180 of the temperature interval between the freezing point and the boiling point of water at sea level.
2. A democracy is a form of government.
3. An umbrella is something used for protection against rain and sun.
4. A garage is a shed in which to keep an automobile.
5. A steel mill is a smoky, noisy place.
6. A coral reef is a reef made by corals.

EXERCISE II

Write logical definitions of the following terms:
1. A machine gun
2. A certified check
3. Photography
4. A beetle
5. A simile

EXTENDED DEFINITIONS

A logical definition is generally a single sentence. The nature of a thing may be made known, however, by details other than the genus and differentia. Such details, as Darrow's definition of *crystal* suggests, may be extensive. Etymology may be helpful in the service of definition, as may other methods already pointed out as useful in amplifying and clarifying one's meaning—may be especially helpful in defining terms. The following quotations show etymology, analysis, comparison, and illustration used in *extended definitions.* Their respective criteria also apply to them when they are used in this way.

ETYMOLOGY

The word 'bore' is of doubtful etymology. Some authorities derive it from the verb meaning to pierce. A bore is a person who drills a hole in your spirit, who tunnels relentlessly through your patience, through all the crusts of voluntary deafness, inattention, rudeness, which you vainly interpose—through and through till he pierces to the very quick of your being. But there are other authorities, as good or even better, who derive the word from the French *bourrer,* to stuff, to satiate. If this etymology be correct, a bore is one who stuffs you with his thick and suffocating discourse, who rams his suety personality, like a dumpling, down your throat. He stuffs you; and you, to use an opposite modern metaphor, are 'fed up with him.' I like to think, impossibly, that both these derivations of the word are correct; for bores are both piercers and stuffers. They are like dentists' drills, and they are also like stale buns. But they are characterised by a further quality, which drills and dough-nuts do not possess; they cling. That is why (although no philologist) I venture to suggest a third derivation, from 'burr'. Burr, *bourrer,* bore —all the sticking, stuffing, piercing qualities of boredom are implicit in those three possible etymologies. Each of the three of them deserves to be correct.

Herbert Comfrey was above all a sticking bore. He attached himself to any one who had the misfortune to come in contact with him; attached himself and could not be shaken off. A burr-bore, vegetable and passive; not actively penetrating. For Herbert, providentially, was not particularly talkative; he was too lazy and lymphatic for that. He was just exceedingly sociable, like a large sentimental dog that cannot bear to be left alone. Like a dog, he followed people about; he lay, meta-phorically speaking, at their feet in front of the fire. And like a dog, he did not talk. It was just your company that made him happy; he was quite content if he might trot at your side or doze under your chair. He did not demand that you should pay much attention to him; all that he asked was to be permitted to enjoy the light of your countenance and bask in the warmth of your presence. If once a week he got the equiva-lent of a pat on the head and a 'Good dog, Herbert,' he wagged his spirit's tail and was perfectly happy.

—ALDOUS HUXLEY, *Two or Three Graces,* 1926

ANALYSIS

1

There appears generally to be a bottom of *clay;* not *soft chalk,* which they persist in calling clay in Norfolk. I wish I had one of these Norfolk men in a coppice in Hampshire or Sussex, and I would show him what *clay* is. Clay is what pots and pans and jugs and tiles are made of; and not soft, whitish stuff that crumbles to pieces in the sun, instead of baking hard as a stone, and which, in dry weather, is to be broken to pieces by nothing short of a sledge-hammer.

—WILLIAM COBBETT, *Rural Rides,* 1830

2

Criticism is judgment, ideally as well as etymologically. Understanding of judgment is therefore the first condition for theory about the nature of criticism. Perceptions supply judgment with its material, whether the judgments pertain to physical nature, to politics or biography. The subject-matter of perception is the only thing that makes the difference in the judgments which ensue. Control of the subject-matter of perception for ensuring proper data for judgment is the key to the enormous distinction between the judgments the savage passes on natural events and that of a Newton or Einstein. Since the matter of aesthetic criticism is the perception of aesthetic objects, natural and artistic criticism is always determined by the quality of first-hand perception; obtuseness in perception can never be made good by any amount of learning, however extensive, nor any command of abstract theory, however correct. Nor is it possible to exclude judgment from entering into aesthetic perception, or at least from supervening upon a first totally unanalyzed qualitative impression.

—JOHN DEWEY, *Art as Experience,* 1934

COMPARISON

Philosophical knowledge is the *knowledge gained by reason from concepts;* mathematical knowledge is the knowledge gained by reason from the *construction* of concepts. The essential difference between these two kinds of knowledge through reason consists therefore in this formal difference, and does not depend on difference of their material or objects. Those who propose to distinguish philosophy from mathematics by saying that the former has as its object *quality* only and the latter *quantity* only, have mistaken the effect for the cause. The form of mathematical knowledge is the cause why it is limited exclusively to quantities. For it is the concept of quantities only that allows of being constructed, that is, exhibited *a priori* in intuition; whereas qualities cannot be presented in any intuition that is not empirical.

—IMMANUEL KANT, *Critique of Pure Reason,*
trans. Norman Kemp Smith, 1929

ILLUSTRATION

A craft union is one which claims membership according to the type of work done. For example, a machinists' union would include all machinists engaged in building, manufacturing, repairing—in shipyards, steel mills, automobile factories. According to this formula of organization, if it were carried out, a thousand workers in one factory might be organized into ten unions of machinists, plumbers, toolworkers, electricians, glass workers, carpenters, iron workers, smelter workers, clerks and watchmen. Each group of employees would owe allegiance to a union including similar workers in all other industries.

        —C. L. SULZBERGER, *A Sit Down with John L. Lewis,* 1938

EXERCISE I

In how many cases are the meanings of the italicized words in the following passages made clearer by etymological definitions? List both the meaning in the context and the etymological meaning before you answer this question.

1

Some maintain that universal active participation in *social service* is an indispensable element in any genuine *democracy*. Where everything is done for the people without effort by themselves, and nothing by the people, not for their individual selves but for the common good, all the *electoral machinery* in the world will not create a democratic community.

        —SIDNEY WEBB, *What Is Ahead for Us?* 1937

2

Neanderthal man was found to be distinctly *human,* but he still retained many features which place him closer to the common *ancestor* of man and the anthropoids than are any of the later races. He shows marked development in cranial capacity over the earlier *fossil* forms, but in configuration of skull he offers no sharp break from *Pithecanthropus erectus,* while his *mandible* is much more like that of Heidelberg man than is found in any of his successors. He is replaced by invading people, Cro-Magnon, and they, in turn, give way before the incoming *Neolithic* races.

        —FAY-COOPER COLE, "The Coming of Man,"
        The Nature of the World and of Man, 1926

EXERCISE II

What methods of defining *advertising* and *man* are used in the following passages? Are any aspects of the terms omitted? If you answer "Yes," name some of them.

1

To saddle the public with useless articles, to create an unnatural demand for them, to scrap the still sound article and purchase the ever less durable novelty, to keep the styles moving—such are the aims pursued by advertisers with an almost missionary zeal.

—EDGAR ANSEL MOWRER, *This American World,* 1928

2

Man is a self-balancing twenty-eight-jointed adapter-base biped. An electro-chemical reduction plant, integral with segregated stowages of special energy extracts in storage batteries, for subsequent actuation of thousands of hydraulic and pneumatic pumps, with motors attached. Sixty-two thousand miles of capillaries; millions of warning signal, railroad and conveyor systems; crushers and cranes . . . and a universally distributed telephone system needing no service for seventy years if well managed. The whole . . . mechanism, guided with exquisite precision from a turret in which are located telescopic and microscopic self-registering and recording range finders, a spectroscope, et cetera, the turret control being closely allied with an air-conditioning intake-and-exhaust, and a main fuel intake.

—R. BUCKMINSTER FULLER, *Nine Chains to the Moon,* 1938

EXERCISE III

What is defined in the following passage? In what way or ways?

If you believe that our civilization is founded in common sense (and it is the first condition of sanity to believe it), you will, when contemplating men, discern a Spirit overhead; not more heavenly than the light flashed upon the glassy surfaces, but luminous and watchful; never shooting beyond them, nor lagging in the rear; so closely attached to them that it may be taken for a slavish reflex, until its features are studied. It has the sage's brows, and the sunny malice of a faun lurks at the corners of the half-closed lips drawn in an idle wariness of half-tension. That slim feasting smile, shaped like the long-bow, was once a big round satyr's laugh, that flung up the brows like a fortress lifted by gunpowder. The laugh will come again, but it will be of the order of a smile, finely-tempered, showing sunlight of the mind, mental richness rather than noisy enormity. Its common aspect is one of unsolicitous observation, as if surveying a full field and having leisure to dart on its chosen morsels, without any fluttering eagerness. Men's failure upon earth does not attract it; their honesty and shapeliness in the present does; and whenever they wax out of proportion, overblown, affected, pretentious, bombastical, hypercritical, pedantic, fantastically delicate; whenever it sees them self-deceived or hood-winked, given to run riot in idolatries, drifting into vanities, congregating in absurdities, planning short-sightedly, plotting dementedly; whenever they are at variance with their professions, and violate the unwritten but perceptible laws binding them in consideration one to another; whenever they offend sound reason, fair justice; are false in humility or mind with conceit, individually, or in bulk; the Spirit overhead will look humanely malign, and cast an oblique light on them, followed by the volleys of silvery laughter. That is the Comic Spirit.

—GEORGE MEREDITH, *The Idea of Comedy*, 1877

EXERCISE IV

Which of the statements below (a) illustrate a confusion between a statement of fact and a definition; (b) differentiate meanings various speakers give the same term; (c) give the exact signification of terms which are similar in meaning.

1

When anyone says, "Liberalism is dead," he may be meaning to assert that the world is done for good with any one or more of the following: (1) the Liberal Party of Great Britain; (2) the doctrine of economic laissez faire; (3) a political method of which the essentials are universal suffrage, free speech, and an insistence upon the maintenance of civil liberties at all times; (4) a philosophy of which the foundations were laid in the eighteenth century and which includes a belief in the natural goodness of man, in the doctrine of equal rights, and in the existence of a natural tendency toward progress wherever freedom is maintained; (5) what may more properly be called the liberal temperament—a quasi-aesthetic preference for freedom and variety over discipline and conformity and a tendency to regard them as ends in themselves.

—JOSEPH WOOD KRUTCH, "How Dead Is Liberalism?" *The Nation*, CXLIII (1936), 297

2

The accused, in committing a libel, acted with malice.

3

Wonder is our reaction to things which we are conscious of not quite understanding, or at any rate of understanding less than we had thought. Strangeness arises from a different kind of *consciousness* from our own.

4

While throughout the world Americanism is today a common expression standing for anything from gum chewing to Behaviourism, any attempt to fix its meaning fundamentally or exhaustively usually ends in a serious and thoroughly unscientific controversy.

Even at home we are hazy about what we mean. The Americanism of the Legion and the Ku Klux is only distantly related to that of the Rotary Clubs and Kiwanis. There is a chasm between the serene appreciation of present America by Santayana and Waldo Frank's lyric dream of a true civilization. . . .

If we go abroad the disagreement is worse. Even so jovial a soul as G. K. Chesterton finds Americanism an appalling danger to contemporary Europe. An acute German, Theodor Lueddecke, sees similar peril in the "rhythm of American economic life." And most extreme is W. T. Colyer, who defines Americanism as a "world menace." On the other side, Jean Georges Auriol believes "American brutality" to be the much needed antidote for Europe's "excessively cerebral sensibility," meaning, doubtless, Europe's intellectual aloofness from fundamentals.

—Edgar Ansel Mowrer, *This American World*, 1928

Exercise V

Definitions for Criticism

Contrast and evaluate the following definitions:

1

A snob is a person who makes birth or wealth the sole criterion of worth. He is cringing to superiors and overbearing to inferiors. He believes in class distinction, yet is himself a social climber. He often ignores those under him as reminders of that from which he has come. He has never learned to value people as such, but merely considers what they can do for him.

2

A snob may be an individual who considers himself superior to others because of some advantage, such as talent, position, or wealth, and lets everyone know it by word and action; or he may be one who tries to conceal a consciousness of inferiority under a haughty, patronizing manner.

—*The Forum*, 81 (June, 1929)

3

A snob is a member of a civilized body of mankind who, by his actions, indicates a consciousness of his supposed superiority to the others in his society.

4

A lowbrow is a person who is lacking in intelligence, knowledge, and refinement of taste if judged by intellectual and aesthetic criteria. Etymologically lowbrow probably developed because it is the direct opposite of highbrow, or one who has a high forehead, which has long been associated with culture, refinement, and social grace. The lowbrow is unappreciative of great music, art, beauty, and philosophy. He is the pie-eater while the highbrow is the cake-eater of society.

5

"Lowbrow" is slang denoting an obvious lack of the essentials of refinement; it is synonymous with taste, attainment, or mentality of an inferior level.

—*The Forum,* 81 (April, 1929)

6

A lowbrow is a person whose aesthetic sense is undeveloped and who has no interest in intellectual speculation.

—*The Forum,* 81 (April, 1929)

7

A gentleman is a male person of ordinary respectability who has a refinement of thought and action. The term comes from the Middle English *gentilman,* meaning a male member of the gentry or noble-born class, who at that time were believed to be almost the sole possessors of these characteristics which include kindness, courtesy, honor, honesty, and morality. Now the word is used to refer to any male possessing such noble attributes.

8

"A gentleman to see you, sir" may mean that the person who awaits is any of the following: (1) a well-bred and honorable man; (2) in Great Britain, a man entitled to bear a coat of arms; (3) also, in Great Britain, a man wellborn though not of nobility; (4) according to English law, a respectable man of independent income, who does not work for a living; (5) probably, a man, for the word gentleman may be used for polite reference to any male member of *homo sapiens.*

WORDS TO BE DEFINED

Snob	Democratic Capitalism
Gentleman	Fascistic Capitalism
Education	Conservative
Civilization	Russian Communism
Science	Chinese Communism

CHAPTER 8

Cause

We cannot know anything of nature but by an
analysis of its true initial causes.
—Joseph Glanvill, *Full and Plain Evidence Concerning Witches and Witchcraft,* 1666

Man's wonder and imagination feed upon mysteries. His desire
to see things clearly and to act wisely prompts him to look for
causes. Once he has found them, much of the unknown remains,
but not so much as before. He has increased his understanding of
events which shape his existence and possibly his power of control
over them.

In the flow of time, events crowd and push together as if the last
prizes were being given away. Automobiles collide, dynasties fall,
chills and fever send men to bed. Radiators freeze, markets col-
lapse, chance and the cook leave the steak too rare.

What causes such occurrences? Men like to suppose that one
thing alone does. Not watching where he was going, the other
driver ran into the oncoming automobile. The ruling family
trusted traitorous ministers whose dark plot overthrew it. Fevers
are punishments for those who think unkind thoughts of others.
The radiator froze because it was left uncovered. Merchandise
produced by cheap labor ruined the market. The carelessness of
the cook spoiled the steak.

Such explanations as those are often untenable. They are oversimplified. Determining rightly the actual cause of any event,
group of events, or state of affairs requires a closer scrutiny of all
the circumstances which may have produced it. Many apparent

causes may have to be rejected before the actual cause is found. The cause may be complex; it may be composed of interrelated factors. It may reach backward in time; it may not immediately precede its effect.

Consider the following paragraph:

> ... The language of natural science is very largely the language of mathematics, and since our rational business is to make the world outlook of science an open bible, it is also our rational business to democratise the art of calculation as the Reformation democratised the art of reading. This means that instead of leaving it out of the curriculum because it is unattractive, we have to make it attractive to the average individual by bringing it into relation with social experience. Taught with that end in view, mathematics might be presented as the mirror of civilisation, exhibiting more clearly than any other discipline the great debt of our so-called Nordic civilisation to its predecessors and the dependence of the most gifted individuals on their social heritage.
>
> Naturally this result will not be achieved as long as most people who teach it both in schools and universities themselves believe that mathematics was invented by idealistic and leisurely Athenians out of sheer fascination with its utter uselessness. So our task implies a much closer cooperation between the teaching of history, of prehistory, and of natural science in school and university alike.
>
> —LANCELOT HOGBEN, *Retreat from Reason,* 1938

This short statement contains several hidden presuppositions about causes and their respective effects. Implicit in it are such questions as these: How may we make an allegedly unattractive discipline attractive? The passage suggests one way. How does the understanding of mathematics affect society? What components of the social heritage of the gifted individual make him depend on it so greatly? Does ineffective teaching result from the ignorance of teachers? May a more effective understanding of history, as a discipline, result from a cross-disciplinary study of it with mathematics?

The foregoing passage shows the possible intricacy of cause. It provides a warning against oversimplification. Historical occurrences are unique. Once a group of interrelated circumstances have produced them, they do not recur. The writer who must explain their causes can only limit his problem, study the records, and guard against hasty inferences and suppositions. When he limits his problem, he narrows both the effect he proposes to explain and the number of factors which produced it. What caused the revolution in England in 1688–1689? That problem is obviously larger than that of the cause of any of the episodes of the Revolution. The Revolution, in general, may have caused the episodes, but each episode had a more specific and immediate cause or causes. Study, for example, the causes named in the following passage:

William did not come over for love of England or for pity of her misfortunes. Neither the country nor its inhabitants made any appeal to his affections, which were all centered on Holland. His wife loved England, but he was not in the habit of forming his policy in consultation with Mary, nor would she have urged him to attack her own father. Her gentle nature felt the whole tragedy of her position, but she silently accepted the decision of the husband she adored, as to the only means of saving England, Holland, and the Protestant cause in Europe.

William, then, was under no personal or moral obligation to risk the fortunes of the little land of dikes and canals for the sake of a country that had often treated both him and Holland very ill. But in his cold judgment, Holland could only be saved from ultimate conquest by France, if England was brought in as an active partner of the anti-French alliance which he had painfully built up in Europe. If he could himself become King of England that object would certainly be secured. Failing that, the object might still be attained if the policy of James were subjected to the will of a freely elected Parliament. For that reason he decided that the enormous risks of the invasion of England must be faced, and he proceeded to make his preparations—military, diplomatic and political—with a combined audacity and wisdom that mark him out as one of the world's great men.

—GEORGE MACAULAY TREVELYAN, *The English Revolution, 1688–1689*, 1939

Notice that in the foregoing paragraph the writer did not explore remote causes. Since all life is commonly a continuing sequence of causes producing effects which, in turn, become causes and produce other effects, the causes of any event may be explored backward in time endlessly. Such explorations, however, are seldom helpful, if ever. They are not informative. No one considers the landing of English colonists in what is now the United States as a cause of the Revolutionary War. Similarly, in the passage just quoted, the marriage of William of Orange to the daughter of James II is not considered a cause. In a causal analysis, immediate and not remote causes are of significance because only immediate causes are directly contributory to the shaping of the event in question.

A causal analysis of historical occurrences, further, may include inciting events, but it must not confuse them with causes. The Boston Tea Party was not *the* cause of the American Revolutionary War, nor the firing on Fort Sumter that of the Civil War. Similarly, in the passage just quoted, William's "preparations, military, diplomatic, and political," were not the actual causes of the invasion.

Historical occurrences cannot be subjected to scientific experimentation. The factors which created them cannot be varied at will until the writer who would explain them can, in every case, prove the exactness of his analysis. For that reason, he must study all the records and guard against hasty inferences and suppositions. Not testing and retesting, but scrutiny and judgment, must, in his case, bring causes to light. And those causes must be causes, not inciting events. They must also be, not remote, but immediate causes.

Observe the precision of the analysis in the following passage:

It is often asked: Why did the Whigs and Tories of 1688 call in foreign arms? Why did they not rise in rebellion as Englishmen in their own quarrel, like the Roundheads of 1642? They had a better case, and the country was far more united against James II than against Charles I. Why then invite foreigners to interfere? The fact that James was introducing Irish, whom the English regarded as foreigners more odious than the Dutch, is an excuse, but not in itself an answer.

The answer lies in the difference of the situation. In 1642 Charles I had no army save what he could raise from loyalist volunteers; in 1688 James had a large regular army on foot. In 1642 a Parliament was sitting as a center of authority round which men could rally against the King; in 1688 no Parliament was sitting. A flag or leader was therefore needed to evoke and organize opposition to James.

There must then be an army of liberation, and there must also be a chieftain under whose banner all sections of the opposition would gladly march. The only army available for such a purpose would be a large draft from the professional troops of the Dutch Republic—a polyglot Protestant force, including a British contingent whose presence would go far to mitigate the sense of a foreign invasion. And the only person round whom Whigs and Tories would rally with equal confidence was William of Orange, husband of the King's eldest child

Mary. By a happy coincidence William as Stadtholder of Holland was the one man who could bring over the desired force. He could also, as head of the European combination in restraint of France, enlist as supporters of his expedition against the ally of Louis XIV, not only the Protestant Princes of Germany, but Spain, Austria and, strangest of all, the Pope himself!
—GEORGE MACAULAY TREVELYAN, *The English Revolution, 1688–1689,*
1939

In contrast to the causes of unique events, those of events which recur again and again may be tested. They may occur naturally or they may be artificially created. Attending factors which are believed to be causes may be varied or omitted and the consequent variations in effect noted. In such instances, the writer may report causes which he has verified by observation. The two following passages illustrate problems of this type.

1

When the house is still at night there are odd creakings, many of which are due to changes of temperature. Parts of the house structure shrink more than others as they cool, and a strain is set up which gives way suddenly. In hot countries, whenever houses have roofs of corrugated iron, the sound due to the contracting roof is very common. A stove creaks sometimes after the gas has been turned off, or the cinders as they cool in the grate. There is a great statue in Egypt, near Luxor, which, about the beginning of our era, used to emit a sound in the early hours of the day, when the sun first shone upon it. Pilgrimages were made to hear it; names of proconsuls and others are inscribed upon the legs of the statue. It was a ruin even then, and it is now suggested that the sound was due to the ringing note of one stone sliding on another, the heat having caused the stone to expand and strain until at last something gave way. Eminent archaeologists differ on the point, some saying that the noise was made by a priest hidden in the stone. But I think that in the beginning the effect must have been natural; though the priest may have assisted nature when some important visitor was waiting to hear, and it was advisable that he should not be disappointed.
—SIR WILLIAM BRAGG, *The World of Sound,* 1922

2

The reflection of sound by the walls of a building leads to curious results in certain cases. One of the best known has given its name to the Whispering Gallery in St. Paul's [cathedral in London]. Any one who whispers to the wall on one side of the great dome can be heard by a listener even as far away as the opposite side, provided that he also is close to the wall. Lord Rayleigh gave the explanation of the effect long ago, and later (in 1904) showed . . . an experiment in illustration of it. He pointed out that sound tended to creep round the inside of a curved wall, being continuously reflected by the wall without ever getting far away from it. We will repeat his experiment. A sheet of iron, twelve feet by two feet, is bent into the arc of a circle, in order to represent a piece of the circular Gallery wall. At one end is a bird-call, at the other a sensitive flame. When the bird-call is sounded the flame flares; and it is easy to prove that the sound is creeping round the inside of the wall and close to it, because a screen, four inches wide, placed close to the wall . . . cuts off the sound entirely and the flame ceases to flare. If the screen is withdrawn a few inches from the wall, the sound gets through between the wall and the screen, as the flame shows. In fact, the screen is no use anywhere except near the wall; but any point along it will do equally well.

—SIR WILLIAM BRAGG, *The World of Sound*, 1922

EXERCISE

After analyzing the cause-and-effect relationships in each of the following passages, determine which events are unique and which are recurring. In the case of the latter, what evidences of testing of causes appear in analysis? Be specific.

1

These, however, are merely symptoms of the decline [of the Roman Empire]. What were the causes? That is a more difficult question to answer. Certain economic explanations have been offered, and are worth considering. The drain of coinage to the Far East to pay for imported luxuries must have had the effect of hampering business by causing a shortage of money. The building-up of great landed estates, worked by slave labor or by dependent tenants who were little better than slaves, undoubtedly had something to do with the decline of agriculture, which diminished the food supply of the empire and so added to the suffering of the poor. But these are scarcely fundamental causes. Those historians are probably closer to the truth who insist that the absorption of the city-states by the empire lay at the root of many of the social ills of the Roman world. The vitality of a large part of ancient civilization sprang from free, independent, and intensely pa- triotic city-state republics. For a long time after they were conquered, the city-states retained their local freedom as Roman municipalities. But gradually they were absorbed into the larger fabric of the autocrat- ic empire, lost their individuality, and with it much of their energy. The extension of Roman citizenship to all freemen tended to destroy the privileged position of the municipal aristocracy, which had been the most vigorous class in the early empire. The extension of citizenship was particularly significant because it filled the army with citizens of the lowest class of society, and the army was now to take over control of the government.

—WALLACE K. FERGUSON and GEOFFREY BRUUN, *A Survey of European Civilization,* 1936

2

Another point of similarity between the tobacco mosaic virus and the virus of animal diseases lies in this: that both may be inactivated and rendered harmless. Thus Pasteur found that by drying the spinal cords of dogs which had died of hydrophobia, he obtained a material which was harmless; and yet it seemed to contain the principle of the hydrophobia carrier, for a person inoculated with the material gained a certain immunity to the disease. Stanley has found that by treating his crystalline protein with hydrogen peroxide, or formaldehyde, or other chemicals, or by exposing it to ultra-violet light, he causes its virulence to vanish. When the virus is rubbed on the leaves of healthy plants, no ill effects follow. And yet the crystals appear to be the same as those of the virulent untreated protein. When they are analyzed by x-ray bombardment they show the same diffraction pattern, when weighed they show the same molecular weight, and, most important of all, when injected into animals they produce an antiserum which when mixed with solutions of active virulent virus is able to neutralize or render inactive such solutions. There are slight chemical differences, however, and it is Dr. Stanley's idea that the effect of the treatment is to alter certain active groups of the huge molecule—to switch certain towers or ells of its architecture, as it were—but to leave the structure as a whole unchanged. These experiments with inactivation of the tobacco mosaic protein seem to promise results that will be helpful to the human pathologist searching the frontiers of immunization.

—GEORGE W. GRAY, *The Advancing Front of Science,* 1937

3

The fear of ghosts has certainly not been an unmixed blessing. Indeed it might with some show of reason be maintained that no belief has done so much to retard the economic and thereby the social progress of mankind as the belief in the immortality of the soul; for this belief has led race after race, generation after generation, to sacrifice the real wants of the living to the imaginary wants of the dead. The waste and destruction of life and property which this faith has entailed are enormous and incalculable. A Patagonian, for example, who has amassed during the whole of his life an estate by thieving from the whites or exchanging the products of the chase with neighbouring tribes, has done nothing for his heirs; all his savings are destroyed with him, and his children are obliged to rebuild their fortunes afresh,—a custom which is found also among the Tamanaquas of the Orinoco, who ravage the field of the deceased and cut down the trees which he has planted; and among the Yuracares, who abandon and shut up the house of the dead, regarding it as a profanation to gather a single fruit from the trees of his field.

While the fear of the ghost has operated directly to enhance the sanctity of human life by deterring the cruel, the passionate, and the malignant from the shedding of blood, it has operated also indirectly to bring about the same salutary result. For not only does the hag-ridden murderer himself dread his victim's ghost, but the whole community dreads it also and believes itself endangered by the murderer's presence, since the wrathful spirit which pursues him may turn on other people and rend them. Hence society has a strong motive for secluding, banishing, or exterminating the culprit in order to free itself from what it believes to be an imminent danger, a perilous pollution, a contagion of death. To put it in another way, the community has an interest in punishing homicide. Not that the treatment of homicides by the tribes or the State was originally conceived as a punishment inflicted on them: rather it was viewed as a measure of self-defence, a moral quarantine, a process of spiritual purification and disinfection, an exorcism. It was a mode of cleansing the people generally and sometimes the homicide himself from the ghostly infection, which to the primitive mind appears to be something material and tangible, something that can be literally washed or scoured away by water, pig's blood, sheep's blood, or other detergents. But when this purification took the form of laying the manslayer under restraint, banishing him from the country, or putting him to death in order to appease his victim's ghost, it was for all practical purposes indistinguishable from punishment, and the fear of it would act as a deterrent just as surely as if it had been designed to be a punishment and nothing else. When a man is about to be hanged, it is little consolation to him to be told that hanging is not a punishment but a purification. . . . Thus, the dread of the ghost seems to have operated in a twofold way to protect human life. On the one hand it has made every individual for his own sake more reluctant to slay his fellow, and on the other hand it has roused the whole community to punish the slayer.

—SIR JAMES FRAZER, *Man, God, and Immorality*, 1927

4

Scarlet fever is an acute, highly contagious disease caused by the exotoxins elaborated by certain type-specific hemolytic streptococci.

THE CRITICISM OF AN ANALYSIS OF CAUSES

The writer who is searching for the causes of an effect and the reader who is reviewing the causes he himself has formulated or that another writer has formulated face a common problem. It is to make certain that the causes are so inextricably linked with the effect that they fully explain it, and hence are not false. Four principles guide them in determining the value of any cause.

First, the cause includes all the essential factors present in the cause-and-effect relationship, not merely one if there are others as well. The person who says, "I sat in a draft and caught a cold," meaning that his sitting in a draft has caused his cold, disregards this principle. Sitting in a draft, as a single cause, cannot produce a cold. Essential to the effect, a cold, are the presence of a cold virus and lowered resistance. Sitting in the draft may have lowered resistance, and thus have been contributory to the state of affairs, but alone it could not have brought on a cold.

Does the writer of the following causal analysis omit any essential, indispensable factors?

The automobile accident on the night of November 3 resulted from natural circumstances, a broken rail, and the negligence of the driver. The road up a long hill, dangerous under ordinary conditions, was covered with ice, and twenty feet of the guard rail broken in an earlier accident had not been repaired. These factors alone need not have caused the accident. Because of the high speed of the car, however, it failed to round a curve halfway up the hill and fell to the bottom of a creek fifty feet below the road.

Second, the cause of an event or a condition can be found only in the essential factors, the indispensable antecedents of the event or the condition. This principle requires a full knowledge of the circumstances under which an effect appears. To say that a phase of the moon produces abundant crops is to disregard the qualities of the seed and the soil, the weather, and the cultivation. All are factors which contribute directly to the yield.

How valid are the causes given in the following paragraph?

Plants growing in a greenhouse are usually larger and healthier than those growing under natural conditions. In the greenhouse, the amount of direct sunlight, or its artificial equivalent, may be measured. The temperature needed for the best growth of different plants may be regulated exactly by a central heating or cooling system. Here also other hardy vegetation which might crowd out the more delicate plant is weeded out and food materials are added to the soil.

The last two points, weeding and fertilizing the soil, are not essential factors in greenhouse culture. As stated, they are not causes of the larger growth of greenhouse plants. In this instance, the writer has included not too few, as in the effect of the moon on crops, but too many causal factors.

Third, the fact that one event follows another does not mean that the first causes the second. A causal relationship exists between the two only when the nonoccurrence of the second after the first can be shown to be inconsistent with natural processes. This principle makes evident the value of experimentation. The consequences of the modification of possible causal factors on the effect helps to isolate the true cause. If the effect never occurs when one causal factor is absent but always occurs when it is present, or varies as the factor varies, that factor is the cause or a part of the cause. In a season of drought, rain may fall immediately after the rainmaker stretches his arms over a body of water or prays. Some may consequently interpret those acts as causes of rain. Stretching the arms and praying came directly before the rain, but for that reason did not cause it. Rain falls when there are no prayers for it and no outstretched arms. And it does not always fall when prayers are said and arms are outstretched. The cause of rain must be sought not in the timing of ritual but in a complex of atmospheric conditions.

Fourth, the cause must not be confused with the inciting event. World War I was not the result of the assassination of the Archduke Ferdinand; World War II, of the invasion of Poland.

In summary, the writer and the reader alike may test the value of an analysis of causes by examining it in the light of these four principles:

1. The cause must be inclusive; it must name all factors essential to the occurrence of the effect.

2. It must be restricted to the essential and indispensable

antecedents of the effect. It must not be expanded to include irrelevant and tangential circumstantial details.
3. The necessity of the occurrence of an effect after a cause and not a mere sequence in time determines a cause.
4. Inciting events are insufficient explanations of a cause-and-effect relationship.

Exercise I

Evaluate each of the following causal analysis. Suggest ways in which those you find faulty may be improved.

1

The First National Bank closed last week because the depositors had withdrawn over 75 per cent of their money. Because of this situation the directors of the bank saw fit to withhold all further payments to depositors. Upon a majority vote, they closed the bank.

2

The First World War was supposed to be fought to make the world safe for democracy. Is it impossible to suppose that it was fought because Germany was taking too much trade away from England? England was getting worried over Germany's increasing navy, and so decided to curb her power before it became too strong.

3

In the spring of 1812 there marched into Russia the greatest armament Europe had ever seen—the Grand Army of France commanded by Napoleon Bonaparte. Lured on by the strange Russian tactics of forever retreating, the French were led deeper and deeper into hostile territory, and farther and farther from their base of supplies. Upon reaching Moscow, Napoleon was in a position so remote that it was virtually impossible to obtain supplies from his Polish bases, and in retreating the Russians had stripped the country of all possible forage. Even so the "great general" committed the final and fatal error by staying on, always hoping for a Russian surrender. When retreat became inevitable, it was too late; the dreaded Russian winter had set in.

4

The causes of conflict among social classes are many and varied.

Primary among them, however, are the jealousies existing over possession of jobs. Also of great strength as a stimulus for conflict are the
prejudices associated with differences in color and race. Immigration
population directly affects the intensity of intraclass conflict. Apart
from economic and racial causes is that of discrepancy in religious
beliefs.

5

The Euglena, a unicellular animal, often encysts and is nonmotile
for a period. This encystment is caused by a change in condition of
natural habitat. A change in the temperature of the water inhabited,
evaporation of this essential compound, or a scarcity of food brings on
the state.

EXERCISE II

The following passage is a criticism of a causal analysis. Summarize
the points made in it. Then name the four standards or criteria of
causal anlysis which the writer has applied to his subject matter. Cite
specific illustrations of their use.

One of the outstanding facts in nature is the mutual fitness of the
organism and its environment. So much impressed have men been with
this fact, that they have commonly explained it as the result of intelligent design. The argument is, according to Paley, somewhat as follows:
A watch is ideally adapted to keep time. Every part has a definite and a
necessary function and all are co-ordinated into a unit. An organism is
in many respects like a watch and it is natural to explain the adaptiveness of both watch and organism in the same way. Since the watch is
obviously the result of intelligent design, the organism is accounted for
as a product of a purposed plan. Now if all nature were adaptive and
every part of an organism were as fit as the parts of a watch, the argument from design might hold. But examples of non-adaptive or even
detrimental structures and functions are extremely numerous. Man is
no worse off in this respect than any other organism, yet man has many
poorly adapted or non-adaptive structures.

Think of man's vermiform appendix that is not only useless but
often a source of grave danger and death; think of his useless ear muscles that are all present but can accomplish no useful function; think of
the functionless breasts of males; think of the vestigial tail, the ill-
adapted wisdom teeth, and many other obviously non-adaptive human
structures. Does it seem reasonable to suppose that these useless structures were designed in their present form? If some parts of an organism
are obviously not designed, is it likely that others were designed and

that the useless parts merely slipped in by mistake? Such considerations as these, and others equally conclusive, make it impossible for us, as seekers after the truth, to accept the view that adaptation in nature is the result of intelligent design.

The over-enthusiastic followers of Charles Darwin are responsible for a greatly exaggerated emphasis upon the adaptiveness of organisms. They went so far as to assume that, because a group of animals or plants is alive and apparently prosperous, every part of the body and all of its responses to stimuli must be adaptive. When critical examination of many species was undertaken, the fact emerged that nature is full of examples of unfitness. Instances of non-adaptive characters mounted up to such an imposing total that some extremists have openly stated that the concept of adaptation in nature is a myth, that man has merely read into nature most of its adaptiveness. The opponents of the idea of adaptation call our attention to the utterly planless course of embryonic development. Instead of proceeding steadily forward as a planned project should, the whole process is one of building up, tearing down, discarding, and remodeling. We are reminded that many insects carry useless and burdensome encumbrances, that many colors are present in organisms that never see the light, that there are many harmful instincts such as that of the moth for the flame. The natural conclusion from this line of argument would be that real adaptiveness is relatively rare in nature, and what little there is, is largely accidental. Such a view leaves little for the evolutionist to explain.

A sounder view is one that attempts to take a well-balanced middle ground between the worship of and complete scepticism about adaptation. Even though every organism possesses some unfit characters it seems certain that in every normal organism there must be some credit margin of fitness, else it could not survive. When we realize that the organic world is only relatively fit and that there exists much room for improvement, we are more likely to be open-minded as to the necessity of a naturalistic explanation of whatever adaptive characters organisms actually possess.

—HORATIO HACKETT NEWMAN, "The Factors of Organic Evolution,"
The Nature of the World and of Man, 1926

EXERCISE III

In light of the four principles named in this chapter, criticize the two following causal analyses.

1

The Greek revival, first introduced into America by Latrobe, was in the beginning simply one phase of a movement which was afoot in Europe. The drawings of the buildings on the Acropolis, by Stuart and Revett, had stirred the English imagination in the latter half of the eighteenth century and had inspired an increasing use of Greek ornament and the Greek orders. In Germany, Winckelmann's studies of Greek art had aroused a widespread enthusiasm and—what was more important—had profoundly affected the development of Goethe, who owed to the writings of the older man much of his large and serene habit of thought. Goethe and Schiller both wrote plays in the classic style, and Goethe chose the classic hexameter for his beautiful *Roman Elegies.* The builders followed the poets, and the Greek revival in the German-speaking nations proceeded with true German regard for scholarly correctness, resulting in a number of monumental buildings which faithfully reproduced the letter of the Greek orders without recapturing even a glimmer of the Greek spirit. In France, Napoleon as Emperor saw in himself a reincarnation of Alexander and sought, powerfully abetted by artists and writers, to impose a whole Imperial art based on a conception of classicism that remained much more French than Greek.

—SUZANNE LA FOLLETTE, *Art in America,* 1929

2

New York has lagged behind the entire country in providing off-the-street parking in the congested area. For various reasons, some of them far from creditable to city officials, open-air parking lots have been rigidly limited in number and this in turn has resulted in high fees—too high for many automobile owners. There is some surplus space available in garages, but these are unpopular with the public for several good reasons: with most of them, parking fees are high, entrance and exit are difficult, locations are inconvenient, their rooms are dark and dirty and attendants are almost uniformly discourteous and careless. Ten years later than they should have done so, the city authorities are now beginning to discuss creating additional parking facilities on vacant lots and in unused buildings. Among the devices at which they are looking is the "ferris-wheel" parking machine through whose use eight or ten cars can be parked in a space not much larger than one of them would occupy resting on the ground.

Trucks and other commercial vehicles, engaged in loading operations, are responsible for a great part of New York's congestion. It is they that cause most of the double parking and slow down traffic by backing into the curb, with the front of the truck extending nearly halfway across the street. To an innocent bystander it is hard to see why the city authorities make almost no attack on this aspect of the situation. A large part of the loading work could just as easily be done at night, or in the early morning, and only habit and inertia prevent this. If the authorities were to issue two types of truck licenses, one of them good only at night and costing much less than the other, or were otherwise to discourage deliveries during the business day, they could clear up much congestion in a short time.

Chicago has solved the traffic snarl in the heart of the city by entirely forbidding curb parking in the Loop district. Although department-store owners in this area protested violently when the plan was proposed, I am informed that after several years' trial they are highly pleased with the result. The owners of New York's stores, however, are still the victims of traditionalism. Although careful studies indicate that less than five per cent of their customers come in private automobiles, and although congestion in the streets is certainly doing them harm, they are fighting vigorously against nearly all proposals to curtail parking. . . .

It is common observation that cruising taxicabs constitute an extremely serious contribution to the overcrowding of New York's streets. The estimate was made some time ago that there are twice as many cabs as the traffic requires. Drivers get miserably low wages and cab users suffer, with everyone else, from the traffic blockade. For this situation the automobile manufacturers are primarily to blame: they produce an unreasonably large number of taxis and dump them into New York streets on almost any terms. It has often been suggested that New York should license only a sensible number of cabs, and follow London's example by requiring these two wait at fixed points for passengers instead of roaming the streets. . . .

All the palliatives enumerated, if applied simultaneously and vigorously, would bring some degree of improvement; but they are not of course the final answer to the question. That final answer is to be found in city, regional and national planning. It is not at all unlikely that New York is larger than—perhaps twice as large as it ought to be, unless it were to be entirely replanned, on an intelligent basis. It is possible that the most hopeful development for metropolitan traffic would be the St. Lawrence Canal project, which would divert a vast amount of business that now goes through New York, and that second to this would be consistent development of the entire port so that freight arriving from midwestern points would be loaded on ships along the Jersey shore and not trucked through Manhattan streets as so much of it now is. Much other decentralization is possible and desirable. Judging, however, from the attitude of the Chamber of Commerce and similar bodies, we are a generation away from having enough collective brains to desire a city of a reasonable size, and in the meantime, we shall go on with palliatives never sufficiently sweeping or applied in time, to give real relief to urban life.

—BRUCE BLIVEN, "The Traffic Catastrophe," *The New Republic,*
LXXXIX (1937), 296–97

TOPICS FOR PAPERS

1. Why _____ bank failed
2. Why _____ was not elected
3. The causes of some specific natural phenomenon: an earthquake, an epidemic; erosion; a cyclone; rain; an eclipse
4. The causes of an historical event: the Crusades; a specific war; the decline of an empire; modification of plans in your own life
5. The causes of a social condition: delinquency among children; migration of workers; a new interest in music; changes in subjects taught in schools

CHAPTER 9

Proof

Life is the art of drawing sufficient conclusions from insufficient premises.
—Samuel Butler, *Note Books*, 1912

In making clear to the reader the significance of any point, the writer may develop it in one or more ways. To avoid being abstract, he may give specific cases which illustrate his main idea. A proper amplification of his subject may require not only illustrations but also a comparison or a contrast. Similarly, as the preceding chapters have shown, analogy, analysis, classification, definition, and causal analysis are methods he may use in expanding his ideas and thus make their meaning fully known. These methods provide answers to such questions as "Can you give a case?" "How are they alike?" "How do they differ?" "What trait may things otherwise dissimilar share?" "What are its parts?" "What is it?" "What do the words mean?" "What causes it?" No less important is another question: "How do you know that what you say is true?" The answer to this question requires *proof*.

A discourse may provide a mere exchange of opinions. Its writer may wish to record his conclusions on varied subjects for what they are worth. The reader finds them interesting in that they reveal the nature of the writer and provide him an occasion to check his own ideas against those of another. Other discourses, however, state conclusions which the reader is expected to accept as true and, when occasion requires, to act upon them. When the writer makes a point or states a conclusion which he intends to be not a revelation of his personality but a contribution to man's store of useful knowledge and, consequently, which he expects his reader to accept and to act upon as a truth, he is obliged to state his reasons for believing the conclusion to be true. When his points are such that readers may justifiably hesitate to accept and to act upon them as true, he must offer proof of their truth if his discourse is to be sound. The reader of a newspaper story of a crime may to his own satisfaction hastily identify the guilty person. If he had to act upon that identification, however, to the point of passing sentence, if he were honest and just, he would first examine the evidence in greater detail and with closer scrutiny and, then, from that examination verify or reject his earlier conclusion. In such instances, the hasty conclusion of the superficial reader of the evidence is obviously less trustworthy as a basis for action than the conclusion of the judge and the jury who have examined it carefully.

Proof is not restricted to the guilt or the innocence of the accused. No assertion need be believed true until it is proved true. No conclusion need be accepted as probably true until evidence shows that it is. Even in the most casual conversation, speaker and hearer alike may recognize statements which are to be accepted as true, others which are to be rejected, and still others to be questioned until further evidence appears. When the temperature is below freezing, no motorist demands proof of the statement "Water freezes at 32°F." "He will live to be as old as Methuselah" is promptly interpreted as hyperbole; its truth, as an assertion to be taken literally, is rejected. The conclusion "The Democrats [or the Republicans] have ruined the country!" may likewise be rejected as an emotional flurry and hence, a proposition not worthy of debate. In contrast, however, the assertion that a particular plan of taxation or schedule of tariffs is desirable may be questioned and a show of evidence in support of it invited.

As he is preparing any discourse, the writer must recognize points which, to be developed effectively, require proof. Such points he must support by the evidence he has. The question "What assertions must I prove?" he can best answer in light of his purpose and the significance which his conclusions may have for his readers. The person who asserts that "Iron corrodes more rapidly than gold" is restating a well-recognized fact which the observation of generations has proved again and again. His readers will find it relevant to other comments he makes; they will not question its truthfulness. They can count on the two metals behaving as the statement says they will behave. In contrast, the person who asserts that "Battleships are an obsolete instrument of war" will have to support his statement, if it receives any series consideration, by the most conclusive evidence he can gather. His serious readers will want to know his purpose in holding such a conclusion. They will anticipate the possible consequences to their navies in battle if, in taking the assertion as true, they propose to build no more battleships.

In contrast to such statements intended as general truths or rules to be followed, stand those observations or conclusions which are not self-evident and established and which do not provide a basis for deciding what direction to take in planning an action. They require no proof because they reflect purely personal convictions and provide no basis for action by others. La Rochefoucauld does not have to prove his maxim, "Men talk little when vanity does not prompt them." He is merely expressing an opinion which he holds of men and not a truth they may follow in attaining desired ends.

EXERCISE

Which of the following statements require proof? Explain the circumstances which make proof necessary.

1. The criminal is guilty and must be hanged.
2. The passions are the only orators that always persuade.
3. The world was originally a whirling mass of hot gas.
4. "I'm not certain, but I'll say anyway that this is an edible mushroom, not a toadstool. Eat it."
5. We have more indolence in the mind than in the body.
6. Racial blending increases the vigor of succeeding generations.
7. The common cold is not infectious.

8. "This was true in our grandfathers' days and hence it is true to-day."
9. Good taste springs more from judgment than from intellect.
10. Environment, not inheritance, determines the characteristics of men.

After he has determined which of his statements require proof and which he can develop advantageously by proof, the writer faces a second question, "How may this assertion be proved?" Three common methods are available. First, he may prove his assertion by quoting or referring to an authority on the subject. He asks his readers to accept the statement as true because experts have found it true. Second, he may show that the assertion has proved to be true in a sufficiently large number of cases and that he has good reason to suppose it will be true in all cases. In this method, he moves from particular facts to a general conclusion or truth: water froze at $32°F.$ last century, last year, last month, last week, yesterday (the number of times the phenomenon was observed may be increased), consequently, he arrives at the general conclusion: water freezes at $32°F.$ This method is called inductive reasoning.

The third method, deductive reasoning, in contrast to inductive, moves from the general truth to the particular case. The conclusion "John is mortal" may be proved, deductively, from the general truth that all men are mortal. In its simplest form, deductive reasoning may be expressed in a syllogism, a scheme which includes three statements or propositions: a major premise, a minor premise, and a conclusion. The major premise states the general truth; the minor supplies a case; and the conclusion applies the general truth to the particular case.

> Major premise: All men are mortal.
> Minor premise: John is a man.
> Conclusion: John is mortal.

The middle or common term in the major and minor premises disappears in the conclusion. In this case, the middle term is man. The truth of this conclusion depends, as in any deduction, on the truth of the two premises. If they are true, the conclusion is true.

The writer, then, may prove an assertion in three ways:

1. By citing an authority or authorities
2. By induction
3. By deduction

The details of these methods may now be examined separately and with them, the tests by which the proof, when completed, may be criticized. If the writer's proof is faulty, both he and the reader will want to know that it is. How may they test any proof? Their own? Or that set forth by some one else? That question the criteria of proof will provide means for answering.

PROOF BY APPEAL TO AUTHORITY

Consider this statement: "The planet Neptune rotates from west to east once in 15.8 hours." In the following paragraph, that conclusion is recommended to the reader as the conclusion of authorities on astronomy:

This planet [Neptune] is 31,000 miles in diameter or about equal to Uranus. It is presumably cloud-covered, like the other three great planets. It rotates from west to east once in 15.8 hours, according to the spectroscopic studies of Moore and Menzel at Lick Observatory.
—ROBERT H. BAKER, *An Introduction to Astronomy,* 1930

In proving the importance of the annelid worm in the study of the animal kingdom, the author of the following passage quotes Charles Darwin:

If one were to be limited to studying a single representative of all the animal kingdom, he had best choose an annelid worm. But earthworms are of much more importance to man than merely as convenient laboratory representatives of this median phylum. Pasteur found that they bring up disease germs from the bodies of buried animals and so start epidemics. Charles Darwin busied himself with their general activities and concludes his readable booklet on *Vegetable Mould and Earthworms* as follows:
When we behold a wide, turf-covered expanse, we should remember that its smoothness on which so much of its beauty depends, is mainly due to all the inequalities having been slowly leveled by worms. It is a marvelous reflection that the whole of the superficial mould has passed and will pass, every few years, through the bodies of worms. The plough is one of man's oldest inventions; but long before he existed the land was in fact regularly ploughed by earthworms. It may

be doubted whether there are many other animals which have played so important a part in the history of the world as have these lowly organized creatures.

—W. C. ALLEE, "Evolution of the Invertebrates," *The Nature of the World and of Man,* 1927

In both these illustrative passages the authorities cited to substantiate the writers' statements have based their conclusions on observations and study. They have checked their conclusions, perhaps inductively, against natural phenomena; they are acknowledged experts in their fields. Their word constitutes a reasonable proof, although, obviously, anyone, the reader included, is free to examine the evidence, to investigate further, and to defend another conclusion if he chooses to do so. The word of these authorities need not be accepted blindly and unquestioningly.

The appeal to such authorities differs from the appeal to authorities who are, in contrast, considered as infallible and unexceptionable. Tyrants, in political systems, for instance, demand of their subjects an unquestioning acceptance of their statements and commands; they assume no obligation to prove them true. They attempt to standardize and stabilize beliefs. With total domination over their subjects, they may perpetuate error as readily and as easily as truth.

THE CRITERIA OF PROOF BY APPEAL TO AUTHORITY

Proof which centers in the judgment of an authority must be viewed in the light of the qualifications of that authority. His experiences and accomplishments must be of such nature that his judgments are respected if the proof is to have any validity at all. The conclusion of a person who is totally ignorant of the subject on which he speaks is worthless. To test the value of proof by appeal to authority, one must answer four questions:

1. What training and experience has the authority had in the field of which he speaks?
2. Is he widely recognized as an expert in the subject?
3. Is he living? If dead, when did he live? Has the body of knowledge with which he concerned himself changed since his lifetime?
4. Does (or did) he view the material as fully and as objectively

as possible? Do (or did) his judgments reflect prejudices and
bias or a disinterested concern with the subject?
Biographical dictionaries will supply the information which these
questions require.

EXERCISE I

Answer the four "value ot proof" questions about both the
American astronomers, Joseph Haines Moore and D. H. Menzel,
and Charles Darwin, the authorities cited in the first two examples
of proof by authority.

When the intelligent reader takes exception to the conclusion of
the authority, he usually presents new evidence, or counterarguments. For example, in defending the view that in *King Lear*
Shakespeare might well have permitted Lear and Cordelia to live,
Bradley says:

When Lamb—there is no higher authority—writes, 'A happy ending!
as if the living martyrdom that Lear had gone through, the flaying of
his feelings alive, did not make a fair dismissal from the stage of life the
only decorous thing for him,' I answer, first, that it is precisely this *fair*
dismissal which we desire for him instead of renewed anguish; and,
secondly, that what we desire for him during the brief remainder of his
days is not 'the childish pleasure of getting his gilt robes and sceptre
again,' . . . but what Shakespeare himself might have given him—peace
and contentment by Cordelia's fireside. And if I am told that he has
suffered too much for this, how can I possibly believe it with these
words ringing in my ears:
    Come, let's away to prison:
  We two alone will sing like birds i' the cage.
  When thou dost ask me blessing, I'll kneel down,
  And ask of thee forgiveness: so we'll live,
  And pray, and sing, and tell old tales, and laugh
  At gilded butterflies?
                        —A. C. BRADLEY, *Shakespearean Tragedy*, 1929

In his Bank Veto message, Andrew Jackson answered in the

following words those who justified the bank by appeal to precedent and the decision of the Supreme Court. The passage is essentially a criticism of a proof based on authority:

It is maintained by the advocates of the bank that its constitutionali-
ty in all its features ought to be considered as settled by precedent and
by the decision of the Supreme Court. To this conclusion I can not
assent. Mere precedent is a dangerous source of authority, and should
not be regarded as deciding questions of constitutional power except
where the acquiescence of the people and the States can be considered
as well settled. So far from this being the case on this subject, an argument against the bank might be based on precedent. One Congress, in
1791, decided in favor of a bank; another, in 1811, decided against it.
One Congress in 1815, decided against a bank; another in 1816, decided
in its favor. Prior to the present Congress, therefore, the precedents
drawn from that source were equal. If we resort to the States, the expressions of legislative, judicial, and executive opinions against the bank
have been probably to those in its favor as 4 to 1. There is nothing in
precedent, therefore, which, if its authority were admitted, ought to
weigh in favor of the act before me.
          —ANDREW JACKSON, Bank Veto Message, July 10, 1832

EXERCISE II

Evaluate the proof given in each of the following appeals to authority.

1

So far are the suggestions of Montesquieu from standing in opposition to a general Union of the States, that he explicitly treats of a
Confederate Republic as the expedient for extending the sphere of
popular government, and reconciling the advantages of monarchy with
those of republicanism.

It is very probable (says he), that mankind would have been
obliged at length to live constantly under the government of a single
person, had they not contrived a kind of constitution that has all the
internal advantages of a republican, together with the external force
of a monarchial government. I mean a Confederate Republic.

This form of government is a convention by which several smaller
states agree to become members of a larger *one*, which they intend to
form. It is a kind of assemblage of societies that constitute a new
one, capable of increasing, by means of new associations, till they
arrive to such a degree of power as to be able to provide for the
security of the united body.

A republic of this kind, able to withstand an external force, may support itself without any internal corruptions. The form of this society prevents all manner of inconveniences.

If a single member should attempt to usurp the supreme authority, he could not be supposed to have an equal authority and credit in all the confederate states. Were he to have too great influence over one, this would alarm the rest. Were he to subdue a part, that which would still remain free might oppose him with forces independent of those which he had usurped, and overpower him before he could be settled in his usurpation.

Should a popular insurrection happen in one of the confederate states, the others are able to quell it. Should abuses creep into one part, they are reformed by those that remain sound. The state may be destroyed on one side, and not on the other; the confederacy may be dissolved, and the confederates preserve their sovereignty.

As this government is composed of small republics, it enjoys the internal happiness of each; and with respect to its external situation, it is possessed, by means of the association, of all the advantages of large monarchies.

I have thought it proper to quote at length these interesting passages, because they contain a luminous abridgment of the principal arguments in favor of the Union, and must effectually remove the false impressions which a misapplication of other parts of the work was calculated to make. They have, at the same time, an intimate connection with the more immediate design of this paper; which is, to illustrate the tendency of the Union to repress domestic faction and insurrection.

—ALEXANDER HAMILTON, *The Federalist,* No. 9, November 21, 1787

2

And seeing God hath said, *He that Stealeth a Man and Selleth him, or if he be found in his hand, he shall surely be put to Death. Exod.* 21.16. This Law being of Everlasting Equity, wherein Man Stealing is ranked amongst the most atrocious of Capital Crimes: What louder Cry can there be made of that Celebrated Warning, *"Caveat Emptor."*

—SAMUEL SEWALL, *The Selling of Joseph,* 1700

EXERCISE III

State the principles or the assumptions on which the critics of authorities in the following passages base their counterarguments. What proposition does Jonson, in the first, oppose to that of the Aristotelian schoolmen? What proposition does Inge, in the second, oppose to the exponents of the ideas of progress and the perfectibility of man?

1

Nothing is more ridiculous than to make an author a dictator, as the schools have done Aristotle. The damage is infinite knowledge receives by it; for to many things a man should owe but a temporary belief, and a suspension of his own judgment, not an absolute resignation of himself, or a perpetual captivity. Let Aristotle and others have their dues; but if we can make farther discoveries of truth and fitness than they, why are we envied? Let us beware, while we strive to add, we do not diminish, or deface; we may improve, but not augment. By discrediting falsehood, truth grows in request. We must not go about, like men anguished and perplexed, for vicious affectation of praise: but calmly study the separation of opinions, find the errors have intervened, awake antiquity, call former times into question; but make no parties with the present, nor follow any fierce undertakers, mingle no matter of doubtful credit with the simplicity of truth, but gently stir the mould about the root of the question. . . .

—BEN JONSON, *Timber, or Discoveries*, 1641

2

. . . we observe with astonishment that many leading men in Queen Victoria's reign found it possible to use the great biological discovery of Darwin to tyrannize over the minds of their contemporaries, to give their blessing to the economic and social movements of their time, and to unite determinism with teleology. . . . Scientific optimism was no doubt rampant before Darwin. For example, Herschel says: "Man's progress towards a higher state need never fear a check, but must continue till the very last existence of history." But Herbert Spencer asserts the perfectibility of man with an assurance which makes us gasp. "Progress is not an accident but a necessity. What we call evil and immorality must disappear. It is certain that man must become perfect." "The ultimate development of the ideal man is certain—as certain as any conclusion in which we place the most implicit faith; for instance, that all men will die." "Always toward perfection is the mighty movement—towards a complete development and a more unmixed good."

—WILLIAM RALPH INGE, *Outspoken Essays: Second Series*, 1922

PROOF BY INDUCTIVE REASONING

Proof by authority makes use of the confidence which readers have in the authority cited. If readers know him to be both learned and truthful, they will accept his judgments as significant and, in all probability, true. They will expect to find in their observations and experiences what he says they will find. They will believe what he says, for he does not assert as fact what he knows is not fact or what he has reason to doubt is fact. They may accept his statements as true without direct evidence, but they take for granted that he has examined the evidence.

Proof by inductive reasoning requires direct observation of the evidence. The persistence of a fact in case after case, observed under varying circumstances, strongly suggests that a generalization which applies to all similar cases, and not merely to the many observed, may be assumed to be true. A generalization arrived at from a study of particular cases may not always represent an absolute truth, but it represents a high degree of probability. Mornings may come when the sun does not rise, but the experiences of generations of men have thus far confirmed the truth of the assertion "The sun rises every morning." The very first men who lived on earth had greater reason to doubt the truth of the statement "All men die" than anyone now living, because they had not observed a sufficient number of cases to generalize from. Less acquainted with the certainty of death than we, they might have supposed that a member of the next generation could live on forever.

Observe in the following passage the movement from particular cases to the general conclusion: "Eating unpeeled fruits and vegetables which have been sprayed with lead arsenate may lead to irreparable injury."

Six thousand poisonings, 70 deaths in England in the year 1900, from beer containing small quantities of arsenic . . . Three hundred French sailors poisoned early in 1932 by wine contaminated with arsenic . . . A girl, aged seven, killed by arsenic fumes from dye in moldy wall paper . . . Six persons poisoned in California in 1931 by greens sprayed with lead arsenate . . . A four-year-old Philadelphia girl dead, in August, 1932, from eating sprayed fruit. With a background of cases like these, are you willing to have even very small doses of arsenic, a deadly poison, administered to you and your children daily, perhaps several times daily? Willing or not, if you eat apples, pears, cherries and berries, celery, and other fruit and vegetables, you are also eating arsenic, and there is good reason to believe that it may be doing you serious, perhaps irreparable injury.

The source of this dangerous poison is the lead arsenate which is sprayed on fruits and on some vegetables to protect them from the coddling moth and other insects destructive to crops. It is extensively used, especially in the Western States, which produce our most attrac-

tive and unblemished fruits. A residue of arsenic and lead remains on the fruit, and when you wash your apple or pear under the faucet you remove only a small part of the poison.
—ARTHUR KALLET and F. J. SCHLINK, *100,000,000 Guinea Pigs*, 1932

What observable phenomena support the conclusion that, relative to landmarks among the stars, the earth and not the sun moves in a great orbit?

That, relative to landmarks among the stars, it is the earth and not the sun that moves in a great orbit is shown by three different phenomena, the discovery of which required exact measurements with instruments that were not available until long after the time of Copernicus. These are the aberration of light, discovered by the English astronomer Bradley in 1727; the annual parallactic displacement of the nearer stars, first detected by Bessel in Germany in 1837; and the annually periodic variation in the radial velocity of stars, which has been observed since the first work of Sir William Huggins on stellar spectra in 1864.   —JOHN CHARLES DUNCAN, *Astronomy*, 1935

How did the American colonists conclude, inductively, that George III sought to establish an absolute tyranny over them? Their reasoning is evident in the Declaration of Independence:

The history of the present King of Great Britain is a history of repeated injuries and usurpations, all having in direct object the establishment of an absolute Tyranny over these States. To prove this let Facts be submitted to a candid world. He has refused his Assent to Laws, the most wholesome and necessary for the public good. He has forbidden his Governors to pass Laws of immediate and pressing importance, unless suspended in their operation till his Assent should be obtained; and when so suspended, he has utterly neglected to attend to them . . . He has called together legislative bodies at places unusual, uncomfortable, and distant from the depository of their public Records, for the sole purpose of fatiguing them into compliance with his measures. He has dissolved Representative Houses repeatedly for opposing with manly firmness his invasions on the rights of the people . . . He has plundered our seas, ravaged our coasts, burnt our towns, and destroyed the lives of our people . . . He has excited domestic insurrections amongst us, and has endeavoured to bring on the inhabitants of our frontiers, the merciless Indian Savages, whose known rule of warfare, is an undistinguished destruction of all ages, sexes and conditions. In every stage of these oppressions We have Petitioned for Redress in the most humble terms: Our repeated Petitions have been answered only by repeated injury. A Prince, whose character is thus marked by every act which may define a Tyrant, is unfit to be the ruler of a free people.

—THE DECLARATION OF INDEPENDENCE, July 4, 1776

THE CRITERIA OF PROOF BY INDUCTIVE REASONING

To test the value of a generalization from a sampling of cases, the writer and reader alike may ask eight questions. The answers to them will indicate the validity of the conclusion. The eight follow:

1. Did the speaker or writer examine the subject matter on which his generalization is based hastily and superficially or carefully?
2. Was the observer prejudiced and biased or disinterested at the time of the observation?
3. Is there, in the record of the observation, any indication of a tendency to disregard, elaborate, distort, or misinterpret the evidence?
4. Have others confirmed the observation? Can they?
5. Are the conclusions of the observation consistent with tested knowledge of the subject? Does new evidence support all divergent or conflicting interpretations?
6. Is the generalization based on an adequate number of cases?
7. Have cases been observed at different times and places under varying circumstances?
8. Have cases which contradict the conclusion been found?

A proper precautionary attitude in generalizing from particulars is evident in the following passage:

Immigration and the consequent mingling of the races in the melting-pot of America, together with the fusion of whites and blacks, presents a problem of great complexity. The eugenist wishes that he possessed sufficient accurate knowledge of the effcts of racial blends to prophesy the outcome, or intelligently to direct its progress. Goddard found from the examination of 148 emigrant Hungarians, Italians, Jews, and Russians, at Ellis Island, that only two scored as high as 12 years on intelligence tests. It is evident that the admission of such inferior classes is detrimental. Eugene Fischer studied the effects of crosses between Boer men and Hottentot women in a hybrid population of 3,000. MacCaughey studied the effects of racial mixtures in Hawaii, Mjoen examined the results of crosses between Norwegian

Nordics and Lapland Mongoloids, Lundberg investigated hybrid races in Sweden. In general, the conclusion is that while the first generation may show increased vigor due to the hybridization, succeeding generations manifest many physical and mental deteriorations that lead to early death, to crime, and to insanity. Admittedly, our knowledge of the whole problem is too limited to prophesy the outcome of particular crossings.

—ELLIOT R. DOWNING, "Human Inheritance," *The Nature of the World and of Man,* 1926, pp. 438–439

EXERCISE I

The eight questions which provide a test for a generalization based on the observation of phenomena may now be applied to a specific case. Can man prove, inductively, that there can or cannot be a spontaneous generation of life in nature? The following passage summarizes briefly the history of speculation on this subject. Observe in it the increasing complexity of cases and the decreasing certainty of the truthfulness of an absolute answer. Questions which refer directly to the eight criteria follow the passage.

The early Greek and Roman natural philosophers and poets agreed that new life is constantly arising spontaneously or through supernatural intervention. Even as late as the sixteenth century Van Helmont, a famous physicist and chemist, concocted a recipe for engendering scorpions. He said:

Scoop out a hole in a brick, put in some sweet basil, crushed. Lay a second brick upon the first so that the hole may be perfectly covered. Expose the two bricks to the sun, and at the end of a few days, the smell of sweet basil, acting as a ferment, will change the earth into real scorpions.

This type of belief was common to all until late in the sixteenth century when Redi disproved the current doctrine that maggots were engendered from the juices of decaying meat. He simply put a screen over a vessel of meat, thus excluding the flies, and found that no maggots appeared on the meat. The eggs of the flies, however, that were laid on the screen hatched out into maggots. Although the experiments of Redi discredited belief in the spontaneous generation of larger organisms, the idea that bacteria and other microscopic organisms developed *de novo* in nutritive media persisted until the middle of the nineteenth century when Louis Pasteur showed its untenability. By simple processes of sterilizing nutritive media by heat and preventing the ingress of spores he proved that, unless bacteria are introduced, nutritive media remain permanently free from them, and that no organisms arise spontaneously in them. The work of Pasteur has been amply confirmed by many other experimenters with the result that it may be said that there is no scientific evidence for spontaneous generation and much against it. Yet it would be dogmatic to deny that any of the very lowest expressions of life, such as the filtrable viruses or even simpler molecular complexes just beyond the borders of protoplasmic organization, may be arising *de novo* today. So eminent an authority as T. C. Chamberlain holds that life may be making new starts even today, but that the available materials for the maintenance of such compounds are everywhere pre-empted by the ever-present forms of life already in existence. Hence new life substances are robbed of their opportunity to realize their developmental possibilities. It is unsafe, then, to conclude that life cannot, under favorable conditions, arise by natural processes of synthesis even today. All we can be sure of is that no such origin has yet been observed in nature nor induced in the laboratory.

The fact that man has not succeeded in making a new living organism nor observed the spontaneous generation of life in nature, does not drive us to a supernatural origin of life. We are frank to admit that as yet we do not know just how, when, and where life began on earth, but we are not yet ready to abandon hope of the ultimate scientific solution of the problem.

> —HORATIO HACKETT NEWMAN, "The Nature and Origin of Life," *The Nature of the World and of Man*, 1926

1. Which of the theorists mentioned examined the problem most carefully: the early Greek and Roman natural philosophers? Van Helmont? Redi? Pasteur? Chamberlain? (More than one may be named.)
2. Would a person who insisted, after Redi's experiments, that maggots were engendered from decaying meat be prejudiced and biased or disinterested?
3. When the microscope was invented, the theory of the spontaneous origin of living matter was revived. By looking at liquids through it observers saw microorganisms, or infusoria, which they said the "putrescible" liquid had generated. Were they disregarding evidence, distorting it, or misinterpreting it?
4. To what extent have others confirmed Pasteur's conclusion that no organisms arise spontaneously in nutritive media?
5. Before Pasteur's experiments, investigators had destroyed living organisms in "putrescible" liquids by boiling the liquids in *closed* tubes. Those who held to the older theory said that the boiling had changed the generative power of the fluids. What new evidence did Pasteur advance to answer this objection? His description of the experiment, which follows, contains the answer to this question. What is it?

I place a portion of the infusion into a flask with a long neck. . . . Suppose I boil the liquid and leave it to cool. After a few days mouldiness or animalculae will develop in the liquid. By boiling I destroyed any germs in the liquid or against the glass; but the infusion being again in contact with air, it becomes altered as all infusions do. Now suppose I repeat this experiment, but that before boiling the liquid I draw the neck of the flask into a point, leaving, however, its extremity open. . . . Now the liquid of this second flask will remain pure. . . . What difference is there between these two vases? . . . The only difference between them is this: in the first case the dusts suspended in air and their germs can fall into the neck of the bottle and come into contact with the liquid, where they find appropriate food and develop. Thence microscopic beings. In the second flask, on the contrary, it is impossible, or at least extremely difficult, unless air is violently shaken, that dusts suspended in air should enter the vase. They fall on its curved neck. . . . if I shake the vase violently two or three times in a few days it contains animalculae or mouldiness. Why? Because air has come in violently enough to carry dust with it.

6. Did Pasteur consider the cases of filtrable viruses or even simpler molecular complexes?
7. To show that "the dusts suspended in atmospheric air are the exclusive origin, the necessary condition of life in infusions," Pasteur examined the air in the streets of Paris, in his cellar, in the country, and on glaciers in the Alps. Why?
8. What types of cases must be demonstrated to contradict Pasteur's findings?

EXERCISE II

The conclusion in the passage given below has been reached inductively. First, state that conclusion. Second, list the cases given to support it. Third, evaluate the proof.

Why was it that the Indian trader passed so rapidly across the continent? What effects followed from the trader's frontier? The trade was coeval with American discovery. The Norsemen, Vespucci, Verrazani, Hudson, John Smith, all trafficked for furs. The Plymouth pilgrims settled in Indian cornfields, and their first return cargo was of beaver and lumber. The records of the various New England colonies show how steadily exploration was carried into the wilderness by this trade. What is true for New England is, as would be expected, even plainer for the rest of the colonies. All along the coast from Maine to Georgia the Indian trade opened up the river courses. Steadily the trader passed westward, utilizing the older lines of French trade. The Ohio, the Great Lakes, the Mississippi, the Missouri, and the Platte, the lines of

western advance, were ascended by traders. They found the passes in the Rocky Mountains and guided Lewis and Clark, Fremont, and Bidwell. The explanation of the rapidity of this advance is connected with the effects of the trader on the Indian. The trading post left the unarmed tribes at the mercy of those that had purchased fire-arms—a truth which the Iroquois Indians wrote in blood, and so the remote and unvisited tribes gave eager welcome to the trader. "The savages," wrote La Salle, "take better care of the French than of their own children; from us only can they get guns and goods." This accounts for the trader's power and the rapidity of his advance.
—FREDERICK JACKSON TURNER, *The Frontier in American History*, 1920

PROOF BY DEDUCTIVE REASONING

In the third method of proof, deduction, the truth of a statement is established, not by particular cases, as in induction, but by general principles. If the statements from which a conclusion is deduced are true, the conclusion is true. Max Müller illustrates the power of brutes to compare and distinguish by citing the ability of the parrot.

A parrot will take up a nut and throw it down again, without attempting to crack it. He has found that it is light. This he could discover only by comparing the weight of the good nuts with that of the bad. And he has found that it has no kernel. This he could discover only by what philosophers would dignify with the grand title of syllogism; namely, "All light nuts are hollow; this is a light nut; therefore, this nut is hollow."

MAX MULLER, *Lectures on the Science of Language*, 1865

The parrot, in this statement, has employed two types of reasoning. He has examined the comparative weights of good and bad nuts in a sufficient number of cases to generalize, inductively, that all light nuts are hollow. With the truth of that major proposition clearly in mind, he need not trouble himself to crack open any light nut he picks up. He can conclude, deductively, even syllogistically, that it will not contain the kernel he wants. Should he by chance, however, discover a light nut with a kernel, his major premise, "All light nuts are hollow," would not be true and his conclusion would not be true.

Observe the deductive method in this passage:

In 1869 the Russian chemist, Mendeléeff, gave the world the first complete expression . . . of the periodic law which, in his own words, stated: "all of the properties of the elements, both physical and chemical, vary as a periodic function of their atomic weights." With the aid of his great generalization, Mendeléeff was able to predict the occurrence of three still unknown elements, their atomic weights, where they probably would be found, and what their properties would be. Within less than twenty years thereafter, all three of these elements were discovered.

—JULIUS STIEGLITZ, "The Nature of Chemical Processes,"
The Nature of the World and of Man, 1926

The following passage employs deduction to prove the value of public education. Point out in the first paragraph the two premises and the conclusion. The second paragraph of the passage below may be reduced to a disjunctive syllogism. The major premise of a disjunctive syllogism states alternatives which are exhaustive and reciprocally exclusive. For example, "This solution contains either lead or mercury" is a disjunctive proposition. The syllogism is completed by a minor premise and a conclusion. Thus, minor premise: "It does not contain mercury"; conclusion: "Therefore, it contains lead." Summarize in the form of a disjunctive syllogism the argument in the second paragraph.

This is my argument. It is the duty of the Government to protect our persons and property from danger. The gross ignorance of the common people is a principal cause of danger to our persons and property. Therefore, it is the duty of the Government to take care that the common people shall not be grossly ignorant.

And what is the alternative? It is universally allowed that, by some means, Government must protect our persons and property. If you take away education, what means do you leave? You leave means such as only necessity can justify, means which inflict a fearful amount of pain not only on the guilty, but on the innocent who are connected with the guilty. You leave guns and bayonets, stocks and whipping-posts, solitary cells, penal colonies, gibbets. See then how the case stands. Here is an end which, as we all agree, governments are bound to attain. There are only two ways of attaining it. One of those ways is by making men better, and wiser, and happier. The other is by making them infamous and miserable. Can it be doubted which we ought to prefer? Is it not strange, is it not almost incredible, that pious and benevolent men should gravely propose the doctrine that the magistrate is bound to punish and at the same time bound not to teach? To me it seems quite clear that whoever has a right to hang has a right to educate. Can we think without shame and remorse that more than half of those wretches who have been tied up at Newgate in our time might have been living happily, that more than half of those who are now in our gaols might have been enjoying liberty and using that liberty well, that such a hell on earth as Norfolk Island need never have existed, if we had expended in training honest men but a small part of what we have expended in hunting and torturing rogues.

—THOMAS BABINGTON MACAULAY, "Education,"
a speech delivered on April 18, 1847

THE CRITERIA OF PROOF BY DEDUCTIVE REASONING

To test the truth of a conclusion which has been reached by use of the deductive method, the writer, in a proof which he has worked out himself, and the reader, in the material he reads, must answer five questions.

1. Is the general premise (the major proposition) from which the conclusion is drawn true of some or all of the things named?

Obviously, the parrot would have relied on chance and not reason in this deduction:

> Some light nuts are hollow.
> This nut is light.
> Therefore, this nut is hollow.

2. Is the general premise true?

Is it true, for example, in the passage just quoted for Macaulay, that the government can protect its peoples and their property only by force or by education? Is it true, from the first paragraph in the same passage, that the duty of the government is to protect persons and property from danger? If these general premises are not true, obviously, Macaulay's conclusions are not true. The truth of the conclusion rests in the truth of the general principle.

3. Is the connecting premise (the minor proposition) true?

To return again to Macaulay, is the gross ignorance of the common people the principal danger to persons and property?

4. Are all the terms used in the major and minor premises given only one meaning? Is there a middle term?

Consider this reasoning:

> Nothing is better than heaven.
> A penny is better than nothing.
> Therefore, a penny is better than heaven.

Obviously, the word *nothing* has one meaning in the major premise and another in the minor. Consequently, the conclusion is false.

    5. May the direct contradiction of the conclusion be inferred from the premises?

> All men are mortal.
> John is a man.
> Therefore, John is mortal.

The contradiction of the conclusion is "John is not mortal." It is inconsistent with the preceding premises and cannot be inferred; therefore, the first conclusion is true. Contrast, however, this reasoning:

> All football players are strong.
> This man is strong.
> Therefore, this man is a football player.

The contradiction of the conclusion is "This man is not a football player." That conclusion is not inconsistent with the premises; consequently, the conclusion may be false. If, however, one reasoned in this way:

> Only football players are strong.
> This man is strong.
> Therefore, this man is a football player.

the reasoning would be correct in its form but the conclusion not proved because the major proposition, "Only football players are strong," cannot be shown to be true.

    An application of these five questions in the testing of a proof may now be observed. In 1775 Jonathan Boucher, in a sermon, criticized in the following way the view, expressed earlier by John Locke, that governments derive their power from the consent of the governed:

    It is laid down . . . as a settled maxim, that the end of government is "the common good of mankind." I am not sure that the position itself is indisputable; but, if it were, it would by no means follow that, "this common good being matter of common feeling, government must therefore have been instituted by common consent." There is an appearance of logical accuracy and precision in this statement; but it is only an appearance. The position is vague and loose; and the assertion is made without an attempt to prove it. If by men's "common feelings" we are to understand that principle in the human mind called common sense, the assertion is either unmeaning and insignificant, or it is false. In no instance have mankind ever yet agreed as to what is, or is not, "the common good." A form or mode of government cannot be named, which these "common feelings" and "common consent," the sole arbiters, as it seems, of "common good," have not, at one time or another, set up and established, and again pulled down and reprobated. What one people in one age have concurred in establishing as the "common good," another in another age have voted to be mischievous and big with ruin. The premises, therefore, that "the common good is matter of common feeling," being false, the consequence drawn from it, viz. that government was instituted by "common consent," is of course equally false.

—JONATHAN BOUCHER, *A View of the Causes and Consequences of the American Revolution*, 1797

An examination of this passage includes two general problems: first, Boucher's own judgment or criticism of the reasoning which he summarizes; and second, an examination of the validity of Boucher's objections. The reasoning under criticism may first be reduced to syllogistic form. It is this:

Major premise: Government was instituted for the common good of mankind. (*I.e.*, "the end of government is 'the common good of mankind.' ")
Minor premise: The common good of mankind can be established only by common consent. (*I.e.*, "the common good is matter of common feeling.")
Conclusion: Therefore, government was instituted by common consent.

Boucher begins his evaluation of this reasoning by asking the second question given above in the criteria: Is the general premise true? He is not sure that it is indisputable. Take for granted, however, that it is true, he says. Then he asks the third question: Is the connecting proposition (the minor premise) true? Is the common good a matter of common feeling? Can the common good of mankind be established only by common consent? The minor premise, he concludes, is, if not unmeaningful, false. Mankind have never agreed as to what is, or what is not, the common good. The minor premise being false, then, he affirms, the conclusion is false: government was not instituted by common consent.

To turn from Boucher's criticism of the deduction to the value of his criticism, one must test the reasoning in the criticism. If the premises do not prove the assertion, as Boucher holds they do not, do his propositions disprove it? One of his objections may have point: the position is "vague and loose." Suppositions as to the historical origin of government—who first instituted government? Why?—seem to have been confused with another problem: the end of government. Contrast the following syllogism with the one immediately after the passage:

Major: The just powers of government promote the common good.
  (The end of government is the common good.)
Minor: What promotes the common good derives from the consent of
  the governed.
Conclusion: The just powers of government derive from the consent of
  the governed.

Without further disentangling the arguments in the passage, however, one may test Boucher's own propositions. Are they true? First, is it true that societies of men have never agreed by common consent on what is their common good? Further, does it follow, as Boucher holds, that the common consent and the common good must be so established that no reasonable adaptation to change may occur? If men's methods of adapting themselves to the world and to one another change, may not the common good of one age cease to be a common good in another? In the light of such questions, has Boucher, in his criticism, either clarified or disproved the reasoning he attacks?

EXERCISE I

Contrast with Boucher's proposition "Men cannot agree as to what is the common good" the following propositions in the Declaration of Independence. Construct at least one syllogism from the reasoning in this portion of it:

We hold these truths to be self-evident, that all men are created equal, that they are endowed by their Creator with certain unalienable Rights, that among these are Life, Liberty and the pursuit of Happiness. That to secure these rights, Governments are instituted among Men, deriving their just powers from the consent of the governed. That whenever any Form of Government becomes destructive of these ends, it is the Right of the People to alter or to abolish it, and to institute new Government, laying its foundations on such principles and organizing its powers in such form, as to them shall seem most likely to effect their Safety and Happiness.

EXERCISE II

By applying the five criteria of deductive reasoning to the following passages, evaluate them.

1

a. Education implies teaching. Teaching implies knowledge. Knowledge is truth. The truth is everywhere the same. Hence education should be everywhere the same.
b. The aim of higher education is wisdom. Wisdom is knowledge of principles and causes. Metaphysics deals with the highest principles and causes. Therefore metaphysics is the highest wisdom.
          —ROBERT MAYNARD HUTCHINS, *The Higher Learning in America*, 1936

2

It is to be regretted that the rich and powerful too often bend the acts of government to their selfish purposes. Distinctions in society will always exist under every just government. Equality of talents, of education, or of wealth can not be produced by human institutions. In the full enjoyment of the gifts of Heaven and the fruits of superior industry, economy, and virtue, every man is equally entitled to protection by law; but when the laws undertake to add to these natural and just advantages artificial distinctions, to grant titled, gratuities, and exclusive privileges, to make the rich richer and the potent more powerful, the humble members of society—the farmers, mechanics, and laborers —who have neither the time nor the means of securing like favors to themselves, have a right to complain of the injustice of their Government. There are no necessary evils in government. Its evils exist only in its abuses. If it would confine itself to equal protection, and, as Heaven does its rains, shower its favors alike on the high and the low, the rich and the poor, it would be an unqualified blessing. In the act before me there seems to be a wide and unnecessary departure from these just principles.
          —ANDREW JACKSON, Bank Veto message, July 1, 1832

EXERCISE III

Evaluate the reasoning in the following criticism:

This popular notion, that government was originally formed by the consent or by a compact of the people, rests on, and is supported by, another similar notion, not less popular, nor better founded. This other notion is, that the whole human race is born equal; and that no man is naturally inferior, or, in any respect, subjected to another; and that he can be made subject to another only by his own consent. The position is equally ill-founded and false both in its premises and conclusions. In hardly any sense that can be imagined is the position strictly true: but, as applied to the case under consideration, it is demonstrably not true. Man differs from man in every thing that can be supposed to lead to supremacy and subjection, *as one star differs from another star in glory*. It was the purpose of the Creator, that man should be social: but, without government, there can be no society; nor, without some relative inferiority and superiority, can there be any government. A musical instrument composed of chords, keys, or pipes, all perfectly equal in size and power, might as well be expected to produce harmony, as a society composed of members all perfectly equal to be productive of order and peace.

—JONATHAN BOUCHER, *A View of the Causes and Consequences of the American Revolution*, 1797

EXERCISE IV

Name ways (authority, induction, or deduction) in which one may prove the truth of those statements that follow which can be proved.
1. Since labor is the source of all value, we must support all wage-earners.
2. The realistic and graphic, not the refined, appeals to the uneducated taste.
3. Deprived of the satisfaction of a triumphant climax to their efforts in life, disillusioned people turn to fiction for consolation.
4. Asceticism can be sustained only by faith, not verified by experience.
5. Feelings, not the intellect, are the springs of human action.
6. Electric power generated by steam costs less than that generated by water.
7. Ugliness betrayed the spirit of man in the nineteenth century.
8. The heroes of the ancient world were cunning, crafty, and deceitful.
9. Advertising operates openly; hidden propaganda works by stealth.

10. Narratives of their deeds written by the crusaders were exaggerated, romantic, and imaginary.
11. The word *highbrow* is an ominous addition to the English language.
12. Expediency often prevents men from acting according to their real convictions.
13. The rise of large-scale advertising, popular magazines, movies, radio, and other channels of increased cultural diffusion from without is rapidly changing habits of thought as to what things are essential to living and multiplying optional occasions for spending money.
14. Satire is a reversal of respect and admiration.
15. One method of commercial propagandists is to instigate an event concerning their company which the newspapers will report as news.

Exercise V

Criticize the proof offered in support of the conclusion stated and developed below. Determine, first, what type of proof is used; then apply the criteria for that type.

The education of most value for guidance must at the same time be the education of most value for discipline. The study of science, as a means of discipline, is superior to the study of language.

One advantage claimed for the study of language is that it strengthens the memory, an advantage believed to be peculiar to the study of words. The sciences, however, afford far wider fields for the exercise of memory. The new compounds which chemistry daily accumulates are so numerous that few, save professors, know the names of all of them; and to recollect the atomic constitutions and affinities of all these compounds is scarcely possible without making chemistry an occupation. When we pass to an organic science, the effort of memory required becomes greater. In human anatomy alone, the quantity of detail is so great that the young surgeon has commonly to get it up half-a-dozen times before he can permanently retain it. The number of species of plants which botanists distinguish is enormous; the varied forms of animal life with which the zoölogist deals is estimated at some two million. To say the very least, the study of science involves as good a training of memory as language does.

Science is superior to language in the kind of memory it cultivates. In the acquirement of a language the connections of ideas to be established in the mind correspond to facts that are in a great measure accidental. In the acquirement of science the connections of ideas to be established in the mind correspond to facts that are mostly necessary.

While language familiarizes with non-rational relations, science familiarizes with rational relations. While the one exercises the memory only, the other exercises both memory and understanding.

Science is greatly superior to language in that it cultivates the judgment. Correct judgment with regard to all surrounding things, events, and consequences becomes possible only through knowledge of the way in which surrounding phenomena depend on one another. No extent of the acquaintance with the meanings of words can give the power of forming correct inferences respecting causes and effects. The constant of drawing conclusions from data, and then of verifying those conclusions by observation and experiment can alone give the power of judging correctly. And that it necessitates this habit is one of the immense advantages of science.

Not only, however, for intellectual discipline is science the best; but also for *moral* discipline. The learning of language tends to increase an undue respect for the authority of the teacher, the dictionary, or the rules of grammar. The constant attitude of mind of the student is that of submission to dogmatic teaching. A necessary result is a tendency to accept without inquiry whatever is established. By science, constant appeal is made to individual reason. Its truths are not accepted upon authority alone; but all are at liberty to test them; in many cases, the pupil is required to think out his own conclusions.

Lastly, the discipline of science is superior to that of language because of the religious culture that it gives. So far from science being irreligious, as many think, it is the neglect of science that is irreligious —it is the refusal to study the surrounding creation that is irreligious. Devotion to science is a tacit worship—a tacit recognition of worth in the things studied; and by implication in their Cause. It is not a mere lip-homage, but a homage expressed in actions—not a professed respect, but a respect proved by the sacrifice of time, thought, and labor. Science is also religious inasmuch as it generates a profound respect for and an implicit faith in the uniform laws which underlie all things. By asserting the eternal principles of things and the necessity of conforming to them, the man of science proves himself intrinsically religious. Finally, science alone can give us a true conception of ourselves and our relation to the mysteries of existence. Only the sincere man of science can truly know how utterly beyond, not only human knowledge but human conception, is the universal power of which nature, and life, and thought are manifestations.

For discipline then, as well as for guidance, the study of science is of greater value than the study of language. Learning the meanings of things is better than learning the meanings of words. Whether for intellectual, moral, or religious training, the study of surrounding phenomena is immensely superior to the study of grammars and lexicons.

                              HERBERT SPENCER, *Education*, 1861

CHAPTER 10

Review:
Methods of Developing Ideas

Each of the nine preceding chapters centered on an examination of one method of developing an idea. Consequently, in each chapter the illustrations were restricted largely to paragraphs developed almost exclusively by one method: definition, analysis, comparison, or another. In the development of an entire essay, however—and even in the development of a single paragraph—a writer may use any combinations of methods that his material requires. Nevertheless, it is likely that in a single paragraph or in an article composed of many paragraphs, one method may become dominant. He is free to use any methods as he sees fit, not forgetting, of course, the criteria which govern it.

Observe in the following essay how combinations of the eight methods of expansion develop a point, which may be summarized thus: *Education should aim at producing men who demonstrate both within themselves and socially the values of culture, expert knowledge, and a religious sense of duty and reverence.* The expansion of this main idea here requires forty paragraphs. Before an examination of the methods of expansion used in the essay can be rewarding, it must be read carefully and its meaning understood. Questions and topics for study are given at the end of the passage.

THE AIMS OF EDUCATION: A. N. WHITEHEAD

1   Culture is activity of thought, and receptiveness to beauty and humane feeling. Scraps of information have nothing to do with it.

A merely well-informed man is the most useless bore on God's earth. What we should aim at producing is men who possess both culture and expert knowledge in some special direction. Their expert knowledge will give them the ground to start from, and their culture will lead them as deep as philosophy and as high as art. We have to remember that the valuable intellectual development is self-development, and that it mostly takes place between the ages of sixteen and thirty. As to training, the most important part is given by mothers before the age of twelve. A saying due to Archbishop Temple illustrates my meaning. Surprise was expressed at the success in after-life of a man, who as a boy at Rugby had been somewhat undistinguished. He answered, "It is not what they are at eighteen, it is what they become afterwards that matters."

2   In training a child to activity of thought, above all things we must beware of what I will call "inert ideas"—that is to say, ideas that are merely received into the mind without being utilised, or tested, or thrown into fresh combinations.

3   In the history of education, the most striking phenomenon is that schools of learning, which at one epoch are alive with a ferment of genius, in a succeeding generation exhibit merely pedantry and routine. The reason is, that they are overladen with inert ideas. Education with inert ideas is not only useless: it is, above all things, harmful—*Corruptio optimi, pessima.* [The corruption of the best is the worst.] Except at rare intervals of intellectual ferment, education in the past has been radically infected with inert ideas. That is the reason why uneducated clever women, who have seen much of the world, are in middle life so much the most cultured part of the community. They have been saved from this horrible burden of inert ideas. Every intellectual revolution which has ever stirred humanity into greatness has been a passionate protest against inert ideas. Then, alas, with pathetic ignorance of human psychology, it has proceeded by some educational scheme to bind humanity afresh with inert ideas of its own fashioning.

4   Let us now ask how in our system of education we are to guard against this mental dryrot. We enunciate two educational commandments, "Do not teach too many subjects," and again, "What you teach, teach thoroughly."

5   The result of teaching small parts of a large number of subjects is the passive reception of disconnected ideas, not illumined with any spark of vitality. Let the main ideas which are introduced into a child's education be few and important, and let them be thrown into every combination possible. The child should make them his own, and should understand their application here and now in the circumstances of his actual life. From the very beginning of his

education, the child should experience the joy of discovery. The discovery which he has to make, is that general ideas give an understanding of that stream of events which pours through his life, which is his life. By understanding I mean more than a mere logical analysis, though that is included. I mean "understanding" in the sense in which it is used in the French proverb, "To understand all, is to forgive all." Pedants sneer at an education which is useful. But if education is not useful, what is it? Is it a talent, to be hidden away in a napkin? Of course, education should be useful, whatever your aim in life. It was useful to Saint Augustine and it was useful to Napoleon. It is useful, because understanding is useful.

6   I pass lightly over that understanding which should be given by the literary side of education. Nor do I wish to be supposed to pronounce on the relative merits of a classical or a modern curriculum. I would only remark that the understanding which we want is an understanding of an insistent present. The only use of a knowledge of the past is to equip us for the present. No more deadly harm can be done to young minds than by depreciation of the present. The present contains all that there is. It is holy ground; for it is the past, and it is the future. At the same time it must be observed that an age is no less past if it existed two hundred years ago than if it existed two thousand years ago. Do not be deceived by the pedantry of dates. The ages of Shakespeare and of Molière are no less past than are the ages of Sophocles and of Virgil. The communion of saints is a great and inspiring assemblage, but it has only one possible hall of meeting, and that is, the present; and the mere lapse of time through which any particular group of saints must travel to reach that meeting-place, makes very little difference.

7   Passing now to the scientific and logical side of education, we remember that here also ideas which are not utilised are positively harmful. By utilising an idea, I mean relating it to that stream, compounded of sense perceptions, feelings, hopes, desires, and of mental activities adjusting thought to thought, which forms our life. I can imagine a set of beings which might fortify their souls by passively reviewing disconnected ideas. Humanity is not built that way—except perhaps some editors of newspapers.

8   In scientific training, the first thing to do with an idea is to prove it. But allow me for one moment to extend the meaning of "prove"; I mean—to prove its worth. Now an idea is not worth much unless the propositions in which it is embodied are true. Accordingly an essential part of the proof of an idea is the proof, either by experiment or by logic, of the truth of the propositions. But it is not essential that this proof of the truth should constitute

the first introduction to the idea. After all, its assertion by the authority of respectable teachers is sufficient evidence to begin with. In our first contact with a set of propositions, we commence by appreciating their importance. That is what we all do in after-life. We do not attempt, in the strict sense, to prove or to disprove anything, unless its importance makes it worthy of that honour. These two processes of proof, in the narrow sense, and of apprecia-tion, do not require a rigid separation in time. Both can be pro-ceeded with nearly concurrently. But in so far as either process must have the priority, it should be that of appreciation by use.

9   Furthermore, we should not endeavour to use propositions in isolation. Emphatically I do not mean, a neat little set of experi-ments to illustrate Proposition I and then the proof of Proposition I, a neat little set of experiments to illustrate Proposition II and then the proof of Proposition II, and so on to the end of the book. Nothing could be more boring. Interrelated truths are utilised *en bloc*, and the various propositions are employed in any order, and with any reiteration. Choose some important applications of your theoretical subject; and study them concurrently with the systemat-ic theoretical exposition. Keep the theoretical exposition short and simple, but let it be strict and rigid so far as it goes. It should not be too long for it to be easily known with thoroughness and accuracy. The consequences of a plethora of half-digested theoreti-cal knowledge are deplorable. Also the theory should not be mud-dled up with the practice. The child should have no doubt when it is proving and when it is utilising. My point is that what is proved should be utilised, and that what is utilised should—so far as is practicable—be proved. I am far from asserting that proof and utilisation are the same thing.

10   At this point of my discourse, I can most directly carry forward my argument in the outward form of a digression. We are only just realising that the art and science of education require a genius and a study of their own; and that this genius and this science are more than a bare knowledge of some branch of science or of literature. This truth was partially perceived in the past generation; and headmasters, somewhat crudely, were apt to supersede learning in their colleagues by requiring left-hand bowling and a taste for football. But culture is more than cricket, and more than football, and more than extent of knowledge.

11   Education is the acquisition of the art of the utilisation of knowl-edge. This is an art very difficult to impart. Whenever a text-book is written of real educational worth, you may be quite certain that some reviewer will say that it will be difficult to teach from it. Of course it will be difficult to teach from it. If it were easy, the book ought to be burned; for it cannot be educational. In education, as

elsewhere, the broad primrose path leads to a nasty place. This evil path is represented by a book or a set of lectures which will practically enable the student to learn by heart all the questions likely to be asked at the next external examination. And I may say in passing that no educational system is possible unless every question directly asked of a pupil at any examination is either framed or modified by the actual teacher of that pupil in that subject. The external assessor may report on the curriculum or on the performance of the pupils, but never should be allowed to ask the pupil a question which has not been strictly supervised by the actual teacher, or at least inspired by a long conference with him. There are a few exceptions to this rule, but they are exceptions, and could easily be allowed for under the general rule.

12   We now return to my previous point, that theoretical ideas should always find important applications within the pupil's curriculum. This is not an easy doctrine to apply, but a very hard one. It contains within itself the problem of keeping knowledge alive, of preventing it from becoming inert, which is the central problem of all education.

13   The best procedure will depend on several factors, none of which can be neglected, namely, the genius of the teacher, the intellectual type of the pupils, their prospects in life, the opportunities offered by the immediate surroundings of the school, and allied factors of this sort. It is for this reason that the uniform external examination is so deadly. We do not denounce it because we are cranks, and like denouncing established things. We are not so childish. Also, of course, such examinations have their use in testing slackness. Our reason of dislike is very definite and very practical. It kills the best part of culture. When you analyse in the light of experience the central task of education, you find that its successful accomplishment depends on a delicate adjustment of many variable factors. The reason is that we are dealing with human minds, and not with dead matter. The evocation of curiosity, of judgment, of the power of mastering a complicated tangle of circumstances, the use of theory in giving foresight in special cases—all these powers are not to be imparted by a set rule embodied in one schedule of examination subjects.

14   I appeal to you, as practical teachers. [This essay was delivered as an address before the International Congress of Mathematicians at Cambridge, England, in 1912.] With good discipline, it is always possible to pump into the minds of a class a certain quantity of inert knowledge. You take a text-book and make them learn it. So far, so good. The child then knows how to solve a quadratic equation. But what is the point of teaching a child to solve a quadratic equation? There is a traditional answer to this question. It runs

thus: The mind is an instrument, you first sharpen it, and then use it; the acquisition of the power of solving a quadratic equation is part of the process of sharpening the mind. Now there is just enough truth in this answer to have made it live through the ages. But for all its half-truth, it embodies a radical error which bids fair to stifle the genius of the modern world. I do not know who was first responsible for this analogy of the mind to a dead instrument. For aught I know, it may have been one of the seven wise men of Greece, or a committee of the whole lot of them. Whoever was the originator, there can be no doubt of the authority which it has acquired by the continuous approval bestowed upon it by eminent persons. But whatever its weight of authority, whatever the high approval which it can quote, I have no hesitation in denouncing it as one of the most fatal, erroneous, and dangerous conceptions ever introduced into the theory of education. The mind is never passive; it is a perpetual activity, delicate, receptive, responsive to stimulus. You cannot postpone its life until you have sharpened it. Whatever interest attaches to your subject-matter must be evoked here and now; whatever powers you are strengthening in the pupil, must be exercised here and now; whatever possibilities of mental life your teaching should impart, must be exhibited here and now. That is the golden rule of education, and a very difficult rule to follow.

15   The difficulty is just this: the apprehension of general ideas, intellectual habits of mind, and pleasurable interest in mental achievement can be evoked by no form of words, however accurately adjusted. All practical teachers know that education is a patient process of the mastery of details, minute by minute, hour by hour, day by day. There is no royal road to learning through an airy path of brilliant generalisations. There is a proverb about the difficulty of seeing the wood because of the trees. That difficulty is exactly the point which I am enforcing. The problem of education is to make the pupil see the wood by means of the trees.

16   The solution which I am urging, is to eradicate the fatal disconnection of subjects which kills the vitality of our modern curriculum. There is only one subject-matter for education, and that is Life in all its manifestations. Instead of this single unity, we offer children—Algebra, from which nothing follows; Geometry, from which nothing follows; Science, from which nothing follows; History, from which nothing follows; a Couple of Languages, never mastered; and lastly, most dreary of all, Literature, represented by plays of Shakespeare, with philological notes and short analyses of plot and character to be in substance committed to memory. Can such a list be said to represent Life, as it is known in

the midst of the living of it? The best that can be said of it is, that it is a rapid table of contents which a deity might run over in his mind while he was thinking of creating a world, and had not yet determined how to put it together.

17 Let us now return to quadratic equations. We still have on hand the unanswered question. Why should children be taught their solution? Unless quadratic equations fit into a connected curriculum, of course there is no reason to teach anything about them. Furthermore, extensive as should be the place of mathematics in a complete culture, I am a little doubtful whether for many types of boys algebraic solutions of quadratic equations do not lie on the specialist side of mathematics. I may here remind you that as yet I have not said anything of the psychology or the content of the specialism, which is so necessary a part of an ideal education. But all that is an evasion of our real question, and I merely state it in order to avoid being misunderstood in my answer.

18 Quadratic equations are part of algebra, and algebra is the intellectual instrument which has been created for rendering clear the quantitative aspects of the world. There is no getting out of it. Through and through the world is infected with quantity. To talk sense, is to talk in quantities. It is no use saying that the nation is large,—How large? It is no use saying that radium is scarce,—How scarce? You cannot evade quantity. You may fly to poetry and to music, and quantity and number will face you in your rhythms and your octaves. Elegant intellects which despise the theory of quantity, are but half developed. They are more to be pitied than blamed. The scraps of gibberish, which in their school-days were taught to them in the name of algebra, deserve some contempt.

19 This question of the degeneration of algebra into gibberish, both in word and in fact, affords a pathetic instance of the uselessness of reforming educational schedules without a clear conception of the attributes which you wish to evoke in the living minds of the children. A few years ago there was an outcry that school algebra was in need of reform, but there was a general agreement that graphs would put everything right. So all sorts of things were extruded, and graphs were introduced. So far as I can see, with no sort of idea behind them, but just graphs. Now every examination paper has one or two questions on graphs. Personally, I am an enthusiastic adherent of graphs. But I wonder whether as yet we have gained very much. You cannot put life into any schedule of general education unless you succeed in exhibiting its relation to some essential characteristic of all intelligent or emotional perception. It is a hard saying, but it is true; and I do not see how to make it any easier. In making these little formal alterations you

are beaten by the very nature of things. You are pitted against too
skilful an adversary, who will see to it that the pea is always under
the other thimble.

20   Reformation must begin at the other end. First, you must make
up your mind as to those quantitative aspects of the world which
are simple enough to be introduced into general education; then a
schedule of algebra should be framed which will about find its
exemplification in these applications. We need not fear for our pet
graphs, they will be there in plenty when we once begin to treat
algebra as a serious means of studying the world. Some of the
simplest applications will be found in the quantities which occur
in the simplest study of society. The curves of history are more
vivid and more informing than the dry catalogues of names and
dates which comprise the greater part of that arid school study.
What purpose is effected by a catalogue of undistinguished kings
and queens? Tom, Dick, or Harry, they are all dead. General
resurrections are failures, and are better postponed. The quantitative flux of the forces of modern society is capable of very simple
exhibition. Meanwhile, the idea of the variable, of the function, of
rate of change, of equations and their solution, of elimination, are
being studied as an abstract science for their own sake. Not, of
course, in the pompous phrases with which I am alluding to them
here, but with that iteration of simple special cases proper to
teaching.

21   If this course be followed, the route from Chaucer to the Black
Death, from the Black Death to modern Labour troubles, will
connect the tales of the mediaeval pilgrims with the abstract
science of algebra, both yielding diverse aspects of that single
theme, Life. I know what most of you are thinking at this point. It
is that the exact course which I have sketched out is not the particular one which you would have chosen, or even see how to work. I
quite agree. I am not claiming that I could do it myself. But your
objection is the precise reason why a common external examination system is fatal to education. The process of exhibiting the
applications of knowledge must, for its success, essentially depend
on the character of the pupils and the genius of the teacher. Of
course I have left out the easiest applications with which most of
us are more at home. I mean the quantitative sides of sciences, such
as mechanics and physics.

22   Again, in the same connection we plot the statistics of social
phenomena against the time. We then eliminate the time between
suitable pairs. We can speculate how far we have exhibited a real
causal connection, or how far a mere temporal coincidence. We
notice that we might have plotted against the time one set of
statistics for one country and another set for another country, and

thus, with suitable choice of subjects, have obtained graphs which certainly exhibited mere coincidence. Also other graphs exhibit obvious causal connections. We wonder how to discriminate. And so are drawn on as far as we will.

23   But in considering this description, I must beg you to remember what I have been insisting on above. In the first place, one train of thought will not suit all groups of children. For example, I should expect that artisan children will want something more concrete and, in a sense, swifter than I have set down here. Perhaps I am wrong, but that is what I should guess. In the second place, I am not contemplating one beautiful lecture stimulating, once and for all, an admiring class. That is not the way in which education proceeds. No; all the time the pupils are hard at work solving examples, drawing graphs, and making experiments, until they have a thorough hold on the whole subject. I am describing the interspersed explanations, the directions which should be given to their thoughts. The pupils have got to be made to feel that they are studying something, and are not merely executing intellectual minuets.

24   Finally, if you are teaching pupils for some general examination, the problem of sound teaching is greatly complicated. Have you ever noticed the zigzag moulding round a Norman arch? The ancient work is beautiful, the modern work is hideous. The reason is, that the modern work is done to exact measure, the ancient work is varied according to the idiosyncrasy of the workman. Here it is crowded, and there it is expanded. Now the essence of getting pupils through examinations is to give equal weight to all parts of the schedule. But mankind is naturally specialist. One man sees a whole subject, where another can find only a few detached examples. I know that it seems contradictory to allow for specialism in a curriculum especially designed for a broad culture. Without contradictions the world would be simpler, and perhaps duller. But I am certain that in education wherever you exclude specialism you destroy life.

25   We now come to the other great branch of a general mathematical education, namely Geometry. The same principles apply. The theoretical part should be clear-cut, rigid, short, and important. Every proposition not absolutely necessary to exhibit the main connection of ideas should be cut out, but the great fundamental ideas should be all there. No omission of concepts, such as those of Similarity and Proportion. We must remember that, owing to the aid rendered by the visual presence of a figure, Geometry is a field of unequalled excellence for the exercise of the deductive faculties of reasoning. Then, of course, there follows Geometrical Drawing, with its training for the hand and eye.

26   But, like Algebra, Geometry and Geometrical Drawing must be
extended beyond the mere circle of geometrical ideas. In an industrial neighbourhood, machinery and workshop practice form the
appropriate extension. For example, in the London Polytechnics
this has been achieved with conspicuous success. For many secondary schools I suggest that surveying and maps are the natural
applications. In particular, plane-table surveying should lead
pupils to a vivid apprehension of the immediate application of
geometric truths. Simple drawing apparatus, a surveyor's chain,
and a surveyor's compass, should enable the pupils to rise from the
survey and mensuration of a field to the construction of the map of
a small district. The best education is to be found in gaining the
utmost information from the simplest apparatus. The provision of
elaborate instruments is greatly to be deprecated. To have constructed the map of a small district, to have considered its roads, its
contours, its geology, its climate, its relation to other districts, the
effects on the status of its inhabitants, will teach more history and
geography than any knowledge of Perkin Warbeck or of Behren's
Straits. I mean not a nebulous lecture on the subject, but a serious
investigation in which the real facts are definitely ascertained by
the aid of accurate theoretical knowledge. A typical mathematical
problem should be: Survey such and such a field, draw a plan of it
to such and such a scale, and find the area. It would be quite a
good procedure to impart the necessary geometrical propositions
without their proofs. Then, concurrently in the same term, the
proofs of the propositions would be learnt while the survey was
being made.

27   Fortunately, the specialist side of education presents an easier
problem than does the provision of a general culture. For this
there are many reasons. One is that many of the principles of
procedure to be observed are the same in both cases, and it is
unnecessary to recapitulate. Another reason is that specialist training takes place—or should take place—at a more advanced stage of
the pupil's course, and thus there is easier material to work upon.
But undoubtedly the chief reason is that the specialist study is
normally a study of peculiar interest to the student. He is studying
it because, for some reason, he wants to know it. This makes all the
difference. The general culture is designed to foster an activity of
mind; the specialist course utilises this activity. But it does not do
to lay too much stress on these neat antitheses. As we have already
seen, in the general course foci of special interest will arise; and
similarly in the special study, the external connections of the
subject drag thought outwards.

28   Again, there is not one course of study which merely gives general
culture, and another which gives special knowledge. The subjects

pursued for the sake of a general education are special subjects specially studied; and, on the other hand, one of the ways of encouraging general mental activity is to foster a special devotion. You may not divide the seamless coat of learning. What education has to impart is an intimate sense for the power of ideas, for the beauty of ideas, and for the structure of ideas, together with a particular body of knowledge which has peculiar reference to the life of the being possessing it.

29   The appreciation of the structure of ideas is that side of a cultured mind which can only grow under the influence of a special study. I mean that eye for the whole chess-board, for the bearing of one set of ideas on another. Nothing but a special study can give any appreciation for the exact formulation of general ideas, for their relations when formulated, for their service in the comprehension of life. A mind so disciplined should be both more abstract and more concrete. It has been trained in the comprehension of abstract thought and in the analysis of facts.

30   Finally, there should grow the most austere of all mental qualities; I mean the sense for style. It is an aesthetic sense, based on admiration for the direct attainment of a foreseen end, simply and without waste. Style in art, style in literature, style in science, style in logic, style in practical execution have fundamentally the same aesthetic qualities, namely, attainment and restraint. The love of a subject in itself and for itself, where it is not the sleepy pleasure of pacing a mental quarter-deck, is the love of style as manifested in that study.

31   Here we are brought back to the position from which we started, the utility of education. Style, in its finest sense, is the last acquirement of the educated mind; it is also the most useful. It pervades the whole being. The administrator with a sense for style hates waste; the engineer with a sense for style economises his material; the artisan with a sense for style prefers good work. Style is the ultimate morality of mind.

32   But above style, and above knowledge, there is something, a vague shape like fate above the Greek gods. That something is Power. Style is the fashioning of power, the restraining of power. But, after all, the power of attainment of the desired end is fundamental. The first thing is to get there. Do not bother about your style, but solve your problem, justify the ways of God to man, administer your province, or do whatever else is set before you.

33   Where, then, does style help? In this, with style the end is attained without side issues, without raising undesirable inflammations. With style you attain your end and nothing but your end. With style the effect of your activity is calculable, and foresight is the last gift of gods to men. With style your power is increased,

for your mind is not distracted with irrelevancies, and you are
more likely to attain your object. Now style is the exclusive privilege of the expert. Whoever heard of the style of an amateur
painter, of the style of an amateur poet? Style is always the product
of specialist study, the peculiar contribution of specialism to culture.

34   English education in its present phase suffers from a lack of
definite aim, and from an external machinery which kills its vitality. Hitherto in this address I have been considering the aims which
should govern education. In this respect England halts between
two opinions. It has not decided whether to produce amateurs or
experts. The profound change in the world which the nineteenth
century has produced is that the growth of knowledge has given
foresight. The amateur is essentially a man with appreciation and
with immense versatility in mastering a given routine. But he lacks
the foresight which comes from special knowledge. The object of
this address is to suggest how to produce the expert without loss of
the essential virtues of the amateur. The machinery of our secondary education is rigid where it should be yielding, and lax where it
should be rigid. Every school is bound on pain of extinction to
train its boys for a small set of definite examinations. No headmas-
ter has a free hand to develop his general education or his specialist studies in accordance with the opportunities of his school,
which are created by its staff, its environment, its class of boys, and
its endowments. I suggest that no system of external tests which
aims primarily at examining individual scholars can result in
anything but educational waste.

35   Primarily it is the schools and not the scholars which should be
inspected. Each school should grant its own leaving certificates,
based on its own curriculum. The standards of these schools
should be sampled and corrected. But the first requisite for educational reform is the school as a unit, with its approved curriculum
based on its own needs, and evolved by its own staff. If we fail to
secure that, we simply fall from one formalism into another, from
one dung-hill of inert ideas into another.

36   In stating that the school is the true educational unit in any
national system for the safeguarding of efficiency, I have conceived
the alternative system as being the external examination of the
individual scholar. But every Scylla is faced by its Charybdis—or,
in more homely language, there is a ditch on both sides of the
road. It will be equally fatal to education if we fall into the hands
of a supervising department which is under the impression that it
can divide all schools into two or three rigid categories, each type
being forced to adopt a rigid curriculum. When I say that the
school is the educational unit, I mean exactly what I say, no larger

unit, no smaller unit. Each school must have the claim to be considered in relation to its special circumstances. The classifying of schools for some purposes is necessary. But no absolutely rigid curriculum, not modified by its own staff, should be permissible. Exactly the same principles apply, with the proper modifications, to universities and to technical colleges.

37 When one considers in its length and in its breadth the importance of this question of the education of a nation's young, the broken lives, the defeated hopes, the national failures, which result from the frivolous inertia with which it is treated, it is difficult to restrain within oneself a savage rage. In the conditions of modern life the rule is absolute, the race which does not value trained intelligence is doomed. Not all your heroism, not all your social charm, not all your wit, not all your victories on land or at sea, can move back the finger of fate. To-day we maintain ourselves. To-morrow science will have moved forward yet one more step, and there will be no appeal from the judgment which will then be pronounced on the uneducated.

38 We can be content with no less than the old summary of educational ideal which has been current at any time from the dawn of our civilisation. The essence of education is that it be religious.

39 Pray, what is religious education?

40 A religious education is an education which inculcates duty and reverence. Duty arises from our potential control over the course of events. Where attainable knowledge could have changed the issue, ignorance has the guilt of vice. And the foundation of reverence is this perception, that the present holds within itself the complete sum of existence, backwards and forwards, that whole amplitude of time, which is eternity.

—A. N. WHITEHEAD, *The Aims of Education and Other Essays*, 1929

EXERCISES

1. The following outline gives only main divisions of the preceding essay. For each main division supply subdivisions: A, B, C, etc. Criticize the outline. If you find this outline faulty, make a new one which follows the organization of the passage more closely.

Main Idea: Education should aim at producing men who demonstrate both within themselves and socially the values of culture, expert knowlege, and a religious sense of duty and reverence.
    I. The development of culture requires, not inert ideas, but the proof and utilisation of ideas. (paragraphs 2–26)

    II. For three reasons, providing specialized knowledge is easier than providing general culture. (paragraph 27)

   III. Culture and knowledge impart an intimate sense for the power, beauty, and structure of ideas. (paragraphs 28–33)

   IV. To be attained, as is illustrated by difficulties in the English system of education, these values must be clearly defined as aims and then supported by a system which gives them vitality. (paragraphs 34–37)

    V. The essence of education is the inculcation of a religious sense of duty and reverence. (paragraphs 38–40)

2. Write a *précis* of the article not more than twenty sentences in length.

3. To determine the methods of development used in each paragraph, first, see whether the main idea in the paragraph is expressed or implied. In paragraph 15, for example, the topic sentence is: "The problem of education is to make the pupil see the wood by means of the trees." If the main idea in the paragraph is expressed, note the single sentence which expresses it. Test your choice by relating the meaning of each of the other sentences to one another and to what you believe is the central idea.

    If the main idea, however, is not expressed, but merely implied, state it in a single sentence. In paragraph 32, for example, no one sentence states the main idea. It is this: "Above style and knowledge is power."

    As further illlustrations, here are the topic sentences of the first six paragraphs:

     1. The test of education is the self-development which it makes possible, the men it produces who possess both culture and expert knowledge.

  2–3. The greatest obstacle in training a student to activity of thought is inert ideas.

  4–5. The best guard against inert ideas is to limit the number of main ideas taught and to teach those ideas so that the student will understand and utilize them.

     6. Literary studies should provide the student with an understanding of an insistent present, which contains both the past and the future.

After determining the topic sentence, observe the relationship which exists between the sentences in the paragraph, one to another and to the topic. The topic sentence of paragraph 30, for example, is "Education should develop the sense for style." The first sentence in the paragraph is merely a longer statement of that topic. The second sentence is a definition of style; the third, a comparison of style in different subjects; the last sentence, a further definition. The paragraph, therefore, is developed primarily by definition.

a. Point out instances of the use of the following methods in the paragraphs named:

Method	Paragraphs
Illustration	1, 3, 6
Comparison-Contrast	10, 18, 36
Analogy	8, 16, 40
Definition	6, 7, 11
Cause	13, 33, 34

b. What methods of development are used in each of the following paragraphs: 9, 14, 15, and 37?

4. After determining the method of development, evaluate the effectiveness with which the writer has used it. Examine the specific case in the light of the criteria for the method used. For example, if the subject matter has been developed by illustration, ask if the illustrations are relevant, specific, concrete, typical, and not exceptional.

Evaluate the use of the following methods in the paragraphs named. For each method, the page on which the criteria are listed is given in parentheses.

Method	Paragraphs
Illustration (p. 220)	19
Comparison-Contrast (p. 247)	26
Analogy (p. 227)	15, 24
Definition (pp. 268–269)	5, 31
Cause (pp. 286–287)	33

5. In the foregoing article might the writer have used to advantage additional methods? For example, what methods might he have used to develop further the subject matter of paragraph 40? Would illustrations clarify the reasons given in paragraph 27? In paragraph 32?

6. In its application to subject matter, a method need not be limited to a single paragraph. It may be extended through a series of closely related paragraphs.
   a. What contrast is developed through paragraphs 3–5?
   b. The analysis of what point extends through paragraphs 8 and 9?
   c. Trace the use of illustration, analysis, and contrast through paragraphs 17–23.

7. The essay is developed largely by analysis. It is an analysis of the aims of education. Trace the analysis through paragraphs 2–26, 27, and 38–40. What topic is analyzed in paragraphs 28–33? 34–37?

8. Evaluate the appropriateness and effectiveness of analysis as a dominant method for expanding the subject of this essay.

9. Write a fully developed paragraph on your own sense of an appropriate aim of education or related aims.